Caryll Houselander

Caryll Houselander

THAT DIVINE ECCENTRIC

by Maisie Ward

SHEED AND WARD – LONDON

Manufactured in the United States of America

Contents

Contents

Caryll Houselander

Introducing
Caryll Houselander

MONSIGNOR RONALD KNOX wished Caryll Houselander could establish a school for the writers of spiritual books. "She seemed," he said, "to see everything for the first time, and the driest of doctrinal considerations shone out like a restored picture when she had finished with it . . . she seemed to find no difficulty in getting the right word; no, not merely the right word, the telling word, that left you gasping."

In 1944 the Winchester Diocesan Clergy School asked her to address them at Oxford. *This War is the Passion* had not long been published and had touched a nerve in wartime England. Deeply aware of the truths that are eternal, but sensitive to atmosphere and very much a woman of her century, she was able to speak of those truths in the idiom of her own generation.

"It is the Week of Prayer," runs a letter from Sydney, Australia, "for the unity of all Christian people. In our University there is so little understanding between the different religious (Christian) bodies. Impoverished" by the constant discussions, by the "fantastically popular Billy Graham crusade" with its emphasis on numbers, "I came home feeling I had lost sight of the Christ I loved and of the love of the Father."

The writer of this letter took up and read aloud to herself Caryll Houselander's *Flowering Tree*. Feeling "blessed" by this reading, she had written to a friend, a missionary in Papua, telling her of the book—"only to find that it is one of her treasured possessions. We are neither of us Roman Catholics—but we both know ourselves to be at one with you. I thought you might like to know that God is able to go on finding people in far parts of the world through your insights—shared."

After every one of her books such letters arrived—from a student for the priesthood in Denmark, from a professor's wife in Indiana, from Europe, Asia, Africa, the Americas, especially from the United States. And her sales were enormous. We published works on spirituality by other writers: Dom John Chapman, Father Steuart, Archbishop Goodier, Father Leen—this laywoman outsold them all. Her books sold like novels, but to people craving for reality, not fiction.

She died in 1954. What she was writing in that last year, and for twelve years before that, does not "date." It is still alive, still contemporary.

Her message can be summarized in a single sentence: we must learn to see Christ in everyone.

2

Tremendous as this truth is, many people might be left cold, or at least cool, by the idea of just another spiritual writer. After all there are so many—we read some of them, we mean one day to read more—but why this particular woman? There is too, I fancy, a slight prejudice (especially among the laity!) against lay writing on theology or mysticism. I remember a deaf and elderly lady in the United States who, told that Gide had been put on the index, cried out,

"Sheed! I'm delighted to hear it. I don't like these lay theologians."

Works of sheer spirituality have very seldom been written by the laity, and we must go back far indeed to find an English Catholic laywoman writing one. Dame Julian of Norwich won for her book the right to stand beside those of Benedictine, Carmelite or Trappist. Priests from many orders welcomed Caryll Houselander instantly, recognizing that she was precisely *not* "just another" spiritual writer. She has occasional echoes of Julian, whose Revelations she loved. But the element which will, I think, make *The Comforting of Christ, The Reed of God, The Flowering Tree,* and above all *Guilt* permanently important was very different and totally her own.

Like Julian she was looking towards God, praying to Him, telling of Him; but the medieval did not think so much about the individual character of those who must be led also to look, also to pray. What she wrote had been given to her as revelation experienced, it was not the fruit of her own contact with her fellow-sinners. Caryll Houselander had a very unusual insight into individual character, quite distinct from her insight into divine revelation, though woven into one vision with it. She could see what was there in the people she wanted to help, and she could say what she saw.

Part of what Monsignor Knox welcomed in her freshness of approach to the oldest of doctrines came from an intense realism about human nature. St. John tells us that Our Lord would not trust Himself to men "because He knew what was in man." Yet the overwhelming fact was to follow that at the Last Supper He gave Himself into the hands of men, said to them, "I am in My Father, and you in Me, and I in you": one of those to whom He said it was about to deny Him. And the risen Christ said to St. Paul, who was persecuting His followers, "Saul, Saul, why persecutest thou *Me?*"

Christ has chosen to dwell in men, and the difficulty of

discovering Him in ourselves and in others is the main test-
ing of the Christian life. "We shall perceive Christ in others
only if we realize that He is *hidden* in His Risen Life; that
we can discern Him only wih the eyes of faith." Only by
faith in Christ can we see Christ in men—"inasmuch as you
have done it to one of these, My least brethren, you have
done it unto Me."

Pretending that men are not men, women not women,
but some sort of sublimated angelic beings adds to the difficulty instead of diminishing it, for it is a manifest contradiction of the reality which is around us, of which we are a part.
Caryll Houselander describes in *Guilt* some of the human
frailties to be found in men and women who are yet called
to be indwelt by Christ.

Life demands courage whether lived in a convent or a
family. There are women unable to face the self-surrender of
a vocation who "invent for themselves a kind of pseudo-
companionate marriage with the Lord in the world, or an
extraordinary mission in life, which precludes fulfilling all
their ordinary obligations, but eludes definition which might
commit them to any self-surrender at all, and is itself a life-
long delaying action."

Marriage, too, demands self-giving—a surrender that may
for many be as difficult as that of the cloister. She noted that
men had been known to commit suicide on the eve of marriage. She became convinced that of the causes of homosex-
uality a potent one was fear of meeting the "far greater responsibility of natural love."

She knew women also who, shrinking from this responsibility, yet find it necessary to have a man in their lives. They
"invariably fall in love with married men, and among the
pious there are those who foster a merciless devotion to a
sympathetic priest."

What she read as well as the people she met helped Caryll
Houselander in the all-important study of the men God had

made and life had played upon to their enriching or impoverishment. This is not to say she was invariably right about people whether in books or in life. For good or evil, she was, like all of us, sometimes mistaken.

I wish that she had written straight literary criticism—for what the distinguished psychologist Dr. Eric Strauss called her "natural genius" in the field of psychology certainly sharpened her insight into trends in literature and the subconscious drives that produce ideas as well as acts, that shape fictional characters as well as those who live and breathe. I give one example of this from *Guilt*. Speaking of the true artist whose voice is the voice of the world, she says:

It is significant that the writing of genius has for some time become more and more concerned with the father-son situation, and this has also filtered into the works of writers on the borderline of genius.

There is scarcely a word written by Samuel Butler on any subject that is not really an expression of the same tortured mixture of hostility to, and identification with, his father which he revealed in *The Way of All Flesh*. It seeps into the novels of D.H. Lawrence, and snarls out of much of his poetry, where it is confused with class-consciousness.

It is present in the fiction of contemporary Catholic writers in the critical attitude they often reveal to the priests who represent the parent Church which they belong to and love. How often a priest in a Catholic book is drawn as a mental fumbler, or almost ludicrous in his purely natural humanness—in fact, the father who represents God and who disappoints the son.

It would be difficult to invent quite so stupid a priest, even for so stupid a penitent, as Graham Greene's Father Rank in *The Heart of the Matter*, without the pressure of that disappointment, and it would be impossible to create Pinkie in *Brighton Rock*, with the agonized twist that makes the juvenile delinquent the pitiful rebel against authority that he is, without having quivered oneself with the universal suffering of the boy's disillusionment.

After such a searching gaze upon the problems of the human race, what a relief it will be for her, one feels, to turn her eyes towards that little group of men and women who alone do not complain of being frustrated in life, who alone have fulfilled their destiny as Christ-bearers—the saints in all their rich variety. And certainly she has written splendidly about the saints—but again from a most unusual angle.

"There is no saint in heaven," she says, "who did not fulfill his human nature on earth." But it was *his* human nature—and about the saints above all she detested what she once called "whimsical unthink." For humanity is almost infinitely various, the fact of sin is universal, and the saint like everyone else has to spend his life in battle. Many faults of character he will perhaps never lose, limitations due to environment or temperament he may never transcend. His human nature is his, not yours, not mine, not always like that of our specially selected friends.

"It would be very difficult," we read in *Guilt*, "to like all the saints." Christ wishes to dwell in every type of human being, and "in spite of the fact that Christ inlives them all, they retain their own characters." Our limitations may be far greater than theirs, but theirs shock us because of the image *we* have formed of what sanctity *ought* to be.

St. Thérèse of Lisieux will use about contemplation imagery suggestive of the "immature romanticism of a genteel French girl for whom a marriage to which she willingly consents has been arranged by an adored father." She "was true in every detail to what she was, a very sentimental little French bourgeoise." The average Englishman tries to escape the dilemma of his distaste for rose petals and his realization of her sanctity by concentrating only on her hard life and her heroism, dismissing as unessential "the exterior things of her personality," being in fact dishonest about the human character which makes no appeal to him. "He imagines he is scandalized by her, but the fact is he is scandalized *by Christ* for choosing to become Teresa Martin."

For someone else the stumbling block may be the dirt and rags of a Benedict Joseph Labre or other saints, perhaps uncanonized, "who are in fact suffering the loneliness and anguish of Christ in Gethsemane."

This unusual approach to the doctrine of the Mystical Body shows it as the startling reality that it is. Caryll Houselander's books, like St. Paul's epistles, dwell on it constantly, and she does not ignore the hardest element in the doctrine —that we must recognize Christ not only in those who appeal to us but in those who do not, seeing in the sinner the dead Christ in the tomb, seeing Him in the saints most remote from us in character and outlook.

"We are reminded of our failure by the fact that there are saints for everyone to dislike."

To summarize what is hard to convey, even in the most suggestive quotations from writing that builds up its effect cumulatively, Caryll Houselander was living in the real world, a world of selfishness and graft, a world of homosexuals and prostitutes, a world of incredible heroes broken on its tough rack, a world of flowers growing on ash heaps and stars illuminating the darkest nights. Because she herself really did live in this world, above all because she did see the stars and the flowers as well as the dirt and darkness, she was able to help men and women struggling with their own sins and hurt by the sins of others.

3

The validity of these insights was proved not merely by the sales of her books but by the people who came to Caryll for help even before the books were written, and got it so abundantly that they in turn sent others. It was proved by the doctors who sought her aid with their patients, by the priests who asked her counsel. From the early thirties this personal vocation became evident: individuals came to her for guidance, those, especially, most conscious of the continual strain of life as we live it today.

In 1942 doctors began to send her patients for social therapy: neurotics and psychotics. First came children, sent chiefly by Dr. Strauss, later President of the British Psychological Society; and presently adults from him and other doctors. Her power of calming an actual lunatic raving in a padded cell has been described to me by the matron of England's largest mental hospital, but the more important part of her work was the steady rebuilding of confidence, the restoration of hope to the despairing, of vitality to those drained of even the wish to live. "She loved them back to life," said Dr. Strauss.

It was a work of love certainly, but of love aided by understanding—and by that strange and interesting faculty, extrasensory perception. People who had tried strange remedies for mental anguish, such as occultism or diabolism, occasionally sought her out and at least once the police asked her aid in rescuing victims of such practices. While I have been lucky in my contacts with priests and doctors I have met no policemen who knew Caryll Houselander, so this remains in my memory only as one of her "good stories," told, perhaps, with dramatic exaggeration. To her it was not an experience of such importance as many far less apparently spectacular. After her books, the fullest use of her special powers is to be found in a vast correspondence. Arising chiefly from the books, the letters were often an expansion of the same ideas—but always specially geared to the character and circumstances of her correspondent. It is amazing how well they too are written—with "the right word, the telling word that left you gasping." They are never scamped or hurried, even when she was writing them at two in the morning and her rather remarkable cat was pushing the pen in an endeavour to send her to bed. For, in the later years, trying to meet all the demands upon her she sometimes cut her nightly sleep to four or even to three hours.

Reading the letters has taught me more about Caryll Houselander than anything else. I hope one day to publish them, but meanwhile readers of her books may be interested to meet the writer, not only through the necessarily incomplete record given by letters but as seen through the eyes of her many devoted friends, and of the few people who ardently disliked her. There seems no middle manner about her.

Determined "unthink" can do much, and there is no doubt that an imaginary Caryll Houselander built entirely of sweetness and light is enthroned in many hearts. This is not the woman I am writing about. Vision may make achievement harder instead of easier. Caryll saw her own shortcomings, sins, insufficiencies with even more piercing clarity than those of others. She was not offering help to her readers as the fruit of her own victory but inviting them to join her in a battle that she was fighting to the very end of her life. It was from conscious weakness, not from strength, that she brought to others the power of God's love.

"Broken across psychologically," as she herself said, quite early in life, she suffered from neuroses, from an overpowering realization of past sin, from struggles against fierce temptation, from waves of near despair. When she had conquered so much else, her keen critical faculty made charity of the tongue difficult: she made nothing of giving "all her goods," her time, her services. During the war and after, she gave away her rations, she "offered her body to be burnt" in voluntary fire-watching by night, shivering with fear and exhaustion after a long day at the First Aid post. She never refused anything—her time, money, energy, sympathy—but for the state of the heart described by St. Paul as the essence of charity she could only pray and strive unremittingly. She was not by nature patient, kind, gentle, but one of those people rather bitterly described as "too clever by half." After some work of charity that missed no delicacy of service, emptied out by a total self-giving, she would be assailed by the longing to analyse the situation and the people; she did this with a singular skill that left little room for the charity that believes and hopes all things.

Yet, too, she often saw the good that was hidden, and one letter describes her discovery of the possible splendour of someone she keenly disliked. It was there to be called forth by prayer and self-sacrifice. Caryll Houselander proved, in fact, her own point about human nature. She had not got rid of the faults inherent in her qualities. Her powers of description brought fantasy and imagination in their train; the poet and the artist in her saw the heart of a situation truthfully, but you could not always rely on accuracy as to the details. She dramatized unconsciously, yet one learnt more from her of the inner reality of things than from the minor facts—what Browning calls their "very superficial truth."

The biographer needs all the facts however superficial, so I have been careful to check her impressions with those of others who lived through the same years in her company and knew all that happened to her as well as knowing her.

There is nothing to explain Caryll Houselander in the background of her childhood, her early experiences and surroundings, unless perhaps profound reaction. Her mother played on the centre court at Wimbledon, her father was a keen huntsman. She herself hated riding and loathed sport of every kind. At two schools she eluded, by luck or skill, any education they had to offer. Both were convents, each in its own way conventional; and while French piety suited her better than English, she was from the beginning, and increasingly all through her life, unable to fit into convention. Dr. Strauss called her "that divine eccentric." Chesterton, who never saw her, might have proved conclusively that she seemed eccentric only because so many of us are off centre; and during the Blitz, and after, she was for many a centre of sanity.

I shall try to tell what is certainly an unusual story, using when possible her own words, those poems especially which she called Rhythms and which meant for her an entering into that vast Rhythm of the Universe of which she had become aware. She saw shapes already present in the wood she carved which only needed to be made visible to others. She saw the image of God in men's souls that only needed to be made visible to themselves and to others. She learnt to carve wood for a livelihood, but very soon she turned from carving wood to shaping language with a skill that I can only envy.

1

Background
for Caryll

CARYLL HOUSELANDER OFTEN dwelt on the dislocating effect for a child of a broken home, and hers was broken when she was still very young.

Yet when Willmott Houselander fell in love with Gertrude Provis on the hunting field their marriage seemed to promise great happiness. Willmott was one of a large family living at a fine old house, Wick Court, not far from Bristol. "A handsome, rollicking family," says a friend, Marguerite Fedden, who still remembers those far-off days. "Willmott was a jolly fellow, full of jokes and very humorous. Old Mr. Houselander, Willmott's father, made one think of the typical English hunting squire. A fine figure of a man—tall and well-built. . . . They were fond of hunting and sport, and hard riders. The mother was gentle and quiet, but the father had a reputation for strong language. One day he was driving down Saltford Hill and met my mother, and began to talk to her. She quietly said, 'Nothing in the B's and D's please, Mr. Houselander!' "

Gertrude Provis Miss Fedden describes as "a horsey, sporting type—fair hair, wonderful blue eyes that looked you through and through, and a fine figure—humorous, good style, a great personality.

"One Christmas she and others came to Midnight Mass with me at St. John's, Bath. She was very much intrigued with the confessionals and peeped in, laughing quietly, and making jokes.

"I could hardly believe my ears when I heard later she had become a Catholic: it seemed so unlikely then."

As Caryll's mother brought her up, she figures much more in the story of her life than Willmott, so I am writing a little about him here, both because I often felt the effect upon Caryll of his influence (even when she revolted against it) and also because he was an interesting and arresting person whose conversation I much enjoyed and who brought back a remote and tantalizing past.

It was after Caryll's death that I first met him; her mother was dead, but they had been apart for nearly half a century. He described vividly how he had fallen in love. She had been, he said, a magnificent rider, and he contrasted her seat on a mettlesome and even dangerous horse with the riding of some of the titled ladies of the Devon and Somerset Hunt. It was, however, her tennis that won for Gertrude Provis the brief but shining fame of the centre court at Wimbledon, where she once won the mixed doubles. Miss Fedden thinks she spent her honeymoon playing tennis, which may not have entirely pleased her new husband.

The more I saw of Willmott Houselander the more I endorsed the description of him as worthy of a place in the gallery of England's eccentrics. He boasted of his descent from a Dutch pirate who ended his life hung in chains on an English dock. Willmott himself lived to be ninety, but he was a mere eighty-seven when he told me of his own boyhood. Sitting in his little flat with a budgerigar perched on his head, he drew my attention to the rather profane language he had taught the bird to utter. Its companion had been schooled by his housekeeper—much to his disgust—to announce, "I'm Elsie's darling," and he was now keeping the birds apart lest this sentimental utterance should contaminate his own pupil.

Yet Willmott did not really lack sentiment, and Elsie was a proof of it. He had sent money year after year to a cripples' home to give one of the children a summer holiday. Elsie had been the one chosen; grown up, she arrived at his flat, bringing with her a wooden leg (which she refused to wear), and offering to work for him for nothing. Willmott, of course, paid as well as employing her, and her skill was astonishing, as she not only stumped about on a crutch cleaning the flat, but even contrived in an emergency to climb a ladder. One friend spoke of her to me as "the performing flea." The wooden leg she always kept in a cupboard.

She provided a sumptuous tea, and Willmott added the choice of gin or sherry, which he affirmed was of a vintage used at Buckingham Palace, got by him at an astonishingly cheap price—for some reason I could not quite follow. He loved to boast of his various bargains.

There were many clocks in the room, mostly picked up at Seton Market—a sort of local Petticoat Lane and also food market—and when they chimed one had to sit silent while Willmott timed them, watch in hand: "Boom, boom, boom; bing, bing, bing; bong, bong, bong," they went, sometimes coinciding, sometimes disagreeing. There was a radio and later two television sets, one labelled B.B.C., the other I.T.V. During sporting programmes he sat in front of both sets with his field glasses up, a woollen cap on his head, and his budgerigar on the woollen cap. Forbidden by his doctor to drink, he liked to ply his friends and it took no alcohol to set him going.

He loved to talk of how pleasurable a life he had had. At the age of three he had (he declared) bought his first mount

—a donkey—for five shillings, at eight he and another boy kept beagles, at seventeen he was a Hunt secretary and not long afterwards Master. He told of driving Mr. Vanderbilt's private coach from London to Brighton and teaching him English ways of coaching—less complicated harness, ostlers less strikingly dressed, heavier horses than in the States. For this one day's work, for him a delightful outing, Mr. Vanderbilt gave him a cheque for £100.

The tide of memories flowed on, interesting, stimulating, amusing—and the budgerigar hopped about, perching now on the window ledge, now on Willmott's head, making its commentaries, which (perhaps fortunately) I found hard to follow.

Caryll used to visit her father every Sunday, usually accompanied by her friend Iris Wyndham. She had an odd shyness of seeing him alone and liked to take a friend with her, and the old man enjoyed an audience for his stories and his birds. When Caryll died he refused to come to her funeral but he sent a cheque for £100 to cancer research. After Caryll's death Iris continued the visits—and also the long daily telephone talks which he used to have with Caryll after he had insisted on installing a telephone in her flat; when she was in the country a daily letter to Iris took the place of the talks. He haunted Seton Market and loved to collect bargains, which he would give to all his friends. Iris would return from visits to his flat laden with improbable objects: a brass door-knocker, a framed picture of the Prussian eagle in bead work, an enormous crocodile-skin dressing case, an umbrella stand, a hat rack shaped like deer's antlers, second-hand clothes, salmon and pork, gin and whiskey, a clock that chimed all the way home.

The stall holders became fond of the old man, and when he was taken ill a Jewish woman came round to see how he was, and finding he really needed a nurse, but absolutely refused to have one, sat up with him all night. Summoned

by Elsie early next morning, Iris arrived to find the stall
holder in the kitchen and Willmott, who had struggled from
his bed to the sitting room, watching television. He was
carried back to bed cursing and protesting by the doctor and
two porters. When Iris came in he said, "Open the cupboard,
damn you; there's a bottle of gin and a bottle of whiskey
there for you."

When I visited him Willmott had taken great trouble to
impress upon me his own atheism—indeed to shock me by it.
But in these last days of his life, when Iris said to him that he
looked better after a visit from his elder daughter, he said, "It
isn't that, it's God."

From the end of Willmott Houselander's life I shall now
go back to the beginning of Caryll's.

2

Childhood

IN A ROCKING-HORSE CATHOLIC, Caryll has told the story
of her arrival in this world (on October 29th, 1901), "so
small and so odd, and so like a tiny red fish, that it seemed
that I should either be drowned in the baptismal waters or
swim away in them." Her mother's brother, Francis Provis,
a gynaecologist, had asked the clergyman to come to the
house, but when he demanded the child's name, both mother
and uncle were overcome by hysterical giggles—for neither
had thought of naming this scrap of humanity "that would
not live for twenty-four hours." Her uncle, who was to be
the godfather, "spluttered out" his own name, Francis, and
the name of a yacht—the *Caryll*—on which her mother had
spent some time. But they could not stop laughing, and the
angry clergyman, refusing to officiate, swept out of the house,
leaving Caryll's uncle to perform the baptism himself.

Caryll's earliest memories were of that loveliest of small
towns, Bath, "ringed with hills, and always in the evening
filled by the sound of melodious church bells . . . too old a
city to grow older."

She seems to have been almost from infancy alive to
beauty: the bells, her father's rose garden: "something apart,
something enchanted and mysterious and unimaginably

beautiful. . . . You came into it by a low and narrow wooden door let into one of the walls. . . . It seemed to me, as a very tiny child, to be miles and miles of roses, and even a roof of roses above my head, through which, when I looked up, I could see tiny patches of blue sky, glimpsed through their red and gold and white and countless shades of cream and orange and pink of a world entirely filled with roses."

Later on she was to see in this door an image of the doorway of humility leading to the Kingdom of Heaven—"a very low narrow door made from the wood of the Cross." But now she was merely enchanted by the roses, and by the multitudinous pets of her grandfather's old groom, Bill: the cosiest of cats "that looked like and purred like round black kettles," a parrot declared by him to be more than a hundred years old, rabbits in hutches, and a very old fat pony kept as a pet and regaled with "beer by the bucketful" and lumps of sugar soaked in whiskey. Bill appeared to Caryll, when later she saw a picture of God the Father cloud-surrounded, to be exactly like Him; only his clothes were different. He had a wife who baked scones and cakes for the children and gave them great packets of goodies to take away.

Partly because when she left Bath this very old man, himself perhaps almost the same age as he attributed to his parrot, was still alive, he seemed to her touched with immortality. "Even now, I can hardly believe that if I went back to Bath, and climbed the little terraced hill to his cottage, I should not find Bill Reynolds there still, with his little pixie wife, his cats and his fat pony; Bill Reynolds, who was the genius of the old grey city ringed with hills and rocked with bells."

As with so many children in those still almost Victorian days, Caryll's memory of the staff, the stern man-servant, strongly disapproving of Catholicism, who escorted them to church, the rosy nurse whose little niece, flaxen-haired and dressed in pale blue, won her heart, are in the foreground of the picture. Next to the rose garden, her keenest memory was of being blown off a pile of luggage at a station and floating briefly through the air—an experience like flying, to be renewed often in dreams in her later life. But, very near it, came that of composing poetry long before she could write, and sitting on her father's knee while he wrote it down for her:

I used to make up and say my "poems" aloud, for my own pleasure, and later as a futile effort to distract my father and stop him from discovering that I had given his dinner to poor men who used to beg at our door! My poor father always wanted his pie as well as my poem, but all the same he wrote a few of them down, as I could not. They were usually stories in verse (of sorts). But the first of all was of an ethical nature. . . .

> Let's all be a jolly lot.
> Let no one be forgot.
> We can't be a jolly lot
> If anyone is forgot.

This effort was when I was three—a horrid, horrid infant prig.

Caryll had no brothers and only one sister, four years older than herself, now Mrs. Morrah, doing most valuable work as a magistrate in juvenile courts. She had written to my husband when Caryll died of having been devoted to her, "though she and I were never very intimate; as I know too well from my experience in juvenile courts, an unhappy family background spoils all happy normal relationships. Consequently she and I were always shy of each other, though in trouble we should always have held together."

In rather a different mood Mrs. Morrah said, when she and I met, "You know I'm the Devil's Advocate." This office is often held by sisters and brothers and is, as I assured her, a very useful one.

"Caryll was a most frightful little exhibitionist," she said. And then, in the same breath, "One of the most amusing and engaging creatures, an unequalled wit. But her bonnet was full of bees."

Her first memory of Caryll is of herself being brought down in a spinal chair to see "Baby," aged two, who was wearing an upstanding bonnet circled with marabout on her red hair, and on her nose the spectacles that she would never be able to do without.

Even more vividly she recalled her at the age of five sitting under a table, crying and crying.

"What's the matter, Baby?"

"It's my husband, he's coming back from the sea and he always beats me."

Despite the age gap the two children would play together, and Ruth remembers especially playing at "church." "It was in the lavatory, and we pulled the chain for the bell."

I think the "feel" of Caryll's childhood is given more fully in an unpublished "rhythm" called "Ghosts and Memories" than even in *A Rocking-Horse Catholic*. This rhythm was not written as biography, but its intensity is that of things experienced:

> Let us walk for a time
> among ghosts and memories.
>
> There was a world once
> painted with primary colours
> out of a child's paint-box
> on a white and empty page.
>
> There was childhood once,
> when the self-love of innocence
> was as bland and shadowless
> as water poured in a white cup.

And there was a father
who was God:
a God who sat in his arm-chair,
smoking his old pipe that was sacred;
a father whose presence
was the rock
that the home was built on.

And a mother,
whose laughter in the distances of the house
was reassurance;
whose kiss was benediction,
accepted,
like a peasant's superstition,
in the defenceless trust
of ignorance.

Dearer than Mother,
and closer than Father,
was Nurse!
She was warmth,
she was a glass of milk and a sugar biscuit,
firelight moving upon the nursery wall,
warm water
and rocking,
the smell of treacle in bread and milk,
the night light, a bulb of gold
in a green saucer.

There was also the young governess,
in whose presence
the wrists became weak with love;
who told us the stories of Hans Andersen
in a voice soft as the summer waves
creaming sands that gleamed
with a lustre of dark pearl.

And the old dog
with inexhaustible patience,
whose friendship exceeded
that of all other friends.

Do you remember tea in the kitchen?
With Cook and Ellen,
and Ellen's young man
when he was home from the sea?—
the brown sugar spread on the bread and butter,
and tea, as sweet as sryup
and strong as beer?

And do you remember
the splutter of light, splashing and sparkling
out of the dining-room door
when it opened and shut again,
while we leaned over the stairs
in our dressing-gowns,
to glimpse the grown-up's world
from a dark well,
and if we were able
to snatch a crumb
from the rich man's table?

Come, let us walk for a time
among ghosts and memories.
Let us forget
that not only home was lost,
not only Father and Mother
(Home,
and Father
and Mother
were God).

Ruth Morrah remembers vividly both their nurse and the
governess Caryll was so fond of, "Miss Dewar. We called her

Dewey. She was a wonderful governess and she protected us to some extent."

I fancy Caryll was not so much aware as her sister of the need for protection in those years before the break-up. The four years difference in age is an immense gap between five and nine, between nine and thirteen. Ruth believes they were both aware of the state of things between their parents —but in *A Rocking-Horse Catholic* as well as in the rhythm Caryll speaks as though it had come as a sudden shock.

Nothing is so mysterious as memory. I have a brother five years younger than myself, and as we talk of our youth we might well, as a listener once observed, have come from two different homes. It is not only remembering different happenings but remembering them in a different atmosphere. So it is with Caryll and Mrs. Morrah. To the elder sister it seems that Caryll, talking of her childhood, "saw the past through the eyes of her present"—but then, who does not? It is a question not only of what happened, but of what you in particular saw. I remember things my brother forgets, he remembers things I forget—yet we both have unusually good memories. We are inclined, too, each to assume that the other *must* remember, must have seen, must have felt the same. Does this mean that it is impossible to get at the truth of anything? I do not think so. Usually the bits dovetail as in a jigsaw puzzle. There may be gaps left, questions unanswered; there need not be substantial contradiction.

Caryll's parents had their hands full enough at this time to induce them to keep the home going. For Ruth's very severe illness was followed by the strange, probably psychological, illness of Caryll herself.

The Houselanders had moved to Brighton, and there, under two very different influences, Mrs. Houselander had decided to have the children baptized into the Catholic Church. Practising no religion herself, she was deeply impressed by Dr. Paley's family. Son of an Oxford Movement

convert, the doctor was bringing up his own children in an
atmosphere of simplicity, unworldliness and charity that she
immensely admired. On the intellectual side came the advice
of Mr. Justice Bower. An agnostic himself, he did not hesitate to tell her that the only conceivable heir to the Christianity of Christ and His immediate followers was Roman Catholicism. He argued the point as if it were a brief, and his own
influence on Caryll was, all through his life, powerful in the
same direction. Could he have accepted the Virgin Birth, he
would have been received then and there! As it was, first the
Houselander children were baptized, and a little later their
mother, under the influence of "Smoky," as they always
called him. Caryll was now six years old, and was baptized
without sponsors, standing on a chair to get her head above
the edge of the font.

Smoky's influence now became paramount; he read poetry
to Caryll, much of it above her head, but stored in her memory; he took her to Shakespeare plays as well as to *Peter Pan*.
He taught her history in story form; he provided altogether a
liberal education, and it was the only serious education she
ever received. In the summer he came to Brighton, in the
winter she was much with him and his wife in London.

But unfortunately, despite his power of apologetic, Smoky
was not versed in Christian theology, and Caryll had the mis-
fortune, so common then and now among the children of
semi-Catholic homes or uneducated Catholic parents, of not
learning those things she needed most to know. She could
spout Shakespeare by the yard before she was nine, but she
was, in the words of Robert Farren, "witless of the Trinity."

Caryll's mother stuffed the children with piety, causing
them to make little altars and to pray long prayers before
them—extra long for the benefit of clerical visitors. Caryll
would, when they had departed, get out of bed and, in front
of her statue of the Sacred Heart, tell God she was sorry for
the unreality of these prayers. Their mother would take the

children to church at this point as often as three time on a Sunday, pouring into her own devotions the energy previously devoted to tennis. But they learnt so little that though Caryll developed a real love of Our Lord, she made up for herself a theology in which He had been cruelly treated and subjected to all His sufferings by a vengeful God the Father. This idea was, she tells us, for many years in the background of her mind, and she makes an impassioned plea for deeper instruction for children, who can, she believes, be taught enough of the mystery of the Trinity to be saved from such distortions.

A proverb can be dangerous with the young—"as a small child," Caryll once wrote to a friend, "I used to eat earth and dirt from the garden path. My nurse frequently said (I was fastidious at table), 'You must eat a packet of dirt before you die.' As I considered death, and Heaven following Purgatory, very desirable, and the eating of dirt, owing to nurse's reiterated remark, as essential to salvation as baptism, I ate it, often resulting in sickness."

A sermon on hell heard at a mission nearly terrified her out of her wits, but with a deep religious sense which she always believed to be innate in children, she was comforted and strengthened by her First Communion, given her by this same missioner's advice at the earlier age just beginning to come in by direction of Pius X. It was the Feast of Our Lady of Mount Carmel, and Caryll was between eight and nine years old.

Between her first Communion and her second came her mysterious illness. Suddenly one day she found herself unable to move, and had to be carried upstairs and put to bed. The doctors could not diagnose her strange condition, which was clearly made far worse by the well-intentioned efforts on the spiritual side of her mother and of a priest who proved later to be himself suffering from mental sickness. She was tormented by a sense of guilt that she could neither explain nor get rid of. She confessed to both her mother and to the priest imaginary sins—and then confessed that she had invented them. This happened daily, indeed several times a day. She begged for Communion, saying that Our Lord would understand what she could not explain to them, but only after the doctors had said she was dying was her request granted. She had been lying, eyes closed, feeling the firelight that danced on the walls to be "like scalding water falling on an open wound. . . . I had realized in a dim, intuitive way that it was not something I had *done* that required forgiveness, but everything that I *was* that required to be miraculously transformed."

The priest asked for no further confession but recited for her the words of absolution, and then gave her the Host broken into fragments in sips of water:

I was instantly at peace—as if I had simply woken from a long nightmare to the security and blessedness of a sunlit morning. For a moment I remained, propped a little on the pillows, lying with my eyes closed; and it seemed indeed that a gentle, golden radiance shone through my thin eyelids and suffused my whole being, as the warmth and light of the sun penetrates and suffuses the earth, quickening the seed to flower.

Then when I opened my eyes I saw that the golden light was from the candles burning on the little altar by my bed, and the firelight that now lit the whole room with dancing flames. But the beauty of fire and light no longer hurt me, I could respond to it, and this response to beauty and the joy of being wholly alive was my "thanksgiving."

I sat up. This seemed to alarm the priest, who told me to lie down again.

I said, "No, I am going to sit up."

"But you *can't* sit up!"

"I *am* sitting up. Please bring my toy soldiers on a tray."

"But you must lie down and make your thanksgiving!" The priest seemed increasingly alarmed.

He went out of the room and called my mother. She was even more alarmed than he, and I was exhorted to say my prayers in case, if I did not, I started "worrying" again.

"I shall never worry again."

In the end, the toy soldiers were brought to me, but they were put on the altar by the bedside, and I went to sleep.

On the following day Smoky arrived from London. He was the only person who accepted the fact that a miracle had occurred. "Damn it all," he said in my hearing to the devout Catholics who were vying with each other in their attempts to explain the miracle away. "Damn it all, it takes an old agnostic like me to believe in God!"

3
School Days

CARYLL HOUSELANDER WAS RELATED to Samuel Butler, author of *The Way of All Flesh*. An old uncle, she told me, used to say that she must have Butler "beaten out of her." Was this, I wonder, the uncle who baptized her, and did he hope to wash her soul of cynicism as well as of original sin? If so, he did not fully succeed.

Caryll often said how valuable her illness had been in teaching her compassion for mental sufferers; but compassionate as she became, with an intensity indeed of compassion, she never lost an equally intense critical faculty. For her writing this was well; at moments it verges on the sentimental, to be sharply saved by an almost icy realism. But her own path was made more thorny by her power of critical insight, and she speaks of herself as having been, when she went to school, "hard and sour as a green apple, eaten up with self-pity, and in revolt against the whole world." The photo of her sent me by the nuns of her first boarding school is the face of one who is looking, weighing and judging. And the only girl who appeared intimate with her at her second school said, "It was only because she seemed so lonely that I made friends with her. She was introspective and inclined to grouse about things in school life."

Caryll had never left home when she learned quite suddenly that her parents were going to separate, and her home come to an end. How deeply she was wounded I only fully realized as I read after her death the long rhythm from which I have already quoted, "Ghosts and Memories." The rhythm does not in its detail correspond with the reality—the Houselander marriage, though in fact permanently broken, did not end in divorce, but in a separation. Mrs. Houselander's friends were, as Mrs. Morrah pointed out, not at all the fur-and-jewel type but outdoor and "horsey"; the nurse had already left and the governess taken her place. In *A Rocking-Horse Catholic* the story is told more prosaically in prose; in the rhythm the sense of catastrophe is overwhelming.

Caryll had told me how she listened silently to discussions of what was happening to her parents—of what *would* happen to her and her sister. Often, she said, people who would be silent when the older sister was there, spoke in her presence—and once she heard, "You needn't mind her. She is not very bright and doesn't know what it's all about." But in silence the child was judging them bitterly:

> There was a whispering in the house—
> "For the sake of the children!"
> There was a whispering on the stairs,
> whispering in the chink of the door,
> whispering in the curtains,
> whispering in the cupboards;
> the house was whispering,
> whispering like the flitter of mice.
> There was whispering in the walls,
> whispering in the tables,
> whispering in the chairs,
> whispering in the passage,
> "For the sake of the children,
> for the children's sake!"

Whispering, whispering, whispering,
like the flitter of mice
the whisper of lies.

The children did not whisper or weep,
they were aloof,
and walked with eyes averted
from Father and Mother
and one another.
They did not speak
of their terrible, shared,
yet unshared secret,
to one another.
They did not mention the fact
that everyone in the house was dead.

Not a word was said above stairs,
but down in the kitchen,
red in the heat of the fire
and damp with the foetid emotion
of relished pity,
Cook wept happily
like a saucepan boiling over
and spilling salty water
to hiss on the stove.

And Ellen grew broody
with envy,

                .   .   .   .

melting until she was shapeless
and her fingers covered with witlows—
longing for carnal love,
and her sailor who was at sea.

Upstairs
the grown-up people were furtive.
They dared not look into the children's faces
and see the accusation

even in the averted,
shadowless eyes.

"For the sake of the children!
For the sake of the children!"
The house whispered with lies.

The grown-up people were guilty.
They started,
when children came in quietly
on sandalled feet.
The ash-trays were filled
over and over again
with obscene cigarette-ends
stained with a red smear,
and the grown-up people's fingers
were yellow with nicotine.

The women who came to tea, in the drawing-room,
fumbled with jewelled fingers
at the the locked doors of the children's souls.
Those women with blue-veined hands,
with soft, white, blue-veined hands,
who are kind to be cruel.
They wanted to stir the stagnant waters
of their exhausted passions
by spurious compassion.
The children were silent,
possessing themselves
in the dignity of their outraged grief.

They suffered the insolent questions,
the overpowering scent,
the odious touch of furs
and the curiosity
and the crass stupidity:
"All little children,
and all little dogs,

love me.
They know who loves them,
you see!"

The children were dumb,
they bled.

Not a word was said
when Nurse packed her tin trunk secretly,
but fear seeped into the house
in a fog—
fear without shape or sound,
fear that they breathed
and felt damp on their faces
and smarting behind their eyes.

If Nurse had said,
"I am going away!"
they would have suffered it
in the clear light of day.
Who can not suffer, and live,
in the light of day?

But Nurse was blind
with her own blistering tears,
and the blindness of those
who spare pain to be kind.
They knew she was going away
without saying goodbye!

They wondered,
without a word to one another,
For how many nights will Mother
kiss us goodnight
with a dead painted mouth,
before she sends *us* away?
On what day
will the sun go out?
on what night

will ashes hang in the sky
for stars?—
when will the flowers
grow already withered
and grey in the woods?

Yes, they were to be sent away, and Caryll wrote several versions of the scene at the station, which ended in the little French convent at Olton:

This is the beginning of a journey
fittingly at a railway station.
We are going a long way,
though to the closed mind
it seems
it is only a child
going to school for the first time.
This is the start.
Heaven or Hell
is the destination.
The platform swarms;
there are girls
overripe in their adolescence
like plums overripe on a tree,
and those
who by a miracle
are slender and lovely
and melt the others,
turning their bones to water
and parting them willingly
from slightly outraged fathers and mothers,
while others,
new girls too, weep unashamedly.
But this,
the child who is dispossessed,
turned out of the garden of Eden,
dry-eyed and hard
goes dispassionately

without a word or a tear,
dressed in the school clothes,
a coat buttoned down the front
and a hard round hat,
like Mr. and Mrs. Noah in Noah's ark,
and legs that are unfamiliar
in long black stockings
hiding the knees
that only recently
Nurse washed in a warm bath.

Well—at last the train is moving
and going;
thank Heaven for that.
The child has gone,
and the others whisper and nudge,
"That new girl's father and mother
are being divorced.
It was in the paper—"

She is alone.

Did she go off all right?
Oh yes, not a tear out of her,
not a word,
not even goodbye.
I fear she's a most unnatural child—
perhaps it is just as well.
After all,
she must fend for herself
on the journey to Heaven or Hell.

To Caryll's account of how she loved Olton Convent her
sister takes strong exception. "We hated it," she says. And
again, "Honest truth, she was not happy at Olton. Really she
was more unhappy than I was. But she was more detached.
She had an inner life she could lead."

Caryll, as well as Ruth, was almost certainly unhappy during the first terms and holidays at Olton. For the holidays too were spent at school, while the other children would go off joyfully with their parents. Mrs. Morrah remembers a line from a hymn she grew to hate, "Take Thou and bless our holiday"; she remembers trying to find convincing lies to hide the facts from their schoolfellows. Caryll and she never discussed it with one another.

There is an early poem in which Caryll pays tribute to the bishop on Prize Day and thanks also

> The Reverend Mother
> Whose children one and all do love her

This is annotated by her: "N¡B. This poem was written to order, it is full of hipocrysy" [sic]. The part about the bishop was "all right," but the other lines should be changed to

> The Reverend Mater
> Whose children one and all do hate her.

But Mrs. Morrah gave me a quantity of Caryll's school-time writings in an unformed hand and astonishing spelling, including other verses which show a change already beginning, but perhaps only completed later. She speaks of herself in *A Rocking-Horse Catholic* as having been only nine, but she was in fact eleven, when she went to school. And the two years that followed are often the most formative in a lifetime. There are verses written to Roosey, her teddy-bear (to whom she remained devoted all her life).There is a spirited account of a parrot who successfully summoned the fire brigade to a nonexistent conflagration. There is a wry but good-humoured complaint of a money present sent her by an aunt —and banked for her by her elders:

> My dear Aunt May,
> I write today
> you for that money to thank.
> But I call it a shame
> and frightfully tame:
> they've put it in the bank.

Besides the papers in Caryll's writing are copies, either typewritten or in an obvious nun's hand, the odd spelling corrected. There must have been a strong friendship between one of the nuns and this child. Mrs. Morrah says she was the only English nun in the convent, in poor health and much in a room of her own where she encouraged Caryll to visit her. But it is certain too, both from what Caryll used to say and from what she wrote about her childhood, that, her initial resistance once broken down, she became devoted not to this nun alone but to the Reverend Mother and the whole convent. Her hatred turned to love, and with that love came healing.

Thinking over Caryll's character lately, I found myself saying, "She was not really reserved, though she was sometimes remote." And in this convent remoteness was respected. As far as possible in the world of school, regimentation was avoided. The Reverend Mother, stern to herself and perhaps to her nuns, brooded lovingly over the children, one as tiny as three years old, many from broken homes or unhappy homes. Personal individual piety was encouraged; the nuns themselves were seen by their pupils as real people— people who could quarrel, whose feelings were known to them. They suited Caryll and she suited them. She saw beauty in the whiteness of the dormitory curtains, in the very plainness of the chairs and tables; she enjoyed the feasts when roses were arranged on the children's tables, and the smell of coffee and fresh baked rolls greeted them in the refectory. She learned the lesson that became a great part of her own special message—that fasts are needed as well as feasts, and that sacrifice brings joy. Later she would lose—or perhaps mislay is a better word—something of what these nuns gave her. But writing of those bitter years she could end her saddest rhythm on a note of joy, because God's presence became vivid once more in the Olton convent.

One learns little from *A Rocking-Horse Catholic* of secular lessons at this convent, but much of heavenly ones, and of the healing of a child's wounded heart. During the holidays, Caryll was much with the community, joining in the Recreations, helping to stone plums for jam, walking in the garden with the Reverend Mother, collecting eggs with the lay sisters. Again the atmosphere is conveyed best in the rhythms, published and unpublished: the blissful First Communion feasts, the calm routine of daily life, the child's outlook on the seasons of self-denial:

> It is November,
> the month of the Holy Souls.
> The Convent children
> are giving up sweets
> and making acts
> for the loneliest soul in Purgatory. . . .
>
> On Sister's shelf in the school shop
> rows of glass bottles of boiled sweets
> tempt.
> Lollipops,
> orange-coloured and lemon
> and raspberry colour,
> and acid drops
> that are sugary, flat and white.
> When you take the red ones
> out of your mouth
> and hold them up to the light,
> they are clear, glowing rubies,

and your tongue is bright
like a burning flower.
This delight
is all foregone
for the loneliest soul of all,
the neglected, forgotten one,
whom no one (they think)
but Form II B
prays for at all. . . .

Sister Martha of the Holy Shroud,
while she does her darning
in the evening,
tells the Convent children
lurid stories
of the suffering souls
in Purgatory. . . .

Imelda,
who is youngest in II B,
bows her head and slowly
takes an orange sweet out of her mouth,
for so can sinners save
a little sorrow for the very holy
people in the grave.

Visiting the Olton convent I found two nuns who remembered the Houselanders—the present Reverend Mother and
a very old lay sister. It is now a vast building—or buildings,
a day school only, with five hundred girls. Only one French
nun is left. In Caryll's first year the numbers of boarders and
day children together reached fifty; before she left there were
eighty, nineteen of them boarders. The dormitories were
tiny, and Caryll would take Roosey to bed with her and talk
through him to the other children. The nun in charge would
hear a voice from her cubicle.

"Silence, Caryll."

"It's only Roosey, Mère, talking to me and me answering him."

The lay sister was in charge of the *boutique,* as the school shop was called, and dispensed the highly coloured boiled sweets which so fascinated Caryll. She remembers her as "very dreamified," always in a world of her own, but "very, very witty: Ruth was the lively one. But once you saw Caryll you never forgot her."

Presently came the First World War—to a convent full of French women, with many French children there and Belgian refugees arriving in a state of excitement bordering on delirium. One of Caryll's patriotic hymns was set to music and sung by nuns and girls, making her head swell, she confesses, "to the size of a Zeppelin." I have seen all these effusions. They no more expressed the real Caryll than the socks or mufflers she so notably failed to complete while the rest of the school poured them off their needles.

Yet in these and other mediocre verses of hers printed in the school magazine lines suddenly stand out:

> The unenthusiastic rave
> The peaceful will to fight

is surely surprising coming from a child. And also:

> A dreamy span of sorrowing years
> Is the passing thing which we call time.

Apart from such flashes Caryll's verse, like her handwriting and her teddy-bear, shows her at eleven and twelve very young for her age.

Food grew scarce and became more and more uneatable. Looking back, Caryll saw the nuns as sacrificing themselves and their children almost too willingly on the altar of patri-

otism. Once at least she let them know what she felt. A voice
was heard from her dormitory:

"I didn't like my supper."

"Hush, Caryll."

"I didn't speak, Mère. It was Roosey. I liked my supper
very much."

Caryll disposed of the uneatable food, passing it under
the table to her hungry neighbours. She was in fact already
ill, though the school doctor failed to diagnose it. He thought
her naughty—or neurotic, which, as she notes, was in those
days regarded as the same thing—and ordered her to eat and
play games. The Reverend Mother, with a deeper insight
than the doctor, kept Caryll with herself a good deal in the
garden, made her stay in bed, or let her work gently at art,
which she much enjoyed. It was only after she returned home
in a state of great weakness that her uncle decided to perform
an exploratory operation which revealed a diseased appendix
of long standing and resultant complications.

But before this happened had come the first spiritual insight of a kind that Caryll would continue to experience all
through her life.

Perhaps it is a pity that she ever used the word "vision,"
although she was careful to put it in quotation marks. And
she explains that she does not mean anything seen with the
bodily eyes—but something intensely realized with the mind.
Caryll was both intellectual, in the sense in which the word is
commonly used for one who thinks things out step by step,
and also immensely intuitive. She would leap to the realization of all that an idea involved, while those of slower mind
would still be plodding along the road of trial and error. I
see I have used again the word realization—and I think it is
the best word for these intuitions which can, too, be called
with profound reality *mental* visions. Her three first experiences brought ever widening realization of a doctrine that
she had not yet learned theologically: Christ's indwelling in

man—the doctrine of His Mystical Body, actual and potential, still being built out of men and women.

Too wide a gulf has perhaps been set between the apprehension of divine reality reached by the ordinary Christian and that of the mystic. The truths of faith are objective realities, and whether we apprehend them by faith, by a process of reasoning, by intuition, or by vision, they remain equally objective and equally true. By all these ways combined, we still cannot *fully* understand any truth of revelation proposed to our faith by the infinite mind of our Creator. In eternity we shall have direct vision, but here on earth, where God graciously gives us a beginning of knowledge, it seems almost ungrateful to worry ourselves about whether that beginning was made along the road traced for us by St. Thomas Aquinas or the road of St. John of the Cross.

The first time Caryll "saw" the indwelling of Christ in man was before she left the French convent, and in rather curious circumstances. The nuns, all but two, were French. There was one Englishwoman and one nun from Bavaria, who knew little English and spoke very bad French. She made no real contacts with the children and had "unhappily no charm." Her loneliness, once the war began, was unimaginable.

The story of this nun, Sister Mary Benedicta, is dramatic. The order, Reverend Mother told me, has now given up the institution of lay sisters. As Peter Maurin said when starting *The Catholic Worker,* the thinkers must learn to use their hands, the manual workers their heads. Based on education, the old division gives to the lay sisters almost all the hard and hidden physical work, while the choir nuns sing or recite the Divine Office, teach in the school, perhaps write books or in other ways make use of the liberal education which they have received. Usually, too, they bring with them a dowry for their support (in the Southern States of America, down to the Civil War, this dowry often included a slave or two).

But Sister Mary Benedicta was an educated, indeed a very cultured woman. Her father had been a professional violinist, she herself played well.

Nuns who had entered after Caryll left the school had vivid memories of this sister. She wore an old habit so patched and darned that nothing of the cloth seemed left. She chose the dirtiest jobs: one of them had seen her push her arm up a blocked and filthy drain to clean it. All agreed when Reverend Mother said she believed her to have been a saint.

"Did you know," one nun then said, "what she told me on her death bed? She had been in another convent and had left. She felt she had thrown away her vocation and decided in reparation to come here as a lay sister."

Perhaps the hardest part of the sacrifice was to have left not only family and home, but native land also. And now the war had brought a situation that must have been almost unendurable.

For French, even more than English, the German was the Hun, *the* hereditary foe, and now he was again invading their land. A map hung on the wall with little flags—moved every day as the German line advanced, marking now the home of one, now another of the community. The nuns tried hard to console their sister, telling her that Bavarian was not the same as Prussian, but even with them a sudden silence must have fallen when she came in, a glance of pity for the shame she was innocently sharing. For in that first war we all got relief in what we held to be a sheer duty. We sang our hymns of hate with the conviction of our own spotless chivalry and our enemy's embodiment of the forces of evil.

Nor did the local police make any distinction between Bavarian and Prussian when they visited the convent to interrogate an "enemy alien." Prejudice against nuns had diminished in this century since so many French exiles (including this community) came over in 1902 and had been teaching local children, but it was by no means dead. A spy dressed up as a Roman nun? What more likely?

Interrogation of a German who spoke no English could not be conducted easily and was not conducted kindly. To one who has given up home and family God does often seem to give in the community another home, and it must have been a climax of suffering when Sister Benedicta learned that the motherhouse of their order had been occupied by a Bavarian regiment.

The child Caryll knew nothing of this story, but she was, says Sister Marie Winifred, an unusually kind child. (Perhaps kind children are in fact unusual.) Certainly one cannot imagine anyone ever wanting to clean shoes: the prelude to this first experience of Caryll's must have been compassion for the lonely woman who was so hard to talk to. And, whatever name we call it by, it was her first lesson in what was to become the chief theme of her writings and the dominant force of her whole life:

One day I was passing the boot-room, the little room where our shoes were kept; the door was open, and the Bavarian nun was sitting alone, cleaning shoes. I can see her now as if it were yesterday—a tall, gaunt woman with brilliantly red cheeks and eyes so dark that they looked black: there she was, wearing her large, cobalt-blue apron, with a child's pair of shoes on her lap.

I stopped and went in, intending to help her to polish the shoes. It was only when I had come quite close to her that I saw that she was weeping; tears were running down her rosy cheeks and falling onto the blue apron and the child's shoes. Abashed, I dropped my eyes and stood in front of her, speechless with embarrassment, completely tongue-tied. I saw her large, toilworn hands come down onto her lap and fold on the little shoes, and even those hands, red and chapped, with blunted nails, were folded in a way that expressed inconsolable grief.

We were both quite silent, I staring down at her beautiful

hands, afraid to look up, not knowing what to say; she weeping
soundlessly.

At last, with an effort, I raised my head, and then—I saw—the
nun was crowned with the crown of thorns.

I shall not attempt to explain this. I am simply telling the
thing as I saw it.

That bowed head was weighed under the crown of thorns.

I stood for—I suppose—a few seconds, dumbfounded, and
then, finding my tongue, I said to her, *"I* would not cry, if I
was wearing the crown of thorns like you are."

She looked at me as if she were startled, and asked, "What do
you mean?"

"I don't know," I said, and at the time I did not.

I sat down beside her, and together we polished the shoes.

After Caryll's appendix operation she had two periods,
almost too brief to be worth mentioning, at non-Catholic
schools before she went to another convent. One was a vast
Council school where the children were known by numbers
instead of names. Caryll refused to answer to her number and
at the end of the week simply walked out, saying nothing to
her mother, but spending her days reading books in various
bookshops.

That she loved writing to the Olton nuns she tells us in *A
Rocking-Horse Catholic,* and during these unsettled months
she wrote (aged fourteen) a poem which appeared in the
school magazine. Two art students agree to paint a picture
which is to be their masterpiece, their subject "Joy." They
will meet again in ten years and decide whose picture is the
best. Roland goes abroad "to the land of all the Arts," and
returns covered with glory but "on his face the marks of
care," while "Raymond, still a happy lad, was shabby and
threadbare."

Roland has painted a marvellous picture, Raymond has no
masterpiece to show. But he takes his friend to a cottage in a
wood full of children, "happy, laughing, poor." He tells him
the story, how, at first:

> I painted, painted, every day,
> And my model, a fair little boy,
>   Sat posing as my "Joy,"
> With tears upon his cheeks.
>
> I sold my paints and canvass then,
> And went about the land,
> Painting JOY in the hearts of men,
>   Helped by God's master hand;
> And finding deserted children on my way,
>   I brought them to this little spot of peace
> To make them joyous here, that THEY
>   Might prove to be my masterpiece.

Caryll must have done a lot of thinking while lying in her bed at the hospital and browsing in London bookshops. The verse is immature enough, but the thought which led her from the crown of thorns seen on a nun's head to the gift of joy to be made to our neighbours would later inspire her work for both children and adults, and would give us all *The Comforting of Christ, The Flowering Tree,* and *The Reed of God.* Caryll was next sent to a small Protestant boarding school where, by doctor's orders, she was not to attend classes. How any school allowed this seems deeply mysterious—it was to happen again at her second convent. Not unnaturally the result was the misery of utter boredom. When her mother refused to remove her she wrote to Smoky, requesting the money for her return fare—which he promptly sent her. Smoky's influence must have been a powerful one. Caryll was not sent back to school, and the old readings with him began again, the old enchantment of his conversation. But Caryll really was a very sick child: despite the removal of her appendix, her old troubles came back: she could not eat; what she did eat she could not digest.

Mrs. Houselander was now living in London, but she decided to send Caryll to a small nursing home in Brighton where she could be under the care of Dr. Paley. His daughter

Molly (now Mrs. Draper) tells me how fond her father was
of Caryll, how concerned about her health: "He said she had
a rotten constitution. He thought she'd never have any
health at all, she had tubercular glands."

Molly Paley, a few years older than Caryll, remembers
her first as quite a tiny child, "a funny little carrotty thing."
They had nursery teas together, and she remembers, when
Caryll was about six, their nanny scolding her small brother
Raymond for getting treacle all over his face—"Nobody will
kiss you with a face like that"—and Caryll saying, "I'll kiss
your tweakly mouf, Way." When Caryll was about nine she
remembers seeing her coming out of church beaming. Molly
asked, "What are you so happy about?" "I've been telling
God a funny story."

It was to Molly's care that her father confided the task of
making this queer little girl happier and better adjusted to
life. For, as Caryll herself says, she had by now become not
only odd but self-conscious about her oddness. With Smoky
she was happy, and with the Paleys, who now introduced her
once more to a household where she could have the things
she loved—poetry, art and books—among people she loved
and was at home with.

The friendship with Molly Paley became later a very close
one, but at this time the age gap meant that, while deeply
admired by Caryll, she could not be her equal companion.
Dr. Paley felt, too, that Caryll must learn to adjust to a
wider life. There was a real risk of her becoming a chronic
invalid. Again her mother accepted his counsel, and Caryll
was sent to the Holy Child Convent at St. Leonard's.

Molly Paley sees Caryll's unhappiness at this period as
almost inevitable, given the immense contrast between her
and her mother. "Gert was as hard as nails: hard and loud,
game for anything. She was not deliberately unkind, but she
stamped on Caryll's feelings."

She was trying to do the best she could at this time for a

child who was not making it easy for her, but her efforts were often unintelligent. Considering Caryll's nostalgia for the Olton convent excessive, she had forbidden her to write to anyone there. Caryll seems to have obeyed, but it was certainly the surest way to start her off with a profound resistance to any other school—and Molly Paley thinks she is unfair to her new one in the sketch she gives of it in *A Rocking-Horse Catholic*. Caryll points out herself that her view was to some degree biased against the English convent by her intense love for the French one, and she speaks of a great main reason for admiring these other nuns and children— their charity. It seemed strange to her that so much should be made of the fact that a nun, entering the convent, kissed a loving goodbye to the horse whose companionship had meant so much of the happiness she was sacrificing. The addition that she had kissed *"not* her mother *but* the soft nose" of her horse means only that the farewell to the horse was what had impressed the school's imagination—and had irritated Caryll. To me it was equally bewildering to read the many, many letters in which Caryll, years later, described the anguish she felt over the death of her cat. I have never loved an animal, but if a cat why not a hunter?

The answer is that for Caryll this incident represented two things she especially loathed; sport, which was her mother's passion, and worldliness which she came to feel deeply permeated English Catholic life.

Was she right? There is, as the Abbé Mourroux has pointed out, an *osmosis,* a sort of atmospheric effect, produced by living in any society; it seeps into us without our being aware of what is happening. During the penal era, English Catholics were outside the national life; they were imprisoned, they died for the Faith, but they did not have to live it as full members of a society whose values are totally different.

It is much more difficult—though less painful—to avoid an atmosphere than to endure a persecution. We have been learning a lot about osmosis lately in quite another context. John Creasey points out in his book, *They Didn't Mean to Kill*, how road deaths have become so commonplace that they are regarded simply as an administration problem, with nobody expecting the administration to solve it, but only to keep the deaths within "moderate" figures. There is no public *feeling* about it, as about polio for instance. Yet, to take one single year, 1957—polio killed 255 people in Great Britain, road deaths were 5,550; polio killed 220 in the United States, road deaths were 38,500. To letters to the British Cabinet, asking for immediate action, only one Minister sent a personal reply. To rouse the public to a situation that *they* could remedy seems to John Creasey like talking to a nation of sleep-walkers who cannot wake up.

May it be that we Catholics are to some extent the same in our outlook towards this world and the next; that the liberty of spirit, of which the safeguard is eternal vigilance, has been at least impaired; that we have become *too* anxious to be full citizens of an impermanent city, and that there is value for us in the occasional sounding of an alarm?

Rightly or wrongly, Caryll felt that false values were seeping into English Catholic education. Sport was becoming primary, standing even higher than study, but both were valued chiefly because they spelt success. And, what seemed to her very serious, was a lack of realization of the position of the poorer children and parents. In those days the heavy burden of school uniforms was barely beginning—Caryll does not mention it; but the many subscriptions asked for quickly emptied her purse of the few shillings she had brought from a home that had become a very poor one.

Children are deeply sensitive, and Caryll was exceptionally so. Looking back, she criticizes severely her own lack of charity and praises that of her schoolfellows. She tells of a nun, prefect of the school, who, after stopping a letter of invective which she had written to Smoky, posted the re-

written letter without reading it and told her that she would
in future allow this correspondence to be sent and received
unread. As I well remember, only letters to parents were
normally thus privileged, and not all children could ask
their mothers to forward other correspondence. Certainly not
Caryll. She deeply appreciated this nun's kindness—but her
view remained, after warmest tribute to the deeply Christian
attitude towards a difficult child, that the school exemplified
in some respects the fact that the world is always seeping into
the Church, and that great vigilance is needed to keep it out.
And she felt rather specially that nuns did not *understand*
money—as that commodity appears to people forced to earn
a rather scanty living.

Some light is cast on Caryll's youth by Butler's *Way of All
Flesh*: like this relative of hers she brought a cool sarcastic
eye to bear on the contemporary scene, like him she was
aware of the ghastly lack of psychology in their elders from
which children so often suffered. Like him she saw how
necessary for the young is some handicraft, some contact with
the realities of matter. Like his hero she suffered acutely
from the financial problem of inadequate pocket money at
an expensive school.

Perhaps Butler's very contempt for the Christian religion
prevented his feeling any strangeness in its being so closely
bound up with the status quo—but anyhow he seems for a
reformer oddly happy with that status quo, as long as his
hero can get on the right side of it. Even simpler than those
of Dickens is Butler's solution of all the troubles of Ernest's
life, and of the lives dependent on him. Sufficient thousands
a year will solve all human troubles!

But what of those outside the magic circle of these thousands, what of the moral state of those inside? Anyone who
(unlike Butler) does believe in Christ and His teaching
must be troubled by a too great conformity with this world

on the part of His followers, and one is apt to become more keenly aware of this conformity when it presses on oneself.

Another memory was haunting me as I read *A Rocking-Horse Catholic*. So I reread *Frost in May*, by Antonia White. The two experiences are very closely parallel. Both girls became aware of an unconscious attitude on the part of nuns and girls, a superiority based on belonging to a "good" Catholic family, not merely good in the moral meaning of the word but in its social significance. Both felt that the world was profoundly present in the convent.

But both also felt that it was *not* the world of art, poetry, ideas. By an interesting coincidence both Antonia White's heroine and Caryll herself had their copies of Shelley confiscated. Caryll felt more strongly (I think) the predominance of the sporting element—but in Antonia's convent also (not Holy Child but Sacred Heart) stories were told of the nun who had ridden to hounds up to the time of entering and kissed her horse a tearful farewell. Entering as a nun the Helpers of the Holy Souls, one of my own aunts behaved in the same way. It is not unnatural for a country-bred girl, but she would have had to be a fairly rich one—and in the eyes of these two all the nuns seemed to come from, all the girls to belong to, rich families. And both felt that this was held, albeit unconsciously, to matter enormously.

Caryll does not analyse as fully as Antonia White another element which is certainly present in all convents—was probably even more present at Olton—which poses another fascinating problem for the Christian artist. The trend of convent education in those days was most certainly against the recognition of positive values in art, music, poetry, apart from their services to religion. How brilliant is the sketch in *Frost in May* of the overwhelming emotion produced in the heroine by Dante and Beatrice acted with power, of the fear induced in the nuns. This fear of artistic emotion and the allied fear of sex do not seem to have been felt by Caryll, apart from the loss of her Shelley: and in this it seemed to her the religious-irreligious issue predominated. Yet, in fact, the struggle between realization as artist or as saint was for her to be lifelong.

These two books could usefully be read by all teachers, which does not mean that they are more than a partial view. Very few adults can look at all sides, probably no single child can do so; yet a child's view is worth noting.

Caryll kept in touch with the Olton convent in later life. She used to go back for week-ends, she has recorded her love of it in her rhythms and in *A Rocking-Horse Catholic*. But in the intimate journal of her spiritual life it is Mother Aloysia whose advice she speaks of asking—the nun who had stopped her letter and given her a lesson in wisdom and charity.

4

Out of the Church

CARYLL WAS ONLY SIXTEEN, and it is an example of her mother's strange temperament that she should have been so suddenly snatched from school—just when beginning to settle down there. The nursing home must have been expensive; Caryll had then been sent to a boarding school to complete her restoration to health, and also to escape the Zeppelin raids. Now she was brought back to London—and to the raids—and turned abruptly into a maid of all work.

Maids were hard to come by in those years of munition-making and war work, and Mrs. Houselander had taken on a job for which she urgently needed help. Partly out of compassion, partly because she had fallen deeply under his influence, Caryll's mother had determined to make a home for the priest who had five years earlier given Caryll the Communion thought to be her viaticum. He had now left his religious order, and was obviously an exceedingly sick man. Della Clifford, now Mrs. Foster, who became an intimate friend of Caryll's, remembers his strange and forbidding appearance, "tall, thin, a face like a skull, unpleasant-looking and unhealthy." She thinks he had pernicious anaemia, and Caryll told another friend how it was her office to give him daily injections without which he could not live. She used to dream of murder by the simple act of omitting the injections, and in her waking hours realized how easy it would be—"a slight prick, and he would fancy I had given it. But I stuck the needle right into him, and that was that."

It was a hard life for Caryll. Her mother had meant her to be a stop-gap as far as housework was concerned, a chaperone chiefly for herself and the priest. But as it turned out, the situation continued for quite a long time. Harder than housework were her relationships inside the house and out. Those were days of narrow conventions, and Caryll's presence was by no means enough to satisfy a censorious world in which Catholics were no more charitable than other people. The unhappy priest was ostracized, and with him his hostess and her daughter. Incredible as it may seem, an old schoolfellow refused to see her on the ground of the scandal, and a Catholic couple who had knelt beside her at Communion ignored her greeting and cut her dead in the church porch.

Letters of abuse came to the house, and out of many converts received by him, only one visited the sick priest in friendship. A few fellow-priests came in reproach rather than sympathy—one alone paid him a visit of true compassion. Psychologically twisted as he already was, the ostracism made him far worse. He forbade Caryll to invite any Catholic friends to the house; but indeed she had none left, apart from the Paleys, who lived in Brighton—and it was only Smoky who prevented her from breaking off the friendship with them from the feeling that they might be injured by her leprous presence.

Smoky, living nearby in St. John's Wood, she visited every Sunday, and he told her she would only hurt the Paleys by a rejection of their very real love. But when he reminded her of his own teaching, that the presence of evil in the Church, and its failure to destroy it, was actually a proof of its supernatural foundation, she would have none of his argument.

The Borgias she could swallow, but those narrow unkind Catholics were seen, not merely read about, and were supposedly the cream of the Church. Always at Mass, heading every subscription list, respected by their fellow-citizens. No, they really *were* the Church, and she wanted no part of them or of it.

Still, for a while she clung to the Mass. It meant the only beauty in her drab existence, and, says Molly, "she had an innate love of Christ too deep to be eradicated."

It was in an effort to assist at Mass that Caryll received her deepest wound. Escaping very late on a Sunday morning from the routine of washing-up and bed-making, at a time long before the evening Mass existed, she had to make her way across London for the nearest midday Mass at a fashionable church where one still had to pay for a seat. There were indeed some free seats at the back, but these were all full, and Caryll, penniless, crept into a sixpenny seat:

I had scarcely knelt down and hidden my face, which was scarlet, when the verger prodded me in the ribs with a collecting bag on the end of a long cane.

"I will go up to the altar of God," said the priest at the altar. "To God, the giver of youth and happiness."

"Sixpence," said the verger and prodded me again.

I looked up and shook my head.

"Sixpence," said the verger and went on prodding.

"I haven't got sixpence," I whispered.

"All right, then," said the verger, "you must go into the free seats."

"There isn't one," I said.

"Well, then, sixpence."

I was scalded. There was a priest standing in the aisle watching the scene. When I sprang to my feet and pushed out of the sixpenny seats, he came forward and put his hand on my shoulder.

"You are not going, child?" he said. I shook him off.

"Yes, I am, and I will never come to Mass again."

I went, beginning the long walk home again, hardly able to stop my tears of rage.

"Thou, O God, art all my strength, why hast Thou cast me off?" said the priest at the altar. "Why do I go mourning, with enemies pressing me hard?"

This kind of story many Catholics find hard to believe. But I knew that church and that verger, given by our family the name of Judas because of his concern for the money bags.

After this Caryll did not, as she says, *want* to be a Catholic any longer. But she did want a religion, and she spent much time seeking—and discovering reluctantly that she was "running away from the thing [she] really wanted—the Catholic faith." She investigated various forms of Protestantism, asked questions of many ministers, was deeply attracted by the Russian Church, had a look at Buddhism, and accompanied a Jewish friend to the synagogue.

The first Buddhist she talked to startled Caryll by reciting to her a poem she had been composing on her way to see him! He on his side was much impressed by her "great psychic powers" and exhorted her to use them in the service of mankind. She went next to a Buddhist priest to get instruction as to what their faith was and found him playing badminton, dressed in his priestly robes. Leaving his game for the moment he told her he could be of no use to her. Western materialism had been too much for him, he said. He had himself become materialized, and it would be impossible for him to teach her his religion.

The Jewish synagogue, on the other hand, made a deep impression on Caryll—and a startling one. The doubt of her own doubts came upon her overwhelmingly:

There was something fierce and terrible, in a way, about the Jewish liturgy, but something familiar too. Deny it as I would,

I could not help being more and more convinced that Christ was a seed that was sown in Israel to flower in the Catholic Church. However, after all these services and all these instructions I was no nearer to what I was seeking. Every creed that I was taught had *something* in it of truth and beauty, but it was always something that, even with my imperfect knowledge, I knew was included in the Catholic Church. Did the Catholic Church include everything? This was the question that began to puzzle and trouble me more and more, for, frankly, I did not *want* to be a Catholic.

What I did want, and with increasing longing, was to join the Russian Church. . . . Most of the Russians were ready to tolerate everything, unready to judge anything. They knew themselves to be sinners, and indeed took it for granted quite happily that we are all sinners, and in spite of the arrogance inherent in the character of the Russian aristocracy they had always a profound humility. Their charity was boundless, and their realization of the closeness and the love of Christ, here and now in this world, an almost tangible thing. They were always extreme, but their extremes seemed to me so much more lovable, even when they were outrageous, than what I· considered the watered-down religious passions and the mediocrities of the West.

I am not clear at exactly what date Mrs. Houselander moved from the flat in Maida Vale to a house in Boundary Road, off Finchley Road, where she began to take boarders.

It was by all accounts a very special kind of boarding house. One visitor, Vivian Richardson, who was devoted to Mrs. Houselander, has told me how she and Caryll often shared a bedroom when the place was overfull, how at times all the guests would help with the washing-up, "even the Colonel" —whose name I did not note. Looking back she sees all this as a joyous scramble. She speaks of Caryll as "a naughty little girl" and begs me not to dramatize her early life. But the visitor shares a room and goes back to one of her own, helps with housework just as much as she chooses. The daughter's room becomes never fully her own, the housework must always be finished. What made it worse was that Caryll was always incredibly slow at beds and dishes. Her friends of later years would watch her with a kind of anguish when she insisted on coping—and to have too much to do probably paralyzed her entirely. One guesses at memories still intensely vivid when she writes, in *The Dry Wood*, of Rose O'Shane washing "greasy dishes, greasy plates, greasy pots and pans in a West End restaurant." Caryll had a shuddering horror of mice, and if the dishes were left overnight the grease, congealed and hard, "had little tracks of the feet of mice all over it, and the fat and gristle left on the plates was always nibbled by mice."

The word frustration was not so much used in those days —but the artist must feel frustration when longing to write, worn out before she can begin and with no solitude to think in.

Mrs. Houselander, whatever her mistakes, had an innate generosity of character that led her to fill the house with other lame dogs besides the unhappy priest friend, sick people too and even those in a last extremity. Caryll, laughing at lunch one day, was startled when her mother said, "How can you be so heartless when there's a dying man in the next room?" She had heard nothing of the dying man, but it appeared that when "Gert," as all her intimates called her, had gone that morning to place a bet, her bookie had suddenly had a heart attack, had begged that his family should not be told—"I don't mind dying, but I don't want to see my family"—and had been brought back to Boundary Road in a taxi to die. Afterwards, his widow and six or seven children all landed themselves on Gert. Perhaps to avoid such embarrassments she later asked Iris to drive her down to see a sick friend in a country place where she didn't want to be recognized, and turned up on the steps of Evelyn Gardens dressed, most unconvincingly, as a man, with a man's appalling old cap on. There are many stories of Gert's openheartedness, but she often made life harder for her own family by the very exuberance of her charity. She was doing her best for their education, and she certainly worked hard enough herself. She was probably stronger than either of her daughters, especially Caryll with her miserable health and tubercular glands.

Ruth had borne the burden at home while Caryll was in the nursing home and at school, but now she was working hard at Oxford. A scholarly career was clearly not possible for Caryll, but she won a scholarship to the St. John's Wood Art School. She was longing to write, but the artistic atmosphere suited her and she made a host of friends among the students. Some of them lightened her labours—Della Clifford especially would now often help her with the washing-up, as she wanted Caryll to go out with her.

"She had high spirits," Della says, "to overcome her miserable surroundings. She enjoyed dancing and all the Art School rags. She had a teddy-bear called Roosey to which she was devoted and which sat on her pillow. It seemed like her Familiar." Della showed me a snapshot of a fattish girl with a quizzical face, hair cut in a fringe and done up in a large "bun" at the back.

"In those days she had a pinky face. She never ate enough, and this worried me. I would sometimes persuade her to have tea and buns with me. I suppose the starchy food, and not enough of anything else, made her plump."

Caryll and Della and two other girls presently shared the expense of buying a wooden hut and having it put up at the end of the Boundary Road Garden. Caryll's was the smallest contribution—but the hut cost only £15 before erection. Mrs. Houselander gave them some furniture, and in those days labour was still cheap. A north light was contrived, and the hut became a studio, christened the Spooky. Here a group would gather, calling themselves the Cheerful Idiots: all from the Art School, all therefore very young, discussing religion and life, all ready to help each other in the struggle for existence. One of them, Eleanor Toy, took Caryll on a glorious trip to Portugal, whence she returned with Apache hats for the whole gang.

"We were a typical art school crowd," says Della. She speaks of Caryll at this time as twenty. Caryll herself is so often inaccurate as to dates, times, and such details, that one cannot be certain she is right even about her own age, but she speaks in a letter many years later of having been "about seventeen" when she went to Portugal. She stayed behind after her friend had gone home, and she mentions in this letter an experience she also described to me. Her money ran out, and she walked from place to place making sketches and selling them to get food. She slept in peasants' houses. They let her wash her clothes and dry them on the stove at night to be ready for her next morning. And they would take no payment from her except drawings of themselves. Caryll was conscious of being too fat and mentions that she had tried "a spell of self-starvation" just before this expedition. But "the food, even the minute quantities I was able to get for many months, was so very nourishing, as of course you know, so many sardines and everything cooked in oil! I never again, after that, was able to get anywhere near the skeleton condition I wanted to."

At one point she found herself in a gipsy camp and was faintly alarmed, but the only notable reaction of the gipsies was to finger with cries of pleasure the long plaits in which she was wearing her red-gold hair as she tramped about.

Caryll had never been pretty, but she was immensely amusing and a first-class mimic. Men students liked her as much as girls, but oddly enough it was not a fellow-student but an Oxford man from a rich family to whom she got engaged in her student years. This man's mother grew so fond of her

that long after the engagement came to an end she took
Caryll with her to Germany and much later still tried to
persuade her to come with her to Australia.

Caryll's friends could never understand this episode in her
life, nor indeed can her biographer. Almost savagely bohemian, she consented to prepare for entry into a very different
world. Her fiancé used to address her as "Little Lady." He
engaged an Italian Countess to teach her deportment! About
this time, her mother, suddenly realizing her shabbiness,
bought her quite a supply of clothes. Della recalls a blue and
white dress, a suit and a very becoming evening dress.

But it would not do. Much as she liked her fiancé—they
remained warm friends—it was all too different from her
ideas of what life should be. Caryll broke off the engagement.
Long after, a friend asked her why she had ever begun it.

"Why on earth did you accept him if you didn't love him?"

"Well, it seemed so awfully rude to refuse."

Caryll was much happier, Della thinks, from the time she
had the Spooky. The others called her by her childish nick-
name of Baby—which she never lost among her early intimates. She was "ready to join in everything unless she wanted
to write. She installed a heater in the Spooky and would
sometimes write there. Or she would go to the Paleys. I remember her spending a week-end with Molly at Fittleworth."

The Cheerful Idiots assembled in the Spooky every Monday. Later they all joined the Hambone Club, of which at
that time all the members were artists, including Augustus
John and Sickert. Then it became fashionable, and the
Cheerful Idiots shook its dust from their feet, leaving together with some of the greater artists. I felt, as Della talked,
that her picture of these years fitted not at all with Caryll's
assertion of her own extreme shyness.

"Oh, she was shy," Della said, "with people who were not
her sort. She made friends easily with those who were."

Caryll tended to identify "her sort" with all bohemians

and with the poor, the weaklings, the down-and-outs. After two or three years of struggling with dishes, she had left her mother's house, and tried to earn her living in a multitude of ways. There was no absolute break, for her first lodging was next door to home, and, as she says in *A Rocking-Horse Catholic,* she could have returned at any time. Her need for solitude was always strong, and I fancy there was a great determination not to give in once she had embarked on a course. She also felt—strangely enough, for she had stopped praying—that God would take care of her. She describes her strange series of professions: house-decorating, charring, writing love letters for various clients—which must have been successful, for they became quite lucrative at a shilling a letter. The only job she ever turned down at this time was a suggestion made by an actress in search of publicity that she should throw herself off a bridge into the Thames. The actress would, she asserted, make the headlines by a heroic rescue. But Caryll doubted the certainty of this!

A story is told which, if it did happen, illustrates the fact that just then she really was in some ways rather "a naughty little girl." When I knew Caryll she was more scrupulous than anyone I ever met about giving full and overfull value for every penny she received. But at this time, having painted a fancy picture of a little naked child standing against a vague blue background looking up at a star, she called it the outcome and representation of a vision and offered it to some spiritualist society. They at once bought it and, deeply interested, asked her if she often had visions. To which Caryll said, "Oh yes."

I find this story exceedingly annoying—just because I am convinced that Caryll did have real extra-sensory experiences for the validity of which she would have gone to the stake. I shall have something to say about these later, but I realize that she made it very difficult by such acts of frivolity for people to take her seriously when she was *very* serious.

But they belong to a time when she *was* frivolous and was also hungry.

The final means of income mentioned in *A Rocking-Horse Catholic,* more lasting but very far from lucrative, was commercial art.

An American friend, startled by the words "commercial art," asked Caryll how she reconciled such a job with her conscience. A little amused at the contrast of such a problem and the reality of her actual problem of living, Caryll explained.

"I had to go to various big stores, draw pictures there of the things they had for sale—hats, corsets, etc.—which were printed the next day in the advertisement columns of the daily papers to show people what the shops had in stock. I also had to draw newspaper advertisements for such things as margarine and powdered eggs, but never for anything I did not think all right."

The pay was fifteen shillings a week but often fell to five shillings through fines for late arrival or failure to think of good ideas. Even paying such miserable wages, the firm went bankrupt and was finally reduced to paying her with chocolates.

Next came a brief incursion into drama, where her contribution was limited to acting such parts as "noises off" for a travelling company. Della says she drew clever strip cartoons of children which she called her "ugs"—short for uglies. They do not seem to have found much of a market. All her jobs were badly paid. And through it all she was watching people, wandering through the London streets, often very tired, almost always hungry, listening to the noises that rose through the silence of the night into her room, even beginning to pray for those to whom her sympathy went out: that great noisy, happy and unhappy world of London.

5
Love Affair

IT IS NOT POSSIBLE to date accurately all the happenings of the years 1917 to 1923, between Caryll's leaving school and her first meeting with Iris Wyndham. But I shall put together here two events which were, I know, at least two years apart, but which are closely connected, and which together changed Caryll's life.

At seventeen, the bitterness of her existence had reached its high point: it was before she had made her many art-school friends; it was after she had rejected the Church—which, to her thinking, had rejected her.

As a child she had been aware of Christ's crown of thorns set upon the head of a poor lay sister; now, at a time when splendour and privilege were most abhorrent to her, she saw Him on the Cross in His kingship. The story can only be told in her own words:

The murder of the Russian Emperor and his family took place in a cellar in Ekaterinburg on the night of July 17th, 1918. . . .

I was on my way to buy potatoes, hurrying because I had been warned that they were wanted for dinner, and so I must not linger. Suddenly I was held still, as if a magnet held my feet to a particular spot in the middle of the road. In front of me, above

me, literally wiping out not only the grey street and sky but
the whole world, was something which I can only call a gigantic
and living Russian icon. I had never seen a Russian icon at the
time, nor, I think, any reproduction of one. I have seen very
many since, but none that has approached this one in beauty.

It was an icon of Christ the King crucified.

Stretched on a cross of fire in a vestment which blazed and
flamed with jewels, crowned with a great crown of gold which
weighed His head down, Christ was lifted above the world in
our drab street, lifted up and filling the sky. His arms reaching,
as it seemed, from one end of the world to the other, the wounds
on His hands and feet rubies, but molten rubies that bled with
light. Everything, even the glowing folds of the vestments,
seemed to be burning and stirring with life and movement as
flames of fire do; the spread arms with the long stretched hands
tapering from the jewelled sleeves were like gorgeous wings
covering the world; Christ Himself with His head bowed down
by the crown, brooding over the world. In the midst of this
splendour the austere simplicity of that beautiful face stood
sharp with grief. But the eyes and mouth smiled with an in-
effable love which consumes sorrow and pain as rags are consumed in a burning fire.

In the same street, shortly after, as she read posters announcing the Czar's assassination, Caryll saw his picture on
the newspaper page, and it was the face of her vision, "but
without its glory . . . between one heartbeat and the next, I
had seen the drama and reality of Christ's Passion in kings. . . .
At the same moment I had a premonition of the things that
were to come, of the vast stretch and anguish of the Passion
of Christ in which the kings of the world, the hierarchies and
the common people would be one, in one terrible glory . . .
I realized that every crown is Christ's crown, and the crown
of gold is a crown of thorns."

The chief effect of this experience was at the time a deep
conviction that it would be through Russia that Christ

"would return to the world to take possession of all mankind. ... The blood of kings was to fall crimson on Russian snows, but mingled with it the blood of peasants, raised by their martyrdom to kingship; and from that great vivifying stream would flow the blood of martyrs all over the world, redeeming the world."

This feeling for light and colour even amid suffering was characteristic of Caryll; the crimson and the white, the molten rubies that were Christ's wounds. The experience did not immediately bring her back into the Church; it started her on a love affair with Russia which helped to draw her into the one great human love affair of her life.

The more people I see who knew Caryll, the more I read her letters, the more I realize her power of loving. She did not only spend herself for her friends; she had for each one a singular concern, what might be called a private face— not just for friends but for each friend. And I imagine this as intensified a hundredfold when she fell in love. He was older than she was by many years, dark and handsome say many of her friends, speaking English with a Russian accent.

Sidney Reilly, forgotten today, was widely known at the end of World War I. He appears in Bruce Lockhart's *Memoirs of a British Agent,* in Captain George Hill's *Go Spy the Land,* in W.H. Chamberlain's *The Russian Revolution,* and more recently in *The Conspirators,* by Geoffrey Bailey. There is, too, his own book, finished by his wife after his disappearance and entitled by her *Sidney Reilly, Britain's Master Spy*—a title widely bestowed on him.

"Pass Comrade Relinsky" are the words with which Reilly opens his own account of some of his adventures: "the soldier did not trouble to examine my papers. He knew me. I was Comrade Relinsky of the Tcheka-Criminel—a Communist and a Comrade."

Born at Odessa, Reilly had spent his boyhood and early

youth in Petrograd. According to Bruce Lockhart, who met him when he himself was the first official British Agent to the Soviet Government, Sidney Reilly had no drop of British blood, was a Jew called originally Rosenblum, naturalized British when and how nobody quite knew. Bruce Lockhart recognized in this man of mystery "the artistic temperament of the Jew," combined with "the devil-may-care daring of the Irishman"—which happens to be the mixture of blood that Reilly himself claimed!

His career had not begun with soldiering or in the Intelligence Service. Born in 1874 he had appeared around 1900 as a partner in the firm of Grunberg and Reilly, timber merchants at Port Arthur, and had amassed a fortune in an arms factory and in commissions from various German shipbuilding firms. Early in World War I he was to be found in Japan, negotiating on behalf of the Russo-Asiatic Bank, and then in the United States, handling Russian munitions contracts. Passing over into Canada, he enlisted as an observer in the R.A.F. and shortly afterwards was sent to London.

Reilly was, to an uncommon degree, a world citizen. His wife mentions his command of five languages—all, she says, talked with a foreign accent—but Bruce Lockhart says he spoke seven, though none of them perfectly. One might well ask what the standard of perfection is when we find a man who passes two years successfully shuttling in and out of Germany, disguised as an officer of the Kaiser's navy, and is next accepted in Russia as a member of the Tcheka! For at the beginning of 1918 the "German naval officer" was recalled to England and dispatched under a code number via Murmansk to Russia.

"He looked amazingly young," Bruce Lockhart comments after their first meeting—and perhaps his age is the most surprising single element in this unusual man's career. The First World War awakened in many of the young a spirit of adventure which had been starved in a too safe, too conventional society. But for a man in his mid-forties, a man who had amassed a fortune and was thoroughly capable of enjoying it, to throw himself enthusiastically into a life of daily discomfort and constant, imminent peril was indeed amazing. His many aliases, his quick-change artistry—in Moscow between M. Massimo (Turkish and Oriental merchant) and Comrade Relinsky; in Petrograd between M. Constantine and Sidney Reilly himself, returning to his old home—were obviously a delight to him. He seems to have revelled in danger. But also he was a man of vast ambition; while Bruce Lockhart saw only too clearly that there was no hope of an effective uprising against the Bolsheviks in Russia, Reilly could write of the masses whose discontent and misery were powerless merely from lack of leadership. "I was positive that the terror could be wiped out in an hour and that I myself could do it. And why not? A Corsican lieutenant of artillery trod out the embers of the French Revolution. Surely a British espionage agent, with so many factors on his side, could make himself master of Moscow."

Bruce Lockhart, with Scotch caution, saw the situation more justly; even had Sidney Reilly been a Napoleon, time must be allowed for this revolution, too, to run its course. Napoleon could not have preceded Danton and Robespierre: embers are found after a conflagration has spent its force. Nor did Reilly take into account all the elements. It is fascinating to set his simple emotional record beside the complex picture painted by a man younger in actual years but far older in his experience of the workings of diplomacy and the complexity of national and personal greeds. Later the anti-Bolshevik Russians were to feel that the Allies had let them down, that each country was fighting for its own hand. Later Sidney Reilly was to feel that the "White" Russians cared only for the recovery of their own property, the re-establishment of what had, in fact, been a thoroughly rotten society. Bruce Lockhart saw from the first how inevitable such suspicions were—and also how much of truth there would be in them.

"Trust the man on the spot" is a slogan commonly used. But in Lockhart and Reilly we see two men on the spot giving totally opposite advice based on contradictory information, the one obtained largely in official circles, the other from an alleged Underground.

When Russia signed with Germany the Treaty of Brest-Litovsk—a Treaty more crushing for Russia than Versailles was to be for Germany—the cry in England was that the Bolshevik government was pro-German, that if it were turned out Russia might go on with the fight. But Bruce Lockhart saw clearly that this peace had been signed for the same reason that had brought the Bolsheviks into power. The Russian army was utterly demoralized, the people were sick of war, and no government could have induced them to go on fighting. Reilly, as we have seen, believed on the contrary that given good leadership the broken forces could be rallied, the army remade.

Bruce Lockhart distrusted all information obtained by espionage, since it set a premium on news stories desired by the spy. Reilly probably felt himself, widely accepted as a Russian, to be in a better position than any Allied official to understand what Russians were feeling. Actually if the Allied High Command had followed the *advice* of either of these observers—and there were doubtless many others, from France especially—it might have worked, but in fact they determined on a miserable compromise.

Although opposed to Allied intervention in the East in 1918 unless undertaken with Communist agreement, Lockhart noted that *if* we were to embark upon it the number of Russians who might join the Allied forces would be in exact proportion to the strength of men sent. The abortive landing of a few hundred men at Archangel reads today like the invasion of Cuba. There was no declaration of war. The landing was allegedly to help Russia—but *which* Russia? Anyhow it killed all hope of a counter-revolution and did more than anything else to strengthen the Bolsheviks.

Meanwhile Sidney Reilly had become deeply implicated in what was (quite unfairly, for Lockhart had no part in it) called The Lockhart Plot. Lenin was severely wounded by a Russian assassin. This was no part of Reilly's plan: he had never intended assassination, but he really believed he could have Lenin and Trotsky seized, and—for their utter downthrow and humiliation—paraded through the streets in their shirts. The idea was typical of the play of his "Napoleonic" imagination. Nor did the Soviets despise him as a danger. The British Embassy was raided in search of him: he saw the raid as he drew near, slipped away, and sought out his friend Captain Hill. "Reilly's bearing," writes Hill, "was splendid. He was a hunted man; his photograph with a full description and a reward for his capture was placarded throughout the town; he had been through a terrible time in getting away from Petrograd; yet he was absolutely cool, calm and collected, not in the least downhearted and only concerned in gathering together the broken threads and starting afresh."

In fact, as he gradually realized, there was nothing he could now do in Russia. Bruce Lockhart, who was in prison, refused Reilly's offer to give himself up in exchange—and Lockhart was, in fact, released after a month and allowed to return to England. Reilly went into hiding in a house for prostitutes in Moscow. Death would have been the women's penalty had he been found, but these houses were, he says, "rarely searched." When he departed "they refused every payment I offered them."

From Moscow to Petrograd Reilly contrived to travel in a reserved compartment of the train as a member of the German Embassy. In Petrograd he learnt that he had been traced, that the man who let him through the barrier had been shot, that his photograph had been circulated every-

where and all the ordinary means of escape from the country
were impossible. His barber, who recognized him in the
street despite a careful disguise based largely on hair and
beard, hid him for a fortnight and then arranged to smuggle
him out. A high price was to be paid to the captain of a Dutch
trading ship. And again it is typical of the man that, instead
of trying to get straight home to England, Reilly managed
to travel via the German naval base at Reval and there to
collect valuable information on the position of the German
fleet.

That year came the Armistice, and there is a gap between
Reilly's own memoirs and the end of the story as told by the
woman he later married—a gap stretching between the
middle of 1918 and late 1922. He had many business interests
and probably spent some time in the States and in Europe.
Reilly had greatly impoverished himself in his ardour in the
cause of what he deemed the true Russia, but he was not a
poor man and when in this country had a flat at the Albany.
     There were many exiled Russians living in London, some
of them friends of Caryll's, and one can imagine what stories
were told of Reilly in these circles, with what excitement she
must have looked forward to meeting him.
     Sidney Reilly's face has been described to me by many
people and I have looked long at his photograph. If he was
as handsome as admirers say, he was certainly not photogenic.
Geoffrey Bailey describes him as haggard and tortured,
"with a high sloping forehead, smouldering eyes and sensu-
ous lips." But had Geoffrey Bailey ever seen him, or is this
simply a description of the photograph, which is certainly
interesting and intriguing? Had he been a woman I should
call him a *jolie laide,* and in a man such looks may be more
exciting than beauty.
     Della Foster knew Reilly, and even after Caryll and he had
grown close, she used to take Caryll's drawings to him at his

flat. He admired them greatly—but Caryll was too shy, and despised her drawings too much, to take them to him herself. Della did not find Caryll's friend attractive. "Very brusque," she says, and she turned the "dark" of other people's descriptions into "swarthy" and questioned the "very handsome." Caryll would say sometimes, "I *must* do some more drawings or he will be angry." Della does not know what happened to these drawings but agrees that he may have sold them for Caryll, or possibly have pretended to do so. There must have been a great many drawings in the end, for it all went on, whenever he was in England, for about two years. Caryll was, Molly Paley told me, "torn in shreds" by her love. "There was a barrier between her emotion about him and her religion." And then, as time went on, "she began to speak less and less about him." He had meant far more to her than she to him; there had been a strong infusion of hero-worship; she was young and hungry for love.

It seems possible that the end of the affair was rendered more tragic for Caryll by arising from Reilly's lightning falling in love with Pepita Chambers, which was swiftly followed by their marriage in 1923. But it is also possible that she had already herself made the break. *A Rocking-Horse Catholic* is a singularly perfect little work of art, but as biography it needs both sorting out and amplifying. Caryll so telescopes the events of many years that it is hard to discover when one experience ended and another began. Here her intimate friends, especially Della Foster and Molly Paley, have been immensely helpful. But also the book is selective; she is telling the story not of her life but of what drove her out of the Church and of how she returned to it. She alludes only obliquely to the love affair which began and ended during the time she *was* outside (temptation sweeping her "as dry grass is swept by a flame of fire") and which no doubt delayed her return.

Had she been fully within the Church when she met

Reilly, supported by daily Sacrament and Sacrifice, the human love story might never have begun. Caryll herself told me—and the book makes even clearer—how all this was linked with the last, and most tremendous, of her three experiences of seeing Christ in man. In a crowded underground train during the rush hour, she seemed to see not only the jostled crowd strap-hanging around her, but all mankind— "not only all the countries of the world, but all those people who had lived in the past, and all those yet to come." And in them all she saw Christ:

This time it was an unimaginably vaster experience than on either of the other occasions; it was not a seeing of Christ in one person, as it had been with the Bavarian nun, or in one particular sort of person, as it had been in the living icon of Christ the King. This time it was Christ in all men. This is much more difficult to describe than the other experiences; I can only do my best to tell it just as it happened.

I was in an underground train, a crowded train in which all sorts of people jostled together, sitting and strap-hanging—workers of every description going home at the end of the day. Quite suddenly I saw with my mind, but as vividly as a wonderful picture, Christ in them all. But I saw more than that; not only was Christ in every one of them, living in them, dying in them, rejoicing in them, sorrowing in them—but because He was in them, and because they were here, the whole world was here too, here in this underground train; not only the world as it was at that moment, not only all the people in all the countries of the world, but all those people who had lived in the past, and all those yet to come.

I came out into the street and walked for a long time in the crowds. It was the same here, on every side, in every passer-by, everywhere—Christ. . . .

The "vision" lasted with that intensity for several days, and each of them revealed the mystery and its implications for me a little more clearly. Although it did not prevent me from ever sinning again, it showed me what sin is, especially those sins done in the name of "love," so often held to be "harmless"—for to sin with one whom you loved was to blaspheme Christ in that person; it was to spit on Him, perhaps to crucify Him. I saw too the reverence that everyone must have for a sinner; instead of condoning his sin, which is in reality his utmost sorrow, one must comfort Christ who is suffering in him. And this reverence must be paid even to those sinners whose souls seem to be dead, because it is Christ, who is the life of the soul, who is dead in them; they are His tombs, and Christ in the tomb is potentially the risen Christ. For the same reason, no one of us who has fallen into mortal sin himself must ever lose hope.

Sidney Reilly later went back to Russia. It needed no special gift of insight to be certain, as Caryll was, that he would be imprisoned and would die there. But to another friend, Charles Scott-Paton, she spoke ten years later of an experience which belongs to and completes this story. She had "travelled far," she said; she had been in a prison cell with someone she did not name and shared his sufferings. And by this she did not mean merely that she had imagined but that she had indeed, in some fashion, really "seen," had in some inexpressible, inexplicable way really shared.

Almost twenty years later Caryll wrote to a young friend harrowed by a similar experience who might be helped by her own story:

Here I can only pray for you. I know what it can feel like to part from a man whom one is in love with, for I too have done so, years and years ago—and the years have not lessened or dimmed the love, even though he is dead now, shot in Russia by the Communists. I know what anguish such a parting can be, but tell you, in case you can find any ray of comfort for yourself in it, that certainly in my case it hasn't brought any sense of waste or frustration, but a kind of completeness and richness nothing else could. I have never had any "feeling" of his nearness or anything since he died, but I have always *known* that he is alive and that one day, I devoutly hope, we shall meet. A few years of grief on earth are nothing compared to being together in eternity in God's presence. Also, and maybe this is more important, *because* I loved that man I have loved many other people, animals and things.

Because of her love but above all because of the inevitable renunciation. Molly Paley saw this love as standing between Caryll and the Church, but we have to remember that she had already been out of the Church several years. The searchings she tells of in *A Rocking-Horse Catholic* were real, spiritual and intellectual, her vision of Christ in man answered her questions as well as strengthening her wavering will. This letter was written on the feast of the Annunciation, 1949. She refers in it to another letter in which her later meditations are reflected—that loving wrongly may shut the soul to God and man, renunciation open it. . . . "The hurt," she wrote,

always remains with one—yet no sooner is such a decision really made than one finds those people and experiences that one has been denying, coming into one's life, like shattering, unimaginable graces—not shattering in the destructive sense, but shattering the walls that any necessarily frustrating experience builds around us, when we foster it.

Maybe while you feel that you have shut the door . . . you have in reality thrown it open to the true happiness which is really your ultimate good.

6

New Beginnings

VIVIAN RICHARDSON OFTEN corresponded with Caryll. Staying in Panama she showed her letters to another friend, Iris Bennett, the daughter of the British Minister there. Iris found the letters extremely entertaining and rather hoped to meet Caryll. Months passed. Caryll by 1923 was back in Boundary Road. Her sister was married. Iris had returned to England, married Richard Wyndham, and was living at the Wyndham family place, Clouds, in Wiltshire. She and Caryll were about the same age, but the odds were heavily against a friendship between them. Caryll had already chosen her lot with artists and poets—especially impecunious ones— with the shabby and the outcast. She almost hated rich and successful people as such. One extraordinary story belongs to this time when for a reason unknown to me she went to make some enquiries, at the request of the police, among the prostitutes of Piccadilly. They received her as one of them- selves and advised her to do something about her dress and her appearance or she would never get a client. On her side her ready sympathy was awakened. She was much moved by one woman who had a daughter in a convent school from whom she had successfully hidden her profession. Perhaps it was this brief experience that made Caryll later look so

closely in the Gospels at Our Lord's tenderness towards prostitutes and sinners, at His promise that they would go into the
Kingdom of Heaven ahead of the (self?)-righteous.

Another element in Caryll's outlook about the rich was
something which she herself later described as a deep-seated
neurosis. She was intensely aware of her own odd appearance,
intensely sensitive about it. Many months later, Vivian being
again on a visit to Boundary Road, Iris Wyndham, beautiful
and well-dressed, drove up to the house in a large car driven
by an imposing chauffeur. The dice were doubly loaded
against her. Caryll glanced briefly through the window and
instantly vanished. To Vivian she called her friend a "ghastly
society girl."

On a second visit "a strange being," says Iris, entered
Vivian's bedroom, her head smeared with strongly smelling
ointment. "I've such a ghastly headache," she said, "I've put
on Bengue's Balsam, which I'm told even cures the pains of
childbirth. I look awful."

Iris said, "I can't see what you look like as I'm too short-
sighted."

Caryll at once became more friendly, and before long they
were, says Iris, "quite matey." She, at least, felt much inclined to develop the acquaintance if occasion offered. She
was, however, established at Clouds complete with baby and
nursery, while Caryll was trying to earn a living in London.

George Wyndham, best known for the Land Act which he
introduced during his time as Chief Secretary for Ireland,
inherited Clouds from his father, Percy Wyndham, who had
built it and had entertained there on a vast scale. From
George it went to his son, another Percy, who was killed in
the First World War. Percy left Clouds to his cousin
Richard, later known as traveller, writer and painter, and like
his uncle George of great personal charm. He and Iris had
one daughter, Joan. Vivian suggested to Iris that she should
invite Caryll to Clouds to decorate Joan's nursery.

Clouds is now a babies' home, and the former rose garden is full of cabbages coming right up to the windows. The library is no more. George Wyndham loved that library, and his last letter, written to my father and received after George's death, was about plans for it, including desks arranged in some ideal original fashion where we were all to sit and write on our first visit to Clouds.

A ghost was said to haunt the house, a "little old woman" who foretold it would be one day a home for children of the poor; I wonder whether today it is haunted by ghosts from the splendid parties given by George's parents, the Percy Wyndhams: Victorian and Edwardian ghosts, with a slight air of bewilderment about them as they look at the babies.

Caryll saw no ghosts there, but she talked to Iris of fairies in the woods around—quite large ones, "all green"! She made drawings and designs for a frieze, illustrating fairy tales, which she completed at home and which was then put up in the nursery. On this first visit Caryll stayed for about a week. The first night Iris had two friends to meet her, and she recalls how amused and fascinated they were by her. "She did not appear shy then or later." At other times they had dinner alone in the immense dining room, and Iris remembers how tiny Caryll looked "sitting at the end of a very long table with the unaccustomed butler padding around her."

On this first visit of Caryll's, Dick Wyndham was away from home and she learnt from Iris that the marriage was not a happy one. Before her second visit things had reached a crisis, and Iris had made up her mind to leave Clouds and to divorce Dick. Her friend Vivian again came to the rescue, suggesting that she take a house called Bacombe Warren near Wendover.

Vivian had often taken Iris to Boundary Road, so that she knew Gert and all the circumstances of Caryll's life. She herself was lonely. From Bacombe Warren she wrote to Caryll suggesting that she should join her there. Caryll had to brace herself to give her mother, as Iris puts it, "long notice, so that she could make other arrangements." There was a row, after which, until Caryll left about two months later, Gert "cast" and never spoke to her again. ("Casting" meant "casting gloom"—a great phrase of Caryll's. And Gert casting was a thing to be dreaded.)

At one time Caryll gave up all hope of leaving: indeed, she wrote to tell Iris that it was impossible, as she had no money for her fare, nor any kind of trunk or case. Iris, now without the chauffeur whose splendour had so irritated Caryll, came to the rescue ("although I was a very bad driver and had never driven in London"); somehow she managed to drive herself up and arrived in the large car before the house in Boundary Road. She didn't dare to get out, but sat in the car while Gert stood silently on the doorstep, plucking her lip and casting. Caryll went in and out of the house, collecting Roosey (the teddy-bear of her childhood), her yellow coat and the armfuls of books that were almost her only luggage. Her mother did not say goodbye.

"When I met Iris," Caryll said later to a friend, "I thought she was the loveliest thing I'd ever seen." She felt that her love and devotion helped Iris, who had been shattered by her painful experiences. "It was like the ice-maiden coming to life," she said.

Much was given, much received on each side of this friendship. To all appearances they were incongruous, coming from backgrounds, formed by educations, totally dissimilar. Yet their partnership wore so well that it lasted for the rest of Caryll's life. A quarter of a century after their first meeting, Willmott Houselander remarked, "You wouldn't find two people anywhere more devoted to each other than my daughter and Mrs. Wyndham."

Opposition to the friendship did not come from Caryll's mother alone. When she divorced her husband, Iris was only twenty-four. Her mother hoped she would marry again. She thought Caryll anti-social, and she feared, too, that Iris would through her become a Catholic and give up all idea of remarriage. Most of Iris's family shared these fears.

Caryll went up every day—or almost every day—from Bacombe to London to work, Iris fetching her by car from Wendover station. Gert presently took a house nearby and used to drive over, dressed in a balaclava cap, trousers and top-boots, tooting all the way up the long drive—a sound, Iris says, at which Caryll grew white and had to be revived with brandy. Still unreconciled to Caryll's desertion, she never spoke during these visits, but sat silent before the fire, "casting." Gradually she thawed, and before they left Bacombe Warren Caryll spent Christmas with her mother.

She told me once the rather macabre story of a later visit which illustrated another element in her mother's character. The neighbourhood had agreed on a simultaneous campaign against the rats infesting the barns and even the attics of their houses (many of them very old). Mrs. Houselander refused to join in what she held to be a brutal slaughter, with the result that many rats took refuge in her house. Caryll, sleeping with her small niece, had stayed awake as long as possible—to be roused from a short nap by the child. "Auntie Baby, there's a pussy with a long nose sitting on my bed and I feel frightened." Her "pussy" was a large rat, and Caryll sat up the rest of the night to keep guard.

What a night it was. At last, unable to bear the strain, Caryll slipped down to the sitting-room of one of her mother's guests—perhaps "the Colonel" of Boundary Road days. He had often given her a drink, and now she took some whiskey from his bottle to keep herself from hysteria. Next day she lacked the courage to tell him, and later suffered much because when she confessed the theft the priest suggested she should try to *give* him a drink as restitution. How awkward it was, she said, to try to coax him into a hotel on a walk—and then no doubt he would have wanted himself to pay for the proffered whiskey.

The main interest of this story is that Caryll had been to

confession and must therefore by then have been back in
the Church. To this period belongs doubtless the story that
she would tell about her General Confession. It was probably hard to speak clearly and collectedly after so many years,
but the priest thought her confession was merely a routine
one and remarked—perhaps incredulously—"And you've
done all this in a week? I congratulate you on your vitality."
It was characteristic of the strange mixture that was Caryll to
tell this story with great enjoyment while grieving deeply
over her sins. From her letters one realizes what an immense
amount this Sacrament of Sorrow meant to her. She loved it
as the embrace of God for the prodigal child, but she feared
always that her own love and sorrow were not enough. In
the years that followed she never missed her weekly confession, but how early this began I cannot tell. All that Iris (not
yet a Catholic) knew was that she took the train into Ayles-
bury for Mass each Sunday.

From Caryll herself as well as from *A Rocking-Horse Catholic* I knew of the link between the end of her love affair and
the vision of Christ in all men. The vision may have had a
delayed action, but I find a difficulty in dating both it and the
beginning of the intense spiritual life revealed by a private
journal which has fortunately survived, written throughout,
not at Bacombe Warren but in London. Bacombe Warren
was very remote for Caryll's daily journeys to London, where
she was working; Iris found it hard to get the large staff
needed for house and garden. She decided in 1925 to move
to London, where she took a house in Evelyn Gardens.

Caryll writes sometime in this year:

Jesus, I praise you because I have known sickness and pain,
I praise you because I have known poverty, failure and contempt, I praise you because I have been falsely accused and mis-
judged, I praise you because I have suffered the parting of
death, I praise you because I have lived in sordid surroundings,

and I praise you for your goodness in bringing me to a happy home and giving the Faith to my friend. Grant that I may always sip from the Chalice I am unworthy to drink from, and support me every moment with the strong enfolding arm of your Love.

This is more than two years after the end of Caryll's love affair, after, it would seem, the beginning of her renewed Catholic life; yet the journal is written throughout as if under the immediate impulsion of some great religious experience. Drawing up for herself rules whereby to direct her life, she resolves to get up every night to pray, however cold it is and regardless of the pain she has been in during the day. She will never lean back in a chair and will do her work standing. She will not drink when she feels thirsty. These things and all else are treated as a stimulus to prayer. She might be back in the French convent as she resolves on the number of spiritual communions to be made in the day, the ejaculations each time the clock strikes, the hours to be worked, the recreation to be taken, the prompt rising and the prompt to bed. Reading both the Journal and the mass of letters, talking to her friends, one realizes again that Caryll's health was always wretched. "Pain" could mean headache, tooth-, ear-, back- or stomach-ache—or a general crippling discomfort. She *never* had normal good health.

The background to her spiritual life was the work of decorating houses, painting lampshades, even making artificial roses. When she was on a decorating job Iris would sometimes carry lunch to her tied up in a large handkerchief like a workman's. They got fun out of much of this, especially when Caryll was working for Grossé—an old established firm of ecclesiastical decorators. She did carvings for them and made cut-outs, especially of cribs, which sold as fast as she could make them.

But, when Caryll took jobs on her own with less honest

employers, she found herself quite incapable of insisting that she be paid properly or even that she be paid at all. Once both girls saw a lampshade she had painted in a large West End shop. It was highly priced, and she had received only a a few shillings.

"Isn't that rather expensive?" Iris asked the shopman, and was told, "Oh yes, we have to pay these artists a great deal."

Nor was this all, for twice Caryll entered into partnership, where the insight that sometimes served her where others were concerned seems to have failed for herself. Her second partner was perfectly honest—though incompetent. But her first venture was made with a man who landed in the Old Bailey, and Caryll shouldered debts for which she was not legally responsible and which for her were crushing. She tells of her unrelaxing effort to forgive the injustice as well as to get free from debt.

Caryll had not lost touch with her old friends of the Art School days. Visiting one of them, she felt "like someone who sees their own country after many years, for to me my countrymen are simply artists. They speak my language, I theirs, we breathe the same air; her room brings memories, all the lovely pictures by John Hancock, the rows of books loved as books ought to be loved. . . . You never hear unkind talk or see unkind deeds among artists, and with them poverty is still honoured, still beautiful. How gladly would I give my life to infuse this gay bohemian spirit into [spiritual] people. Why does spite, envy and cruelty thrive in the porches of churches when love and goodwill and content go hand-in-hand in so many studios?"

Caryll herself really was married to poverty, and abounded in kind deeds, but in kindness of speech she was often lacking, and on this her journal is illuminating. "St. Peter," she begs, "dear saint of impulses, pray for me that I may stop cutting off people's ears."

And on another page " 'He who is without sin among you,

let him cast the first stone.' How often do I cast it and why? Alas, to show off; it seems brilliant and amusing before men, but how does it seem before God?

"I often cast the first stone just for fun, horrid wanton fun, like boys who tie tins on cats' tails. . . . I never have to accuse myself of unkind thoughts but always of unkind words, so I must speak without thinking. Now I will reverse it. My *thoughts* are kind, so I will think without speaking."

Her friends say that while Caryll in those days still appreciated her food—they mention oysters and hot chocolate with whipped cream!—she would in Iris's absence feed on a bit of cheese, or on roast chestnuts—she kept a string hanging in her room and would pull one off when she felt hungry. It was not only asceticism or even the need to pay her debts, it was also absorption in her work, that carried her away from considerations of time and place and of the need for food and sleep. Also when she did not specially like a food she actively disliked it—and one resolve in the Journal is to "eat all I can however distasteful."

I have tried from a typewritten volume called by her *Young Green Poems* to identify which poems belong to the early years at Evelyn Gardens. About one I felt almost certain—"Father William Doyle, S.J." For, magnificent as was Father Doyle's courage, his minutely counted practices of prayer and asceticism were so much the kind of thing that Caryll came to dislike, that she would hardly have written it later. She had obviously been also reading a very different person, Gerard Manley Hopkins, as she saluted his fellow Jesuit:

> How guess (when love's spear pressed
> Startles us—hardly a dart!)
> How he took the point to his breast
> And Christ drove home to his heart.

The Journal reflects her outer as well as her inner life for about four years. Sometimes the entries are long, sometimes very short, sometimes close together, sometimes with months between. At first she tends to use the terms as well as the methods taught her at Olton, but bit by bit the Caryll emerges whose one spiritual principle was to put love into everything to the uttermost limit and to distrust too much counting of acts, to dislike much of the advice in spiritual manuals. In fact this Caryll is really present from the first. She soon realizes that getting up at night to pray makes her irritable next day: when overworked or in pain she must give it up. But there are other ways. An early, undated entry runs:

The most unpleasant things become delightful if they are done with Our Lord, and especially things done through poverty. I used to hate washing clothes and even cry over it, but since my last final financial ruin I find great joy in it. First of all I try to think of Our Lady washing for the Holy Family and how carefully she would have done it, and so try to do mine well. Unfortunately I do *not* do it well, however hard I try, as all the coloured things run onto the white ones. Also I never can get anything clean however hard I rub! However, I rub as much as I can without making holes; then I think how lovely it is to *have* to do it, so it is a little devotion to her to love the necessity.

Then I think how Our Lord washes our souls clean and offer it up to Him. . . . Also I must remember to clean the bathroom when I have done as I splash soap all over it. . . .

Another time which God makes sweet is the times when I have no bus fares and I must stay in Kensington when Iris is away.

A break in her labours came when the mother of her fiancé of long ago took her for a tour in the Rhineland. "Everything was silver-grey and mysterious," she writes of her first evening, "with a kind of silver sun shining through

. . . most enchanted-looking rocks and little riverside towns with sloping, crooked roofs like pictures in story books." But in this land of comfort as well as enchantment she must not forget her rules; she must get up from the too comfortable bed, she must limit her cigarettes to ten a day. She decides not to spend on learning German the time that might be given to prayer.

Neither prayer nor efforts at self-denial are allowed to subserve her own spiritual life alone. A German woman had struck her as "rather offensive" against England and

full of bitterness. Troubled by my own sin in forming this opinion, I got up and prayed very earnestly for her the same night; and whilst I prayed it seemed as if I saw her (only inwardly) in a room, and one by one changes came. First the room was rich and then all turned shabby and poor. Then her personal treasures were taken one by one, then her friends and relations were taken—then I saw Germany stretching before her, and I saw how she was consumed with love for her country, and I understood how *torn* her heart was when Germany fell. Lastly I saw her with Germany in the form of a child, trying to hide the child's faults with one hand and to bind up his wounds with the other.

I was filled with pity and love for her, and when I saw her again we talked of the war without the least ill-feeling and were greatly drawn together.

I have since learned that she has indeed lost riches, position, friends and relations and is now leading a heroic life of suffering.

The sure cure for bitterness, Caryll comments, is to pray and do penance for the person; love will grow in proportion. "It is not according to how *much* penance I do or how *many* prayers I say, but how much *love* I put into it."

She met on this trip a Hungarian with "a note in his voice" like that of the man she had loved. "I am obliged to talk to him often, and it twists my heart to do it. After all these years of driving back the thought of Sidney, I cannot see the faintest likeness to him in anyone without feeling as if my whole life were an open wound."

She had been "homesick for Iris" too, and a few pages later she writes, "Heavenly to be home once more." Human love meant an immense amount to Caryll, but she seems to have felt almost from the first that she must not lean upon it, that she must learn to live in dependence on God alone:

Now I expect nothing of myself, just nothing at all, or of anyone else: the result is I expect everything of God. . . . I do not crave for sympathy any more—I am so overfull of it to give, and this is Our dear Lord's gift to me—His latest precious gift. . . . I have read too much, made too many useless rules, considered too many theories; now I must abandon all except the thought of Our Lord. . . . I must study Him more closely, with an empty heart without restrictions. I must go back to Nazareth, I must follow Him in Jerusalem, see Him with His apostles and learn to imitate Him, not from spiritual books but from Himself.

It is the beginning of Advent when she writes this, and many pages follow setting down "in their lovely confusion" some of the thoughts that crowd upon her and which we find developed later in her various books. Clearly she had often intense joy in her intercourse with God—she meditated on the Trinity, she let herself "sink into God," she thought of Our Lady with her Son: "But what is between Our Lord and His mother is out of my reach." But there was also great suffering: the human trials of her life, darkness and dryness which she felt amounted to a purgatory on earth, and just plain human temptations.

About temptation she said at this time to an intimate friend that when heavily assailed, it helped her to get up and walk about the room, knowing that the trial would pass. To another friend she said that we are all like people trying to drive a team of powerful horses with a thread of silk. The only thing to do is to put this thread into God's hands, and He will control the horses.

And in the Journal she records two dreams:

I was tempted, and after praying for strength I sat down by the fire and let my soul sink into God.

I think I fell asleep, and what followed was a vivid dream. I saw a great plain before me, and there was nothing but rocks and cold and darkness, and in the middle was the source of my temptation represented like a little glowing warm castle.

I was struggling whether I would go to the castle or not, when Our Lady stood before me with the Infant Jesus in her arms. She told me to take Him and carry Him across the plain and on the other side would be Heaven. His face was covered, and she told me not to look at it.

I started, and as I went I felt I *could* not do anything to hurt Him because He depended on me, so I was able to pass the castle easily. When I got to the other side Our Lady was waiting; I gave her the child and asked to see His face. She smiled and shook her head, answering "In Heaven" and disappeared. When I woke up I no longer had any temptation.

Another time when I had suffered a lot I dreamt (this time really asleep) that I saw the child, about four years old, lying in a kind of basket with His feet resting on the world and behind Him a great field of blue, but His face was turned away. I said, "Shall I see your face?" and an angel came and said, "Seek to see it in Heaven."

A thing that has fascinated me in these pages is Caryll's steady conviction that she has a special vocation not for herself alone but for others.

At the end of 1926 she was very unwell. She wrote on Dec. 26th:

Lord, the child whom Thou lovest is sick.

I realized today how very sick she is; at first I was a little afraid, then I knelt down and offered myself anew to God, and now I am ready to live a long while or a short while. He is here and He is there, and wherever He is I shall be content to be. . . .

I *know* that every time I try for a job and fail, every time my headache comes violently and makes me lie up useless, every time I try to show out God's meaning and it all goes wrong, it is none the less on every occasion a complete and a successful thing instead of a failure; it is a finished action because it is God's will. Nothing is complete but His will, and that completes all our seemingly unfinished, interrupted, useless actions on earth "All things pass away and thou along with them." "And He shall wipe all tears from their eyes."

And on January 14th, 1927:

Prayer and meditation I can no longer do much of, and I can do little and very poor work, but I can offer Him long patience, content in seeing the gradual crumbling of my hopes. Faith in my vocation in spite of all that seems to disprove it. . . .

A month later things had worked up to a climax of despair. It cannot have been easy for Iris, surrounded by bitterly disapproving friends and relatives; for Caryll it appeared desperate. Naturally enough, they attributed to her the lowest motives for living, as they felt, on Iris's charity. They did not believe in her deep affection, they heartily disliked the religion which was her greatest treasure and which she had thanked God for giving to her friend. Caryll, deeply sensitive, was well aware of their attitude. She had, too, a special resentment towards someone whose name she never told me when speaking of those days. Nor does she tell it in the Journal, but we see her applying the Gospels to the healing of her own hurt and the forgiveness of whatever it was she had to forgive:

February 1927

At last I am finding poverty terribly difficult to bear, not having **no** money but having no paint to earn it with, no bus fares to go to fetch the work, no materials to make samples; every side hampered, every way shut off, and sneers and comments on my debts from the very person who has deprived me of my own money.

These were the months in which by some confusion, or simply because she thought Caryll no longer needed it, her mother was not sending on to her an allowance made for her support by Mr. Houselander. Iris, on her side, was not aware of the situation, and asking her—or indeed anyone— for financial help was something Caryll could never face. Nothing made her happier than being able later to contribute a share to housekeeping expenses. But at this time, Iris says, "She had a roof over her head, she had meals, but I did not take in how often she had not a penny to pay a bus fare."

The Journal goes on (in February 1927):

It is an opportunity to practice patience, to ignore the sentimental substitute held out to me and practise *real* charity. I must try not to dwell on things, to love poverty and look on it as a gift from God's hand. I do realize it and in that way love it. I must smother my hatred of injustice when it is personal.

Remember Our Lord's teaching: if a man contend for your cloak, give him your coat also.

Refuse to be bitter, to sink to the world's standards.

Trust God. I have His promise.

Della, Kath, Jimmie and Mickie all out of work, but God will provide.

I must study the Sermon on the Mount. All its teaching is above the silly resentment I feel. Now what is really the matter is this: I haven't enough trust in God. I want to help my friends, to buy my own medicine, to keep my clothes neater and please Iris, and to do this by work.

Our Lord will give me the means to work if I seek His Kingdom first. I must not faint now, it is the critical part of my vocation—days like this, days of fierce fighting with myself, always give me faith in my vocation. "Something bitter to suffer," my heart calls out, and it calls finally rejoicing because the cross is the sign.

Now that's better, first of all seek His Kingdom and trust Him, for myself and the others, for today.

(1) Don't worry, forget cares; they are as dangerous as riches —more so, for they are more subtle. Our Lord said that the seed was choked by the cares and riches of this world.

(2) Since work is impossible, *pray*, and pray in peace. God is working for me. He is going on gently with His plan.

(3) Thank Him. It is the real thing, it is glorious, it is the lovely entrance of the will of God.

It was the proverbial dark hour before dawn for in the same month comes a cry of gratitude:

It would be strange if I made no note of God's goodness since my last entry. First of all He put right the matter of my allowance in the way I would have chosen, had it dawned on me to choose a way.

Secondly He gave me so much work that I hadn't a moment to record anything. He gave work to Della, Tim, Kathleen and Eve.

I've been thanking Him and thanking Him. Cannot cease to believe in my vocation even in moments of blackness. In God's way, in God's time, I know it will arise, and many souls will be drawn to Christ.

13th March, 1928
Received as a novice of the Third Order of St. Francis.

15th March, 1928
All desire for the few things awry to be set straight has left me—with God's grace I intend to enjoy them for His Glory; they are after all my only treasure; a greater love of the poor than I had ever known has come to me, and a new, different light as to poverty, God's will and so on.

July 1928

It is time to stop *playing* at love and to love with a will, to lay my hand on the steel that I have never dared to wield, to use the knife on self-love. No more high-flown ideas now, only Charity, the curb on the tongue. . . .

My heart is cold, my thoughts are cold, my soul is cold, but my will is on fire; in that fire I will forge a sword of service . . . [as to other people] ask myself every day . . . what have I given, taken, expected, how used for God, how sharpened, real kindness?

20th January, 1929

What a gap—and in it Smoky has died. I am happy for him and *long* to die and be with him again.

6th March, 1929

After all these Holy Communions, Masses, Confessions, books, rules, resolutions—*nothing* is done.

No, God forgive me, His grace works silently, secretly; in the hour of trial I shall know that it is so—I need to trust.

But alas I know *this:* I am as unkind as before, my tongue as violent, my mind as melancholy, my will *more* weak, my fervour died out, my self-indulgence grown as I could never have imagined, my spirit of prayer fading—and all this in the very sight and faith of God.

"Self-indulgence" seems always to mean smoking. Caryll resolves to fine herself a penny for every cigarette in excess of the allotted daily ten. She exclaims (in her own odd spelling): "Tobbaco! what a thing to put before God."

But it was a good many years before she succeeded in breaking this rooted habit—and I always wonder how she managed to get cigarettes or to do without them in the period when she had no pennies to spend even on bus fares. One difficulty in dating the events of Caryll's life is that she lives so intensely in each period or episode that one tends to imagine it as going on endlessly.

Considering again the question of a rule of life, Caryll seems to see deeper in 1929 than she did earlier:

. . . the Will of God [she writes] is my devotion, and when I consider that the very things which seem to hinder are manifestations of His will, I may say that the beginning of my rule must be to fling myself wholeheartedly into managing my hindrances for God's glory.

The Journal ends in this month with the words "Oh Blessed, Blessed peace of God! How little I deserve it now, and yet knowing His mercy I dare to hope for it."

And she wrote in *Young Green Poems*:

The Refusal

I found Him dear to whom I prayed
  Who did my prayer withstand,
And all my want forgot I stayed
  To kiss His open hand.
Wherein there was not my desire
  But one sharp wound that glowed
And from the burning of its fire
  Love flowed and overflowed.
I blessed the heart I could not move
  To give for my distress
The thing I asked, who being love
  Refused to give me less.

7

Life at Evelyn Gardens,

1925-1935

TAKEN BY ITSELF, the Journal of the years in Evelyn Gardens might be misleading. All her friends remember Caryll as gay, amusing, ready to join in any fun that was going and often initiating it. Louis Billaux and his cousin Jacques Doneux, both partners in Grossé's firm, used to come often to the house, and although one entry records that she sat up talking with Jacques about God till 1 A.M., his memories are mostly of gay parties when they all brought musical instruments, and Caryll would bang a drum. He remembers, too, her teaching their office "boy" (actually an illiterate forty-year-old) wood-carving and with endless patience building up his self-confidence.

She was now regularly employed by Grossé and sent to decorate churches in various places. She tells with delight of a decorating expedition to Eastbourne.

"The downs were full of welcome, and coming home they were crowned by great columns of dark cloud, like the pillars of a huge doorway leading to a hidden city. The sea-air, a blessing to me like God's grace, filled me with love and joy."

But decorating, says Jacques, "was not her strong point. She would accept any criticism, but she got bored finishing things off. She was just arriving at success as a wood-carver when she gave it up for writing. Her cut-outs were wonderfully successful."

She did, too, a good deal of painting and mentions with pleasure in the Journal visits to her sister at which she painted "under difficulties" the portrait of her little niece—"Deirdre not still a second, portrait going on pretty well in spite of it!!" The same day the baptism of Deirdre's baby sister is recorded —"Bridget Viola Mary, she cried lustily."

After the baptism Caryll went back with her sister to tea, met the priest ("very nice but rather 'hearty' for my taste") and bathed Deirdre. She had a great affection for this niece and wrote two poems to her, the first beginning "Thou atom in thy mighty bib. . . ." In the second, "To Deirdre Five Years Old," she sees the child, unspoilt image of God, trying to give to her doll the love and life the Father gives to us:

> When I return, most sweet,
> To sit at thy small feet
> And teach thee 1, 2, 3, and a, b, c,
> I learn my lesson, yes,
> From thy huge littleness;
> I learn the lore of Heaven, Child, from thee.
>
> Yes God, and only He,
> Is one, child soul, with thee:
> Thou hast thy silly doll of nothing worth,
> But since thou lovest this
> A living thing it is
> Born at thy will, a never-ending birth.
>
> Worn out a little now
> With kisses on its brow,
> A little flattened by thy tight embrace,

Yet even I behold
(Grown in thy presence bold)
The shadow of thy spirit on its face!

So is our Father, just
As tender unto dust
As thou to sawdust; so do Christ's Hands cling,
Seeming to hurt the toy
Of God for sheer sweet joy
Of giving life to His poor lifeless thing!

Oh! Life of God in a child
Unbroken and undefiled,
I believe in the Kingdom of God in thee!
Thou hast Christ's brimming cup,
But canst not lift it up.
I come to drink the chalice on bended knee.

Caryll was the godmother of the Billaux's child, David. She loved this family, calling them "the dearest imaginable trinity." As a wedding present she had painted the front hall of their house with sky and trees and birds. She stayed with them one summer at Lyme Regis and another at Angmering and delighted in giving David the pleasures suitable to his age—his first ice cream at eighteen months, his first outing in a boat, and later vast schoolboy teas. She carved for him a Christ child in wood with twelve companionable lambs.

Elizabeth Billaux did not become a Catholic for many years after her marriage, and Caryll wrote her long letters answering her problems. When this correspondence drew her closer to the Faith, Caryll wrote joyfully:

You know that I do literally love Louis as if he were my brother—people sometimes say that of a man but don't really mean it, they mean that they feel sentimental to some man but are afraid they ought not to. But in this case I am genuine, I

think of him as I would of an only brother. . . . Well, naturally
it fills me with joy to imagine his happiness.

I think the long time you have been pondering things good,
because I am sure you are too fine, too big and genuine and too
capable of real holiness, to become a Catholic except as the result of your own experience, and your own experience does of
course include loving and marrying Louis, being David's mother,
and so on.

Louis, after seeing Joan's nursery, asked Caryll to paint a
cot for little David. No doubt they wanted the cot, but I sus-
pect they wanted also to help Caryll financially, and they
must have felt the despair attaching to any such attempt at the
very typical letter she wrote to Elizabeth:

I shall be overjoyed to paint David's cot and certainly I will
put on it the sort of very young things you suggest. I agree they
are the most suited to a baby, and in any case you are the one
to know best what suits *this* adorable baby!

I think Louis only thought of knights because he has seen
some on our nursery at Evelyn Gardens, and they are decorative,
but that nursery was for a little girl of five or so, and I agree
that the simpler and the younger and the brighter things are for
a tiny, the better—so we will leap and frolic!

Dear Elizabeth, I do deeply appreciate your kindness in
suggesting that you would like to pay, but I could not *dream* of
it, it will be my greatest joy to *give* David *all* I can, and all you
will let me, for so long as I live, and I hope even a little after I
am dead!

This indeed she did—for during the last years of the war
when her books were making Caryll prosperous she sent
David's parents a cheque for £100 towards his education. In
her will she left him £50 to be given to him on his twenty-
first birthday.

Caryll's problems in earning a living were certainly made

more acute both by her attitude to money and by her relentless honesty about her own work. Speaking in the Journal of
her fight with her ex-partners' debts, she says how strange it
seems that God "has put in my heart the hatred of money and
yet made it my duty to struggle so hard for it."

She would often, says Jacques, say of some job she had done,
"That's simply frightful, you can't possibly pay me for it."
Another letter to the Billaux after the war had started brings
out this same quixotic attitude. She had done a set of Stations
of the Cross for a customer in Manchester, which owing
largely to war conditions had not been thought satisfactory.
Caryll writes, "You could point out that now the artist is
conscripted, the paint unobtainable. . . . So far as money is
concerned, forget what's supposed to be owing to me, use it to
get someone else to do it, if they will."

It must have been easy for those who did not *want* to pay
Caryll when she made it so difficult for those who did.

Caryll's apprenticeship as a house decorator turned out to
be lucky for herself and her friend. They decided to decorate
the Evelyn Gardens house themselves. Caryll covered the
walls of the day nursery with fairy tales and painted the night
nursery ceiling the dark blue of a night sky spangled with
stars. Iris remembers her on a ladder singing, as she painted,
"Oh Mary, we crown thee with blossoms so gay"; Jacques less
poetically recalls her painting with her right hand and holding a "potty" in her left to catch the drips. The smell of paint
was not mitigated by the skills of today, and both girls got
painters' colic rather badly.

Iris and Caryll were not alone either at Bacombe Warren
or at Evelyn Gardens. There was first the all-important only
child Joan whom Iris adored and Caryll accused her of spoiling, though she too worked in Joan's service: painting her
nursery and playing with her in the early days, sending her
long letters when she was away at school. Iris's mother, Mrs.
Bennett, came to live with her daughter after the move from

Bacombe Warren; there were the cook and housemaid; there was Jessie, who had been first Mrs. Bennett's maid, then Iris's, and finally Joan's nurse.

Caryll seldom lost a friend, and the fiancé of her early youth still often took her out. When she engaged an impecunious dancing teacher just to give her employment he insisted on paying for the lessons. Caryll, in fact, danced very well and loved going to dances.

Countess Paoli—her former mentor in deportment!—also came to Evelyn Gardens, and almost all Caryll's friends became, as time went on, friends of Iris also. To some extent this was reciprocal—but Caryll was apt to put up a resistance against the more wealthy and worldly element whose invitations are recorded in an old diary of Iris's showing daily lunch and dinner parties, balls and theatre parties. ("Awful," said a friend fascinated by this record, "to think that every one of these moments will have to be accounted for!") Caryll had not the time, the clothes or the inclination for a full social life, but she did share some of her friend's friends and could have shared more had she chosen.

One day a friend with whom Iris was staying in the country rang Caryll up begging her to join them for the night. Caryll was working some way from home and had not even a night-gown with her. This objection was brushed aside and the loan of a nightgown promised. But late at night, left in her bedroom, Caryll realized this had been forgotten. She got into bed naked to find an electric blanket—not self-regulating, as it would be today—which she had no idea how to manipulate. She spent the night alternately grilling and freezing and got up unrefreshed, hoping for a restorative lengthy bath, but no towels had been provided! Too angry to take the obvious course of ringing for the housemaid, she recklessly poured a whole bottle of bath salts into the water, dragged a sheet from the bed and dried herself on that. And so back to London and the day's toil.

As time went on, both mothers softened towards their daughters. Mrs. Bennett once dressed Caryll up in a golden wig of her own, made up her face, and decked her out in a smart hat and veil, when she wanted to go somewhere unrecognized. Another time, she gave Iris and Caryll her tickets for the second act of a Wagner opera, tightly wrapping a gold cloak around Caryll's everyday clothes ("like a cocoon," says Iris) and sending them in her car. Caryll loved Wagner, but was nearly stifled by the cloak, which she had to keep tightly fastened to conceal the dress. They had gone off in a hurry, forgetting the problem of returning; between them they had only fourpence, so they took a twopenny bus-ride and walked the rest of the way, Caryll kicking off the high-heeled shoes Iris had lent her and walking home in stockinged feet. Getting near the house, Iris too took off her shoes, and they both began to run, passing a policeman on his beat who looked much startled as two golden figures came up noiselessly behind him.

Every summer Iris took a house at the seaside or in the country to which the whole household migrated. Caryll often went with them. But a letter one summer shows that she had stayed behind and was worrying about her friend. "Joan darling," she writes to the now schoolgirl daughter,

do please make it *your* job to look after her and make her fatter. You know that for you there is nothing she won't do. . . . Take the cream pot and pour a *lot* on her plate first, don't let *her* give *you* all the tit-bits; also don't let her get too tired, and don't *jump* on her. You are big and heavy and she is so brittle, so breakable, as there is so little fat on her bones. . . . When Peggy told me she is thinner I felt so miserable. I can't have a decent holiday like you, but I was happy as I thought it was doing Mummy good, and now I'm not too sure, I feel wretched. . . .

Maybe I worry too much, but I love her so much and you know how one feels when one loves anyone. Well, I thought to myself, "I will write to Joan and tell her how I feel, she is understanding and wise, and so long as she does not forget she will do this looking after Iris for me". . . .

To impress all this on Joan's memory, "for summer holiday memories are not too good," Caryll sends a rhyme which ends:

I mustn't jump upon her like a silly nine-stone ass,
For Mummy is a brittle thing, six foot of shining glass,
But I must fill her up with cream and bread and sweets
And pat myself upon the back each time she sits and eats.

Another year, the entire family—Iris, her mother, Joan, Joan's nurse, Caryll and two maids—all stayed in a chalet at a kind of super-Holiday Camp on the east coast. Caryll would not take part in the endless organized amusements, except for one fancy-dress dance, to which she went as a savage, dressed in sackcloth and carrying a shinbone.

Reconciliation with Mrs. Houselander had, as we have seen, come earlier, and Iris and she had long been on the best of terms. Gert had a great sense of fun, and there was something gallant about her which those who knew her best still salute, speaking of her as "the old war-horse." "If you went to Gert with a hard luck story," one friend said, "she would never turn you away."

One day Iris had received an invitation for a week-end at a famous country house. As she read the request for information about the time she *and her maid* would arrive, Gert said, "I'd love to see that place. Let me go as your maid." Iris tried in vain to dissuade her; she appeared in neat black dress and stockings and carried out the part perfectly. It was Iris who was nervous, not she.

"This is the bell into your room," their hostess said, "in case Mrs. Wyndham wants you."

"Yes, my Lady."

"There is coal for her fire out there on the landing."

"Yes, my Lady."

Left alone, they burst into helpless giggles. "Don't you dare to ring," said Gert. And later, "Damn you, why haven't you got a title? I had to sit at the bottom of the table in the servants' hall."

But she brought it off triumphantly, and was highly delighted by the adventure. Years later she told Charles Scott-Paton that she knew some members of the house-party and feared she might be recognized. Iris, who after all was there, is convinced this was not so—and Gert may very well have put it in to heighten the drama.

Sometimes Willmott Houselander invited Caryll and Iris or some other friend to his yacht, and fed them on pink gin and lobster. One visitor remembers an expedition when the rain poured outside, and over the drinks Willmott handed Caryll a letter for her opinion on the writer's character. Iris remembers his taking them on the river in a small boat and recalls Caryll as petrified with fear. Iris herself loved boats and on one occasion was caught on a friend's yacht between France and England by a bad storm and was lashed to the mast for twelve hours. The yacht lacked ballast and had been taken by Iris's friend without her husband's knowledge. Over and over again Iris recited the rosary while Caryll, at home, spent the night in a "terrific sweat," praying for her friend— and read in the morning reports of yachts lost in the channel. They were met by the owner in the towering rage that so often succeeds fear. When Iris got back to Evelyn Gardens, preceded by a reassuring telephone call, she found Caryll and Joan waiting for her with bunches of flowers.

Peggy O'Reilly (now Mrs. Muller), who had known Caryll earlier, had been away for several years, first trying her vocation as a Holy Child nun and then living in the West Indies. She was now back in London and often came to Evelyn Gardens. She remembers how at first Caryll's little sitting-room was rather a place apart from the rest of the house. "Impecunious creatures drifted in and out. At first we didn't mingle, later we were one home. . . .

"Baby," she says, "was always painting. She never stopped working for one moment while we were all prattling. She was determined to be a saint—I said, 'Why not become a nun?'

"Caryll loved Mother Aloysia, but she said, 'No convent would have me, certainly not the Holy Child. And I don't know how you could endure sleeping in a dormitory with all those novices.'

"But," Peggy goes on, "Caryll wanted to give everything. It was a definite principle that she would keep nothing she could give away. She became what she was by daily and hourly austerity. She never let up on herself, she never gave in to physical weakness, she worked endless hours."

Peggy said once to her, "I wish, Baby, I had your gift of repartee."

"Oh, Peggy, it's a curse. My mother and I both have it and at a party we egg each other on."

"She had *terrific* remorse after a rash conversation"—and Peggy remembers arriving after a long journey to find a letter from Caryll abasing herself for a harsh judgment and begging her friend not to repeat it to others.

"She adored Iris, but she criticized even her."

In this happier atmosphere of "one home" Caryll found energy for other activities besides her work, including writing plays, producing and acting in them. There was of course a good deal of gagging. No manuscript has survived, but Iris has keen memories of her own mother as one of an audience all convulsed with laughter when Caryll's mother acted the Genie of the Lamp while Caryll herself played Aladdin. Mrs. Houselander had, as we have seen, already shown herself a pretty good actress; she boasted of showing this again when one day in Bond Street she almost collided with a chauffeur who had been at the country house of her masquerade, and whose recognition changed into bewilderment as she unblinkingly met his gaze.

Caryll had a good deal of her mother in her. Infinitely more sensitive, she had the same instinct for fun, telling tall stories, using strong language, making sometimes Rabelaisian jokes. Willmott Houselander had educated her before educating his budgerigars, and some of the words had stuck. The Caryll of the Journal, later so sought after as a spiritual guide, was unrecognizable by some of her early friends. Those who did not share her faith suspected hypocrisy, but in fact the two Carylls both existed all her life. I had written "side by side," yet this is hardly accurate, for they were deeply fused. Caryll had perhaps a touch of vanity about herself as "woman of the world"! My son, sitting at her request for his portrait at the age of eighteen, was amazed at learning from me that she had only been out of the Church and leading a bohemian life for such a few years. He had somehow got the notion of a long and varied experience. But like all those who got to know her intimately he carried away the double impression of someone enormously and endlessly amusing and of someone continually aware of the divine. It is a rather unusual mixture, in so strong a measure, of each element.

Poplar was and is one of the poorest areas of London. What was called a Settlement had been started there when these schemes were in vogue at the end of the nineteenth century, and was now under the care of the former pupils of the Holy Child schools. A photo shows Caryll and Iris dressed as rosebuds and obviously enjoying themselves in a mock ballet at the Settlement. Only one performer knew anything about ballet, and she wisely persuaded the others to try to dance properly, adding that they would certainly do it so badly as to be far more amusing than if they guyed it.

Iris often went with Caryll to Poplar, but her first Catholic good work was nearly her last, for a Settlement child whom

she held on her lap gave her measles, of which she almost
died. Caryll nursed her through the crisis of a desperate illness—a crisis in which Iris's personal maid, also a Catholic,
refused to help, as she said that she could not miss her Children of Mary meeting at the church. The doctor was on a
confinement case and could not come, and the terrified Caryll
was left to deal single-handed with her apparently dying
friend. "She saved my life," says Iris. "She sat up with me all
night, bathing me in tepid water to reduce the fever."

In thanksgiving for her own conversion, Iris took Caryll
to Lourdes on a pilgrimage led by Archbishop Goodier—
£24 a head, she recalls, and this sum covered the return
journey and a week in Lourdes. The journey was not very
comfortable: food was only provided on the platforms where
the train halted. Water gave out in the lavatories, and the
pilgrims had to sit up all night, growing steadily dirtier with
the smuts and grime of the train. But in Lourdes they witnessed the cure of a five-year-old boy who, as a baby, had been
kicked in the face by a horse, disfigured and blinded, the
optic nerve (as his mother told them) being destroyed. Iris remembers the moment when the child received his sight: never
having seen—as far as he could remember—he screamed with
terror, and his mother fainted, while the priests ran about
calming the crowd and (said Caryll) assuring them that nothing had happened! Iris remembers seeing the boy that night
walking in the torchlight procession, carrying a candle; and
Caryll saw him at the Grotto, taking the candles which pilgrims handed to him, lighting them, and sticking them in the
sconces. She had told stories to him on the boat, and after the
miracle said to his mother that no doubt she would now send
a telegram announcing the news to her husband; but—"That
was faith, if you like," Caryll commented—she replied that a
telegram would only frighten him: they had both known the
child would be cured, and had, in fact, now that he was five,
entered him for a school.

Rosamond Batchelor, avid reader of her contributions, can date the beginning of Caryll's connection with *The Children's Messenger* from the fact that in many of her drawings she used Joan as a little girl for her model. She probably met Father Bliss through Father Steuart, who was her confessor for a short time after her full return to the Church in 1925. This meeting had an immense effect on her future. "He was the first," says Rosamond, "to tell her that she was primarily a writer and must give up everything for this. He saw the unique quality of her thought and expression, encouraged her enormously . . . helped her by his understanding and praise to develop her writing in a direction which, but for him, it might not have taken. It was he who gave the name 'rhythms' to her unrhymed poems. . . . And Father Bliss's mysticism, his deep humanity and charity under so shy an exterior, his love of poetry, especially Hopkins . . . all played a great and long-lasting part in Caryll's life."

Soon Father Bliss became her spiritual guide and Caryll on her side worked hard for him, seeking for themes for her many stories, and illustrating them herself. She wrote for *The Messenger of the Sacred Heart* and for *The Children's Messenger,* both edited by him. For the first she did articles as well as stories, some of a mystical turn. Iris had lived in Rumania with her grandparents up to the age of eleven, and the Russian influence so noticeable in Caryll was now supplemented by Iris's memories of Rumanian legends and traditions. The Eastern Church is constantly present in her writings of this time, and one sees too, I think, a struggle going on in her to find expression for her own originality where it conflicted with the conventional shape which Catholic writing had largely taken. It is greatly to Father Bliss's credit that he usually helped Caryll to break the mould—a mould already partly set for her in a convent-school childhood. But in her letters one finds an occasional doubt expressed as to whether he will accept an article which, by the standards of conventional piety, is over-bold. And in her own writing one still notes occasional traces of an early bad manner.

Caryll was living in a number of worlds which in those days were far more rigidly divided than they are today—not certainly *as* rigidly as before 1914, but far more so than after 1940. There was the fashionable society of Iris's family, the bohemian world of her own artist friends, mixed of necessity with that of the commerce in which many of them must earn a living. There was the world of the poor, who were at this moment *very* poor, which she was always trying more and more to belong to.

There were, too, in the personal sphere, the separated worlds of her father, her mother and her sister. There was the Catholic world of her school friends and the pagan world of most of the people she was meeting day by day. I remember a girl out of that pagan world who, coming into the Church, came out of a welter of discussion, questing, analysing, that would amaze and bewilder most Catholics. "We talked of religion," she said, "until we were sick." At the back of her Journal Caryll wrote:

We live in a time that is tortured

> "Between two worlds,
> One dead
> One powerless to be born."

Some people cling to what is past; some, the fewer and braver, face the future; but to live harmoniously in the present is an almost superhuman task.

The modernist writers are not the contemptible egoists which they are too often supposed to be. They refuse to write anything which is not an integral part of their own experience, and most of them have no experience of Faith as we understand it. The problems tormenting those of the modernist sort outside the Church are a thousand times more terrible to those within it.

My position is that I am obsessed by the spirit of this age, with all its faults I love it and believe in it.

I believe that it is the most serious duty I have, to see, to *recognize* Christ in it and to go on, never to go back; that all our modern inventions and conditions are to be used, cleared of abuses and lifted up but not swept away, that compromise with the present and a looking back to the past is a sin.

I find no sympathy with this view in the thought of my fellow-Catholics, who seem to me to be always striving to return to the past and to set fierce limitations on the uses of the present.

I find in this attitude a deadlock, a deadening and choking of effort.

I do not trust myself to stand alone, I will not range myself among those who, though they clearly share my desires, do not share my faith in Christ.

Consequently I am tortured.

I desire supremely and above all to be in perfect harmony with the whole world.

How exactly did she propose to be in harmony with a *whole* world patently inharmonious—indeed at fierce war with itself?

In Caryll's eyes the greatest of all obstacles to harmony was the gulf dug by society between the respectable and the outcast—whether cast out by society for wrongdoing or merely dropped for the sin of failure and poverty.

"She wanted," a very intimate friend told me, "to make herself one with prostitutes and drunkards—to go to pubs and get drunk with them. Father Steuart thought this too extreme."

Caryll certainly sought the extreme in all things, and, as we have seen, whatever her experience of pubs, she had already adventured onto the shady side of Piccadilly and was not merely imagining the sort of people she would find there.

It is a far cry from Piccadilly Circus to the Ladies of the Grail—but it was actually her search for a union of all classes and for an extreme expression of this as a union with Christ that led Caryll to welcome the Grail enthusiastically when it first came from Holland to England.

"She had read," says Rosamond, "a somewhat misleading account of them, which led her to think that their work was a kind of counter-blast to Communism in that it established Christian 'cells' in working-class milieux—that their object was to *share* the lives of working-class women and girls in factories and other places of work, and deeply Christianize this background from within. When she found that, although they did some work among the poor, they did not seem to regard it as their main mission—and in fact separated the two classes among whom they operated—she saw how completely she had misunderstood their aims."

Most English Catholics know the Grail today both as a Secular Institute and as a lay Movement. At this date the scope of the Movement was less widely conceived than it is today. It was solely for youth and was directed mainly towards the alumnae of such schools as the Sacred Heart and the Holy Child. It is hard to put the two elements of the inner Society and the outer Movement into one definition or to list all the activities undertaken—study weeks, the planning of liturgical and theological lectures and retreats, a monthly magazine, religious art and drama.

When I first met the Grail I noted chiefly the colourful quality of their displays: *Everyman* in the Albert Hall was an outstanding example, but even with smaller groups and less ambitious pageantry the appeal to both eye and ear is striking. As a Youth Movement it appeals to the love of music, dancing and colour inherent in the young and increasingly directs this love towards the Liturgy. Perhaps the most important success of this side of its work has been the introduction to England of the Gelineau Psalms.

The Ladies of the Grail were the inner circle and are now known as the Grail Society. They direct the outer circle or Movement, which now includes, besides youth groups, family, parish, and college groups, individuals and even

schoolgirls—known as Links. All these vary in the degree
of their dedication. The Society itself is one of those group-
ings of people totally devoted to the apostolate and living
a life similar to that of religious, for which the name Secular
Institute has been found and consecrated by the Church.

Obviously for the lay members too an intense spiritual
life is necessary. When Baroness Yvonne Bosch van Drake-
stein, the Grail leader who came to England from Holland
in 1932, first met Caryll she realized her unique quality and
did all that she could do to foster this life. "Caryll was a
natural mystic," she says.

Caryll on her side felt a deep sympathy with the Baroness,
and even when she fell out of sympathy with the Grail itself
her affection for its leader persisted. Although she never
actually joined the Grail even as a member she did, down
to the war years and through them, help it as much as she
could. Even if it was not doing exactly what she wanted, she
felt that it might have something of value to offer in developing a spirit of faith and enthusiasm in the young. In little
groups of two or three many of the girls came for her advice
and help. She painted the back scene for the performance
of *Everyman* and enlisted her friends to help with pen and
brush other Grail displays and also the magazine.

Above all she made for them one of her best sets of
Stations of the Cross. This is now in the chapel of the Sloane
Street house, but it was, the Baroness tells me, originally
intended for something Caryll longed for: just a room, a
place of peace in London filled with beautiful things where
anyone could come and "could find Christ." A chapel was
needed for Grail members and for those who can worship
with them, but this other room was just to be an oasis for
the weary, the heart-sick, the *non*-believer or the doubter,
a place of rest and quiet. The idea was abandoned from lack
of space, but it had been for a while accepted and had
called out all Caryll's energies.

The Baroness speaks of Caryll's "immense vitality." It was,

I believe, partly through this encounter that she fully discovered her vocation. She had to decide just where she stood
on many aspects of the apostolate. With Fr. Bliss she had
been a disciple—she was never a disciple of any Grail
leader, although devoted to Yvonne and lavishly generous
with her own abundant ideas. "She would give me several
versions of the same thing, all written in a night or a night
and a day. She would say, 'You can do what you like with
them.' She would come down in the early afternoon and
stay till *very* late. We would give her dinner, but she would
only peck at her food."

It is clear from the masses of essays, rhythms, fragments
which the Baroness still has after choosing out those she
liked best for the magazine, that Caryll was in a highly creative state just then. And she wanted, she needed, other minds
to co-operate with hers. The type of discussion she loved does
not suit everybody, and Yvonne says frankly, "My brain
was whirling before she left."

Enclosing a delicious drawing of chestnut buds Caryll
wrote to her one spring:

When I came in last night Iris called me to her bedside and
said, "Go quickly and draw our chestnut buds; their little hands
are folded in prayer, and tomorrow they will spread them out
and say, 'Dominus vobiscum.' "

So I went down to the sitting-room and drew them, and sure
enough they are tiny hands, with little thin wrists, praying. . . .
It is so *lovely* to think that all over England they are opening
these small green hands and saying "Dominus vobiscum" to the
world. . . .

. . . That is our "Message." The Lord be with you and with
your spirit!

I am happy that you feel strongly for this Christing of the
world.

It seemed to Caryll that almost worse than the menace of

Hitler, which was just beginning, was "a great wave of spiritual Naziness . . . sweeping through England and in a yet more deadly fashion driving people out of the inward kingdom of their souls—out of their home—Christ."

This undated letter is curiously interesting, for it not only puts Caryll's point of view more strongly than any other I have seen—it also assumes that her friend is in fundamental agreement with it. She expresses her amazement that they *should* agree so fully, coming as they do from different countries, very different backgrounds of education, environment, circumstance, occupations. Yet "we are in such agreement over what is really inexpressible . . . we meet . . . in the Crucified Christ."

There had been a quarrel—"over which," says Caryll, "I shed many tears"—arising from Caryll's "sense of rage and frustration" with the Grail. But this had, she believed, ended by bringing Yvonne and herself into a new and deeper unity. "Your words, 'to believe in our message even when it seems impossible,' have in fact made me believe at times when I saw no light. Now I see light." She blames herself bitterly for talking too long, too much, too "violently" and "exhaustingly." She ought to have persuaded Yvonne to do all the talking, "but that is not easy to do." One pictures an exhausted Yvonne listening as the night wore on, less and less attentively, to a vehement Caryll!

Here was the crux. The two friends held ardently to the same ideals, but were far from being in agreement as to methods. Caryll believed Catholic Action as too often practised to be a menace, desire for visible results an immense danger: "so long as we believe that our activities, our vocations, are going to have an effect which Christ's own life on earth did *not* have, so long as we 'organize' for a *visible* kingdom, we shall not be at peace."

But she had now come to believe that Yvonne was going "to stem the advance of over-organization. To begin to

simplify; to begin, so to speak, to tidy out, to throw out
the rubbish. . . .

"England is the house that you are to spring-clean."

It is the paradox of the Gospel: to work secretly, looking
only to "the Father who seeth in secret," yet to let our
"light shine before men." It is the problem of every Christian
organization, including the Church itself, which after all
was founded by Christ to gather in all the world, yet to re-
ject worldliness. And any organization can be helped im-
measurably by having a devil's advocate on the doorstep.

At this time one of Caryll's favourite literary forms—
abandoned later—was the Dialogue. Several were sent me by
the Baroness. The interlocutors are always anonymously A.
and B., and the form is used as a way of putting the different
sides of an idea from the angle of different minds, both to
help each to clarify his own thoughts and to develop the
subject more completely. There is "A Dialogue on Adoration," a series of three called, "Should We Understand?"—
with further subtitles—"Understanding the Apostolate,"
"Idols or God," and two dialogues on the way of approach
to a Communist.

The three on understanding are the most interesting, and
they mark a divergence already beginning between Caryll's
ideals and what she believed the nearly universal tendency
of any organization, now becoming visible in the Grail. One
might put it simply that people of the same kind tend to
coalesce—but to Caryll it appeared that the Society wanted
to bring about its unity by shaping people of very different
kinds into an unnatural uniformity. She felt also rather
strongly, as she had in her convent days, that this uniformity
was based on a class ideal—a "Catholic lady," with some
slight doubt as to which word was more heavily emphasized.

"What most enriches the world," she writes as A., "is that
every individual, having first of all respect for the rights of
others, holds fast to his own integrity." We must "come to

understand the great diversity of being that needs must be if the community is to come to the full flower and fruit of the fullness of Christhood."

A. urges also a knowledge of the faith that enables the ordinary Catholic to explain it when called upon. B. says that example is all-important and that "arguing puts people off."

A. "Off what?"

B. "God."

A. "No, I think stupid arguing puts people off you. . . ."

And the reason is because the world thinks that Catholicism has been tried and failed; "we have not only got to *give a message, we have to redeem a past.* And what are we doing?—instead of telling people what God is really like, that they may be attracted to God, we go on holding up our *own* ideas about Him that they may be attracted to us!"

B. "To *Him*, through us."

A. "And you think your soft voice and your smart suit will actually draw men to the *Cross!*"

These three dialogues are more positively arguments than any of the others, and at one point they show, in the light of the sputnik and other recent developments, an insight not common so early. Talking of false gods, B. suggests that Communists worship the State.

A. "No, don't believe it—machinery. . . . They pay to it the one form of worship that *is* worship, sacrifice of self. Many a Communist doubts the government, many a Communist in Russia doubts the ideal, but none doubt the machine."

Through it will come their food, in it they become aware of power—one of God's attributes:

The machine, to an ignorant peasant—and believe me the Soviet is careful to keep many ignorant peasants in Russia—the machine is mysterious—it is vast . . . more powerful, much more

* Italics mine.

incomprehensible, than men. We all tend to endow what is big and mysterious with personality . . . and the machine with its huge, relentless personality has for the Russian the gigantic power and mystery of a god. . . . If you doubt it, get a record of Mossolov's Steel Foundry music and play it. It is not a symphony, it is a hymn, a hymn of passion and adoration. Would to heaven there were half the splendour in the hymns that we drearily moan from our security.

A. has declared that Catholics also worship idols, and B. demands to know what idols these are.

A. "Money, respectability, health, to name only a few of the perhaps less harmful ones—they are a trio of demi-gods in the service of the great God Ego."

B. disagrees, pointing out that these three things are all given by God: "only a fool is deliberately disreputable, and we have a duty to protect our health. As God put gold in the earth he meant us to use it."

A. suggests they go on to consider "the more pernicious idols."

B. "I can hardly imagine what they will be!"

It is certainly hard-hitting, and it almost comes as a surprise to many besides B. that there are false gods far worse. These are false ideas of the true God and of His Christ. "The gentle, doting, characterless man" so many hymns depict, the Stern God, "waiting to pounce on poor little human creatures for their least failing," the Morbid God whose followers cultivate "a kind of gentle dreariness . . . a pleasurable grief."

What is the answer? B. asks. And A. gives two.

As a child's whole life is coloured by a stern or a loving father we, if we truly follow the command "Love one another," will give to all men some notion of a loving God. "All through life the hard Christian drives people from God, and the warm ardent Christian leads to Him."

But the *mind* too must be trained, indeed the mind *first* must be trained. "Learn, as the Catechism says, to know Him, then the rest will follow. If you *do* know God as He is, you can't help loving Him and serving Him—and it is so for others, for the blind, hungry, desperate, human race, looking to us for the knowledge of God."

It was not the social outcast only that Caryll tried to help by showing forth God's love. Spiritual needs had as deep a claim on her—perhaps even deeper—than material. Iris has told me how her mother, whose life had been almost wholly social, the fading of whose beauty with the coming of old age had been so deeply tragic to witness, came to love Caryll, to depend on her company more and more. When she was dying it was Caryll she asked for.

Caryll told me about this death bed, and I found recently a story she wrote for the *Messenger* a few years later. Surely in this story Caryll herself is Jane, the granddaughter of the dying woman, praying beside her and seeing in one of those strange insights of hers the return of childhood to the immortal spirit of an old woman. But it was Rumanian, not Russian, that the dying woman was talking:

There was the rattle of a child's scooter in the street below; and then a few shrill, sweet cries of the last playtime before bed. For a moment Jane had an impression of children all about her, of liveliness and sweetness of life. And she thought: "How strange that is, 'Unless you become as little children you cannot enter the kingdom of heaven.'" How could anyone like grandmother become a child? If only they could, Jane felt she would not be afraid. For it was not really this first experience of death that she feared so much; it was that other dread, the dread of knowing that she disliked the old lady, that she simply could not imagine loving her even if they were both together in heaven! And coupled with this the conviction that she must pray and pray for this soul: that perhaps her very charity would make the soul haunt her! . . .

Grandmother was talking again. Jane went over to her and leaned down to hear. She was speaking in Russian, which was her first language when she was a little girl. Jane understood little of it, but she knew the word for "mother," and that word fluttered on the failing breath like a candle flame blown to brief spurts of brilliance by a wind that is extinguishing it. "Mother" and "wolves" and "snow" and "cake": what strange words! The only ones Jane understood out of the rushing gusts of whispered speech. And now from the closed lids tears were flowing. "She is speaking of her mother," said Jane, "and I think perhaps of her early home in Russia. She says 'wolves,' and 'snow,' and 'cake.'"

Nurse came over and wiped the tear-covered face with curiously beautiful skill. Whenever she stopped reading and moved, Jane saw a kind of wonder of impersonal compassion and love flow from her skilled hands. "She has a sort of general love, something I can't give," she thought. Nurse said: "They always seem to go back to their childhood at the end; it happens over and over again". . . .

Grandmother was calling upon her mother with heartbreaking urgency: "Mother, Mother, Mother"; and then there were other words, and among them "river" and "Easter" and "empty" and "house" and "darkness." Timidly Jane took the hand she had thought cruel. Now she saw only its littleness, its terrible frailty, its helplessness to beat on the door of Eternity. She held the cold little hand and she was afraid still, but now less afraid, growing a little in love. She was so tired that, despite the tension, she nearly slept, and it seemed to her that she was watching a little girl who was running about in an empty house, calling, searching for her mother. And the mother was not there. She had been dead for fifty years. All round the house, the white silence of snow; on the table the flicker of candles round the tall white Easter cake. The little girl is wearing a white muslin dress for a party; but she must go on a journey; she must cross water, although the lake is frozen outside and the wolves can cross it from the forest beyond. One river still flows. It may be the Styx, it may be the waters of birth. The little girl must cross it. She is weeping through the house, all alone. She has come back after fifty years and everyone has gone. A little child, she must go on her journey alone.   . .

"The change has come," said Nurse. And when it did come it came so gently that Jane could not say precisely at which moment grandmother died. . . .

So empty was the body on the bed that it seemed not to be there at all. Beyond it there was a stillness of light like well water, and in the light a little girl with imploring hands. Her hair hung down to her shoulders, gold that is nearly silver. Her eyes were grey and gentle and full of tears. She wore a white muslin party frock, corals round her neck, blue bows on her shoulders, long frilly drawers down to her blue dancing-sandals. Her mouth trembled, uncertain whether to smile, imploring like her hands. And she was the smallest girl imaginable, with fine little bones, and tiny pitiful wrists, fragile and lovely.

The ghost had come to haunt Jane, just as she had known it would. Only it had come in the power of littleness, and Jane was not afraid. She began again the *De profundis*, wrapped about in an air of very grave sweetness, like that of a church in Holy Week, when the Good Friday Mass draws to a close.

.

8

Milborne Grove

TOWARDS THE END of her tenancy of the house in Evelyn Gardens, Iris, alarmed by the estimate for "complete redecoration," started a drastic economy drive. The two younger maids, both engaged to be married, were given tremendous wedding receptions, in defiance of the economy drive; Jessie retired to her own cottage: no new servants were engaged; most of the house was shut up; a stove was installed in the dining room, and Iris bought a cookery book.

Before they left Evelyn Gardens, Jones was given to Caryll—a small, very fierce tabby kitten, a "cellar cat," as she used to say. She had always longed for an animal of her own: Iris had a whippet and a Sealeyham, Joan a succession of pets, whose deaths Caryll recorded most feelingly, and with elaborate detail—real minute-by-minute death-bed scenes—in letters to her at school. A pet of her own—and that a cat, likely to keep mice away—meant a great deal to Caryll.

Iris remembers, when George V was dying, how Caryll sat up half the night, holding Joan's pet mouse in her hand, offering for him what must to her have been the most appalling penance imaginable.

They moved to Milborne Grove in 1934 or '35. Milborne

Grove is a row of attractive little whitewashed houses, off Bolton Gardens—a secluded little street, with something of the country about it—trees and gardens in every direction. All the houses had small front gardens and longish, narrow back ones, reached by a flight of steps from the hall. At the bottom of Iris's back garden was a shed, which became Caryll's workshop, containing two chairs, a table, a bench at which she carved, and in winter an oil stove. There was no insulation, and several friends describe it as bitterly cold about the legs and generally uncomfortable. Caryll never cared about comfort anyhow, and above all would not have noticed its absence when she was working.

In the early days at their new home, Iris and Caryll went to Bruges—for £4 a head, on a Cook's tour, the £4 covering the return journey and several days in Bruges, which Caryll had long dreamed of visiting. The food provided ·by the little hotel where they stayed, though good, was inadequate, and after early Mass Caryll and Iris used to devour the hot doughnuts bought off barrows in the streets. Caryll loved Bruges—the drives by horse-drawn cabs, the boat-trip through the canals, the churches, the pictures (the Memlings especially), the Béguinage, the old houses—one house in particular, the House of the Pelican, which inspired her to carve the pelican feeding its young which now hangs over the front door of Iris's cottage.

The Milborne Grove period was perhaps the happiest in Caryll's life. Most of her friends fuse in their memories the last years in Evelyn Gardens with the time in this new house, but there was one huge difference for Caryll—the shed at the end of the garden.

It was the same pattern as earlier at Boundary Road and later at Nash Lee Farm Cottage. Iris had given her a room for a studio at Evelyn Gardens, but now she had a tiny place of her own just slightly removed from the house. And here she cooked sausages, served beer, made coffee for her friends, worked frenziedly and talked endlessly. Anybody with a problem, anyone seeking for religion, was sent to her by her growing circle, and each one sent made the circle wider. "She had a wonderful knack for converting people," Jacques Doneux says: "one evening did it when others had been bashing at them for years." And he went on to give the reason: "She gave herself up completely to other people. She didn't live her own life enough. Yet she didn't *need* other people: she could have been a hermit."

To another friend she said: "When I met you, God said to me: 'I must have that soul. See to it.' " This man, Henry Tayler, owed his conversion, he says, entirely to Caryll, and he tells how she accompanied him to church for his first Confession. As he was uncertain what to do, she whispered, "Go where you see the red light." A red light held entirely different suggestions for Henry, who went into fits of laughter, while Caryll, also laughing, knelt beside him. Henry had covered his face with his hands, and a pious old lady, mistaking his emotion, was scandalized by Caryll's levity, tapped her on the shoulder, and muttered, "Why don't you try to comfort the poor young man?"

If Jacques is right about Caryll's hermit nature, her hermitage would certainly have been thronged by the multitudes on whom she already wanted to pour the compassion of Christ. She was quite intensely aware of people, and I believe really needed them, even if not as much as they needed her. She was still more intensely aware of God. It is hard to convey with what unselfconsciousness she would talk of the need to pray and to do penance for those people who asked for spiritual help. If God said, "I must have that soul," it was because He trusted her to get it for Him.

Some of the friends Caryll made at this time have written of what knowing her meant to them. "Dickie" Orpen (daughter of the painter, now Mrs. Olivier) first met Caryll when she was literally on the move: going to Evelyn Gardens she found the house empty but saw her next day walking up Milborne Grove "clutching a pint of milk." For years she had supper once a week in the hut.

Wisdom, kindness and love plus, plus, plus, this revelation of Christ in a person! In Caryll chain-smoking furiously with a dandelion-yellow upper lip, standing over her drawing or engraving on the high, narrow carpenter's bench, her hair in its childish cut flowing liquidly from the fine bone of her cheek in this simple waterfall of pale orange. Lit by the lamp, her finely articulated hands appeared curiously transparent but very capable in an innocent and effortless way; when not holding a pencil or graver she relaxed them and they lay quiet, slightly flexed on some scrubbed surface of plain wood or a sheet of paper. She used to cover her face with some abominable chalky-white substance which gave it quite often the tragic look one associates with clowns and great comedians. The great beauty of her eyes was often hidden by her glasses, and by the fact that she didn't often look at one, as she worked while she talked, and I think was always frightened that she might send one to sleep by hypnosis. It only once happened to me. I was concentrating very hard on what she was telling me and fell asleep in an instant. She caught the cup of tea from my hand, and when I "came round," or woke, was visibly rattled and at pains to tell me I had fallen asleep of my own accord. Her powers of that kind, of hypnosis, of telepathy, were very great and alarmed and frightened her.

That "abominable chalky-white substance" exasperated Caryll's friends. "Have you spilt the flour bin on your face?" Molly Paley asked her the first time she saw it. "Oh, don't you like it?" said Caryll.

And when I once asked her *why,* she said, "I don't like a pink face."

Perhaps she hid behind this clown-like whiteness as behind a mask; perhaps, as Iris thought, she didn't want to look like her mother; perhaps, as another friend said, her skin was *too* pink: all those, and probably only those, who knew Caryll will realize how much it exercised us that she should by choice make herself look so strange.

"Surely," said an uncritical admirer, "it was part of her asceticism, to make herself ugly." "No," said one of her critics, "it was sheer exhibitionism—to make herself looked at" (which it certainly did). I was suddenly reminded of a man to whom I think Caryll bore a marked resemblance—the Dominican friar Father Vincent McNabb. Once, speaking outdoors at Parliament Hill Fields, he lost his temper with a heckler. After the meeting he knelt down and kissed the heckler's feet. The crowd stood half stunned. But the heckler said, "Get up, McNabb, that's nothing but play-acting." And as he dusted his habit, Father Vincent said reflectively "Well well, it's hard to know, isn't it?"

To me the strangeness of Caryll's whitened face was not off-putting, but it was bewildering. Dickie first meeting her in the early thirties took her for a very old woman. I, twelve years later, could not have guessed her age: clown or gnome or witch, behind her mask of white one felt her ageless.

It was the hungry 1930's and Caryll, tormented by the troubles of others, felt them even more when herself secure in a job. One day she and Jacques and Louis and two girls of their staff were sitting round a table discussing especially those people they knew whom it seemed most impossible to help. There were two problems: how to find the money and how to bestow the help. They talked of Our Lord and His multiplication of five loaves and a few small fishes, of the boy whose small basketful fed all that crowd, the apostles whose hands distributed—*in* whose hands were multiplied—the lad's little lot. Suddenly Caryll said: "Let us put down a penny each. If God wants us to do something He will multiply it."

At this point Louis' father, Charles Billaux, came into the

room and looked for a puzzled moment at the coins on the table. "Whatever those are for," he said, "I will multiply them," and he laid down five shillings.

It seemed a happy omen—and it was decided, despite Caryll's dislike for organizations, that a small society should be started—"The Loaves and Fishes." They were five already, and with two more completed the "five loaves and two small fishes" of the Gospel. These were the anonymous committee called "The Loaves and Fishes." Working members were known as Sprats, the Chairman was the Red Herring. He is described as "leaving the house heavily disguised, as his identity is kept a secret." There was truly need for a considerable amount of secrecy in the work done by Sprats, for almost every Sprat had sea-horses of his or her own. These receivers of help were so christened because they cling and entwine themselves round something for support. There were many difficulties in approaching them, finding ways to give that would not offend, bringing friendship to them that should make it easy for them to receive. "While with St. Paul," Caryll wrote, "we shall often be fools for Christ's sake, we must aim at that rarer state of being intelligent for Christ's sake."

It was chiefly the "unofficial poor" the Sprats wanted to help: those who, brought up in fairly good circumstances, "are faced with dire poverty, sometimes destitution, and who feel constrained to keep the fact secret"; those, untrained in any skill, who in the Depression especially could get no work; the sick and the old who had never earned enough to save; those still young but with no family to fall back on; refugees in a foreign land—all those unfortunates who might be saying in their hearts "to dig I am unable, to beg I am ashamed."

Such people tell their story only to each other. To help them you must look for them, learn to understand them, give help with delicacy and tact. Caryll says, "Money is needed, understanding is needed; but money and understanding seldom go together."

A Sprat gives a regular subscription, small or large. And "each Sprat will, if a chance occurs, catch a mackerel. A mackerel is a rich person who is willing to give a large single donation or even a small single donation through a Sprat, but who is not a regular subscriber." All the work must be done "in a secret and individual way," no names of those helped being divulged unless absolutely necessary. When sea-horses are "supersensitive," fairy godmother methods must be employed. "In selecting sea-horses for help, the only consideration is their *need* for help; worthiness and such things are of no importance."

As soon as £10 had been collected the work began. The first case was an elderly man in desperate circumstances, and the help given just "managed to bridge a crisis at the end of which permanent and unexpected help came from another quarter."

Even the official poor slip only too often through the net of public assistance and become sea-horses. Iris remembers two cases that came to Caryll and herself. In a train from Marylebone to Wendover they met a weeping woman with a baby, which had a complaint needing constant nursing. She could not get it into a hospital, there were other children at home and she was at the end of her tether. Money was at once sent to the District Nurse to get her a home help. Another day, rushing to catch a train in Leicester, they glimpsed through a window partly covered by a rag a room of unimaginable poverty, lit by a single candle, and a solitary woman looking unutterably wretched. Back home they began sending parcels through the local vicar, who had not known of her existence and began to look after her.

At the other end of the scale was the more typically Sprat case of a Russian refugee countess.

"We dragooned our friends," Dickie writes, "into wanting

Russian and/or German coaching and paid for it out of Sprat funds.

"I painted her and repainted her so that she should have her model's fee plus as many meals as we could fit in before and after the sittings.

"Spratty visits to her murky basement were dreadful ordeals to us all, as, to her, the room was illumined, as if by neon lights, by her late husband's aura, and a species of Aurora Borealis played round her ikons and her husband's photograph and one distressed her by inadvertently bumping into these phenomena."

Another sea-horse remembered by Charles Scott-Paton suffered from pyorrhea and resultant bad breath which made it hard for her to get teaching work. She needed but could not pay for false teeth. "Let the old girl have her teeth," Caryll urged, and they invented an imaginary competition of which she was to emerge winner, with a sizeable money prize.

Sprats were not infallibly tactful, and the dire phrase that one had sometimes to murmur to another was "She has taken offence." But a great deal was accomplished. Jobs were found for the unemployed and a shop was opened at the top of Iris's house to which Sprats sent things they could or couldn't spare. Gifts were made to sea-horses and purchases were made by helpers, the money going into the general fund—of which, despite the looseness of the organization, most careful accounts were kept.

Caryll had dreamed of hundreds and thousands of Sprats. Actually by the end of the year there were ninety-eight, which really seems remarkably good. As many were Catholics Father Bliss became their unofficial chaplain; he said Mass for them and for their work every month. Gert was much interested, and she and Caryll's sister both joined. A magazine was started, but the first issue was also the last. In it appear two lines of a limerick:

> A sea-horse from Bloomsbury said
> Were I not so extremely well-bred—

I wish I knew what concluding lines won the prize. But
Caryll in her editorial capacity remarked, "Strict fair play
will be observed and the editor's indecision will probably be
final."

The apotheosis of the sea-horse was witnessed when the
war came and one of the most unemployable got a commission in the army, proving perhaps that it was more the
shape of our society than innate incompetence that had
created the problem. Nevertheless the Sprats still go on and
still find secret needs that they alone can meet.

The most interesting thing in the magazine is Caryll's
poem "Philip Speaks," which so greatly impressed Professor
Mackail when he read it a little later reprinted in the *Grail
Magazine*. For this poem was inspired by Sprat work. From
the Gospel the title of loaves and fishes had been chosen for
resources, which, however slender, always proved to be just
enough:

> The Lord blessed the bread.
> He put it into our hands
> and it multiplied,
> not in *His* hands but in *mine!*
>
> Even now remembering this,
> my thoughts shut like a folding wing;
> my mind is a blank sheet of light
> in the mystery of the thing.
>
> For me the miracle was this:
> that a clear stream of the Lord's love—
> not mine—
> flowed out of my soul,
> a shining wave over my fellow men.

Caryll had been for Father Bliss the answer to an editor's prayer, for she could both illustrate her own stories and fill the spaces with verse. In the desperate later days of the war she wrote whole numbers of the *Children's Messenger.* I have been surprised to find that children still like her stories. She certainly gave them something better than the young usually got in those days: she tells a good story, even if it is a "moral tale." (I wonder, however, whether children mind this unless it is also dull.) There is a good deal of atmosphere and a touch of fantasy which appeals to the young and imaginative, but I could never feel she was really a children's writer.

My opinion is not shared by a friend whose memories I have already quoted—Rosamond Batchelor—who came to know Caryll at Milborne Grove. Rosamond became both a Sprat and a contributor to the *Messenger* and much admired Caryll's work for both.

"I never willingly missed," she writes, "reading her stories and poems—so concise, so perfectly finished, so full of atmosphere and spirituality, even mysticism. Even before I knew her, she was an influence in my life."

Dickie Orpen, knowing Rosamond and also thinking highly of her poems, suggested a meeting between her and Caryll. As with the first approach to Iris, Caryll recoiled "NO, NO," she said. "I admire her work, but I'm sure I should dislike her *intensely.*" At last, however, she agreed to a meeting, and both were invited to supper at Dickie's studio. "I don't think," Rosamond says, "I quite knew what to make of her at first." And to Dickie it seemed that "they didn't hit it off at *all!!*"

But later, looking for Dickie, Rosamond ran into Caryll, who took her down to the shed, which was full of her paintings—Father Bliss, "startlingly like him," Henry Tayler, and a beautiful, emaciated girl against a gold background. This girl had been a neurotic who, Caryll said, had starved herself to death, yet in whom she discovered a hidden well of sanctity typified by the gold background. To look for the inner reality of a person was always a challenge to Caryll, especially if the person was a neurotic. Besides painting this girl she wrote about her as she most profoundly was, a short story transforming her into the sister of a martyr in Elizabethan England.

There too was Jones—already lame from an accident. Caryll had taken him to a vet, saying miserably, "I suppose he'll have to be destroyed?" The vet replied, "Would you destroy your father if he broke his leg?", set the leg and gave Jones many years more of life.

People [writes Rosamond] had not yet begun to harass and besiege Caryll, and although she had her work—her writing and drawing for Father Bliss, and her crib figures and decorating for Grossé—she was not yet the overdriven Caryll of the war and post-war years. In fact, what I chiefly remember of the Milborne Grove period was the extraordinarily happy, serene and friendly atmosphere which at once enveloped one, with "Mother Iris"—as one friend used to call her—looking after the little party (but a mother who looked so young that my brother and I both thought she was Joan's sister).

Caryll strongly disliked the bulldozing, insensitive, almost domineering apostolicity of many well-intentioned Catholics: and I think that one of the reasons for her making so many converts was that the non-Catholics who met her knew that she would continue to like them as people, whether they became Catholics or not. She disliked all group-mindedness, and, with the exception of the Catholic Evidence Guild, almost all associations within the Church. And I think she disliked them because she thought them unfunctional, out of touch with life and the crying needs of people round us, and apt to set up little enclosures of fundamentally self-seeking piety. In rather the same way, I have heard her criticize the lives of nuns who go to such trouble to invent penances and mortifications—who don't know the *real,* uncontrived anxieties of some unemployed father of a family, or some mother who can't feed her family properly, and doesn't know where the rent is coming from.

About Catholic societies, another reason why Caryll approved fully only of her own Sprats and of the C.E.G. is illustrated by a sentence marked by her in his daughter's Life of the founder of the Salvation Army. Speaking of the importance of women officers, General Booth says, "to eliminate them would mean not only the loss of their influence and work, but the loss of the influence resulting from the combination of men *and women,* which is different from and more potent than, the influence of either sex by itself. 'Male and female created He them.' "

This Caryll felt very keenly. She disliked the segregation in parishes—Boys' Clubs, Children of Mary, Catholic Young Men's Society, St. Vincent de Paul. She specially believed that not only dances and social occasions should be shared, but that apostolic work also should be done by both sexes together. Despite what the Salvation Army lacked of the full Christian life—the Mass, the Sacraments—Caryll had an immense admiration for them. Their work among the real outcasts, their refusal to care about being respectable, was after her own heart. Heavily marked, too, is another passage in that admirable biography: "I should say that *if* the idea of doing a big thing for the world is impossible without sacrificing its quality—we had better drop the idea of a big thing!! All the past goes to show that the *few* out and outs in any cause have done the most."

This indeed Caryll felt intensely—and did not Our Lord call His disciples a "little flock"?

Dickie was not a Catholic when she first met Caryll—"She spoke to me as if I were, and when I told her I wasn't she said, 'Oh, but you soon will be.' " She and Rosamond had both been art students, though not at the same school as Caryll.

Dickie now had a studio of her own and engaged a model once a week, inviting Rosamond to share these sittings and to supper afterwards. "One of my memories of those delightful evenings is of the model sitting stark naked on the sofa and primly deploring the immodest fashions of the day."

"During those years, 1932-39," Dickie writes, "if you asked Caryll how she was, she answered, 'Ow, riddled with guilt and toothache; sometimes one and sometimes the other and frequently both.'"

The toothache ended dramatically. One day in desperate pain Caryll said to St. Thérèse, "They say so much about you! Can't you do something about my teeth?"

And Thérèse did. Almost miraculously the pain ceased.

One last passage must be quoted from Caryll's journal, especially interesting because of its affinity with the revelations of Julian of Norwich. The book of this uncanonized anchoress has an immense appeal for our troubled world, more especially her assurance from the silence of her anchorhold that God holds our world in His hand and that at the end of all our troubling He has promised that "all shall be well." There are passages in these revelations which make me almost sure that Caryll had read them when she wrote of her own prayer. Later she had the book on her shelves and she refers to it in a war-time letter. But it is hard, despite Jacques Doneux, to conceive of Caryll in an anchorhold. "I could kiss the paving stones," she said rapturously when returning to London. And is not the nightly prayer of the priest in *The Dry Wood* as he sets open the window and lifts the great city up to God Caryll's own? In her journal she says:

Something took place in the church which has given me great consolation in prayers at night. I was kneeling one evening before the picture of the Holy Face meditating on the emblems of the Passion when I thought Our Lord said, silently, to me to cease from my meditation and pray for sinners. Having given way to discouragement I was very loath to do so, but I began to pray mechanically and timidly nevertheless.

Presently I thought that the cross was in front of me and Our Lord suffering on it, I did not *see* it, neither did I hear anything, but it was like a deep knowledge of what was going on, it was as if it was quite dark, but I was aware without seeing.

On the cross Our Lord bled, His Precious Blood poured from His veins in rivers, it poured from the crown of thorns and flowed over His body like a shining cloak, and from all over His body like a garment.

I knew that at the foot of the hill a multitude of souls stood and were nearly drowned in the abundance of Our Lord's Precious Blood.

Then I thought Our Lord said that these were the souls of those who love Him, and that His Blood was flowing very freely without travail.

Next Our Lord hung on the cross and a great dryness was in His Body as if all His blood had gone from His Sacred veins, and I knew that He thirsted with a most bitter thirst.

Then Our Lord groaned and seemed to be in bitter travail, also He lifted His Head to His Heavenly Father and seemed to be in supplication.

He then (so I believe) made known to me that He had left in His Sacred Body a single drop of Blood which He must shed for the redemption of the most abandoned sinner in the world, and that only through unimaginable agony could He shed it—

It seemed as if His Blessed Body could not shed this last drop of His Precious Blood without a prolonged and terrible struggle and most fearful anguish, and as if He bade me to remain at the foot of the cross all my life and travail in my soul for sinners.

I understood from this how Our Lord agonized for us and how complete was His immolation for us and for His Father's glory.

I understood how earnestly we ought to pray for sinners and how tenderly we ought to love our Blessed Lord. Since this I have found it much more easy to face the cold nights and the discomfort of praying at late hours; indeed I could weep to think how I count the cost, which is really nothing—and *I* may be that worst sinner for whom Our Lord shed His last drop of Blood.

Her vocation, Caryll did not doubt, was to draw men to Christ, but she did sometimes doubt the manner of it—active or contemplative. She was not as yet overdriven, as she became later, but life and friends already made big demands on her; and her own urge to creative writing, to silence, prayer, contemplation, was correspondingly strong. She told Dickie a story that made a profound impression both in itself and in the manner of its telling:

Caryll's dream was a nightly one for a period of some months in the late '30's (1938 or possibly early 1939), at a time when her waking hours were consumed by "callers," many of them in genuine need of her insight and charity and help and the light she could shed on the murky problems of personality and behaviour. BUT many of them came to indulge in what she called "an orgy of self-think-on"—people who had no intention of taking the advice they asked for. She felt at moments that everyone was conspiring to stop her doing anything creative: they consumed her time and left her feeling exhausted.

It was against this background that she began to dream, nightly, of being in a wonderfully peaceful library—she knew it was in a house in Regent's Park, and it had french windows opening onto lawns and trees. There was always a companion there, a man with whom she talked; they read and discussed books and philosophy and poetry and writers. They were *en rapport*, and their silence was as good as their talk. (I don't know if Caryll told me they sat each in an armchair on each side of the fire or whether that was my visualization.) She said the room was entirely lined with books and unutterably peaceful. After some time Caryll found that she was looking forward with intensity to this dream—thinking of it often during the day.

She was startled to find that she and her dream companion

had been discussing books as yet unpublished: a shock to read reviews and criticism of work with which she felt already so familiar. She began to feel guilty that her joy and peace lay in a dream world and less and less in daily contact with her fellow-creatures. (I don't think she ever at that time withheld her time or counsel or prayers from *anyone*—despite the "Oh, she is the most dreadful bore" and "I've had a series of visitors, you simply can't imagine, self-obsessed BORES"—in double paren-thesis. I can't help thinking that what you called her biting tongue was sometimes almost a camouflage for a burning char-ity towards all sorts and conditions of men; done almost to lessen the loneliness of her own vocation by talking like this to her friends and of her friends?)

Then one night in her dream—no warning, the man said to her very seriously: "Caryll, you know that you cannot go on like this, you must make a decision, it is one which you must make by yourself, I won't attempt to influence you one way or another. You can stay here always, but if you think you must go back to these people you worry about during the day, you must get up, don't say goodbye, just walk across and out into the garden—don't say anything—don't look back—indeed you will never come back. Now you must make up your mind." Caryll said she was weighted with sorrow, the temptation was enormous, but she was in some fashion aware that should she decide to stay she would die in her sleep. She longed to stay, and still longing she got up and slowly walked over to the french window and out—and she never dreamt the dream again.

It was perhaps after the ending of this dream that Caryll wrote one of her loveliest rhythms, "Afternoon in Westmin-ster Cathedral." In its final form it can be read in *The Flowering Tree*. She copied out a first draft for Yvonne Bosch with the note "all this rhythm arises from short medi-tations (consisting of that most valuable form of distraction, looking at other people)," and in a covering letter (unfor-tunately not dated) she says:

. . . last September Our Lord told me that He wished that I would look at Him much more in people, that He would like to be loved and reverenced more in people and "discovered" and recognized even in very unlikely people. He would like people to be told and shown "their glory"—which of course is Himself.

I did try to do as He said and shall go on trying, but I found in it one great source of pain, namely that when I am alone I am no longer alone with Him, but people are present to me very much as He is, only not so dominantly. . . .

Now this rhythm, "The Cathedral," is the result of trying to carry out His request, and it is intended as a gift to people, simple, ordinary people, to show them "their glory"—you will understand it better if you read it knowing this . . . it has been done in scraps of time and has been a dreadful effort, one which I would have abandoned, were it not that I felt Our Lord would like it as a present to Him in the people He loves so absolutely.

Entering the shed one day Yvonne found Caryll prostrated on the ground.

"Caryll, are you ill?"

"No, but a friend of mine is going through a fierce temptation and I must suffer it with her."

It is not only material help that Christ desires to give through human hands. For we are all one and

"We are only syllables
Of the perfect Word."

9

Extra-Sensory Perception

THERE ARE TWO elements in Caryll that I find almost impossible to convey, elements so strong that any picture of her that omits them would seem to those who knew her hardly to be a picture of her at all. One is her quality as a wit, a conversationalist always with a feather-light touch, a contagious sense of fun, an altogether delightful companion whose friendships were immensely various because she could enter into so many different minds, could sympathize with so many kinds of problem and personality. But the many letters sent me were written to people with distressing problems: they are letters of help and advice and do not at all depict Caryll's lighter side. She was one of the most amusing people I ever knew—but this does not come out in the letters. Nor is her conversation *repeatably* amusing—she did not utter epigrams, her humour was diffused through her conversation; and the effect of mimicry can never be conveyed.

The other quality difficult to convey is her habit of totally matter-of-fact reference, in conversation with friends, to experiences lying well outside the normal, her own special varieties of extra-sensory perception. To one who does not believe in E.S.P., as it is popularly called, she would be impossible as a witness. First because she never bothered to establish that she had any such powers—you either believed her or did not; the matter did not seem to her of primary importance, her real work lay elsewhere. Second because in conversation she was both inaccurate—about time, place, the measurement of distance and such matters—and greatly given to exaggeration—comic exaggeration, poetic exaggeration.

A mildly funny story became under her treatment wildly amusing but certainly less exact. She said once that as a child she would be eager to produce the same intense impression on her hearers as some happening had had on her—a huge dog had terrified her, but a dog however huge would mean nothing to a grown-up, so she called it a tiger. Grown-up herself, she would see the absurdity of this, but there is no doubt the tendency to exaggeration was always in her. Not only that. She was an artist, and had her own kind of pleasure in telling some odd incident, not photographically as it happened, but as a small work of art, trimmed here, expanded there. And she still indulged in occasional fantasy—as when she was painting fairies and talked to Iris of seeing them in the woods. And if anyone asks me how I should distinguish Caryll telling seriously of what she believed to be a real experience from Caryll indulging in fantasy, I can only say that I knew—as one does know such things with a close friend. And obviously such knowledge has no value as evidence to others. The result of all this is that even if one is as sure as I am—and all her intimate friends—that she had powers outside the normal, I can only relate, I cannot prove. It is not because of them that I am writing this book.

The vocation, mentioned so often in her journal, was the vitally important thing in her life, not only for her but for thousands of others, and it was just beginning to make itself clear. With the coming of the war it became more definite and increased in range, but she was already exercising it. This vocation was to bring to men the truth that Christ is *in* men; and it involved bringing alive in them the great truths about Him and about their own souls.

Caryll had an unusual insight into people, an unusual sympathy with their difficulties. Her long hours of prayer were deepening her own spiritual life. But these two elements did not give her the complete equipment for her task. She had to study—to read psychology and grow in understanding of the human mind (especially the human mind off-balance), to read theology and grow in understanding of Christ's revelation, to read above all the Gospels and meet Him in them.

One reason for the crashing failure of many well-intended missions—to the young, to the workers, above all to the unbelieving, wavering, or uncommitted—comes from lack of courage to undertake this arduous labour of preparation. It is possible to lose oneself in plans and schemes and organization, to "make contact," to gather people in clubs or camps with the idea of bringing them the one thing necessary—and then find oneself with empty hands. What you have not got you cannot give, you cannot get the needed knowledge without learning it. Neither piety nor extra-sensory perception will teach you the Christian religion!

Caryll knew this. Certainly she did not think of her curious powers as having any bearing on her vocation in its direct application to others, though they sometimes helped her in a minor way to understand the people she was helping. As a reason for accepting the truth that Christ is in men, she *never* used the visions she believed she had on three occasions seen. She used the Gospel, she used theology, she used her insight into men's minds. As a reason for believing in immortality, she never used the contact she would tell her friends she had had with a saint or a soul in Purgatory. She gave the Church's teaching about the soul, about Purgatory, and about Heaven.

But, though it is in no way essential to her spiritual teaching, extra-sensory perception is relevant to her personality, just as her sins and struggles are. Like them it must be looked at.

2

Many books have been written on the working of extra-sensory perception, now more commonly called *psi*. This is not the place, nor am I the person, to discuss the whole problem of its reality or functioning. Anyone wanting to go into it could begin by reading Rosalind Heywood's *The Sixth Sense*. For a fuller examination of *psi* phenomena, the investigations of Dr. Rhine at Duke University, North Carolina, partially recorded in *New Frontiers of the Mind*, will be found invaluable. In *The Hidden Springs* Renée Haynes has fascinatingly opened the enquiry into the relation between *psi* and mystical experience: she gives a useful bibliography.

The phenomena studied occur widely and are vouched for by many witnesses. They appear to fall into two sections, according to the meaning attached to "extra-sensory."

It may be taken as meaning that some people have an extra sense, operating in the same material universe as the standard five (sight, hearing, smell, taste, touch), belonging to the same order, though as different from them as each of them is from the other four.

On the face of it there seems no reason why five ways should exhaust the possibilities of the material universe making itself known to us. We cannot *imagine* what a sixth way would be like. But then a person who happened to be born without one of the standard five could never imagine what that one is like. There is simply no way of conveying to a man born blind what seeing is. If on some remote island there were a tribe stone-deaf, then not only would a visitor of normal hearing be unable to convey to them what hearing meant, but the perceptions of material reality it clearly brought him would be regarded by the tribe either as extra-sensory, or as supernatural (diabolic probably).

Or again "extra-sensory" may be taken as meaning awareness of a whole field of reality altogether beyond that which reaches the brain by way of the five senses, or could reach it by any sixth (or seventh, or eighth!) channel of the same order.

Present awareness of things long past as if they were actually happening is one phenomenon for which a mass of evidence is presented; another is the awareness of things that have not happened yet, whose later happening confirms the exactness of the first awareness. Telepathy may come within one meaning or the other of the key word "extrasensory." And of course there are "visions" wholly spiritual, mystical experiences, which suggest some kinship with the second sort of perception but have elements special to themselves which seem to place them in a different category.

If we confine ourselves to the first meaning of E.S.P., *psi* would seem to be a natural faculty which, like other natural faculties can be used for good or evil, and which (again like other natural faculties) often appears to act where no purpose at all can be ascertained, acting simply because the appropriate stimulus has been offered. It is highly developed in some, less in others, not at all in, perhaps, most. Some hold that everyone is born with it, but that the majority lose it under the pressures of a mechanized society. Others hold that it is more akin to the special gifts of genius—in music, for instance, or painting—natural, but not found in every man's nature.

For reasons we have just noted, it is almost impossible for those who have this faculty to convey to those who have not how it works or even what it is. The language in which men's experiences must be expressed—even to themselves—makes no provision for experiences so rare, so abnormal, as these.

One simply has to use the words that are there. With the first kind of E.S.P.—where a sense other than the standard five is functioning—the difficulty even of describing what has been experienced is very great. It is not so obviously great with the second—where things not present *there* or not happening *there* are seen or heard—because it seems like normal seeing or hearing. Yet the problems raised are even greater, as to time and space and human cognition. However clear and detailed the sense experience feels at the moment, an uncertainty remains in the mind whether the eyes and ears of the body were, in fact, in operation.

Rosalind Heywood describes herself as saying to a fellow psychic who was testifying to what she had "seen":

"But, of course, you didn't *see* it."

"Of course not," the other replied, to the exasperation of an incredulous enquirer who was demanding evidence. Caryll Houselander, too, speaks of many of her own experiences as of things seen not with bodily eyes but with those of the mind.

She had always been interested in handwriting: she had several books on graphology, collected newspaper cuttings and other material and made a serious study of it as a science. From the books she could point out the formation of the letters and the accurate results of a wide application of the rules. But her own perceptions went much further than this. She could read character, and sometimes both the past and the future, not merely from handwriting but by holding in her hand a paper so folded that she could not see the writing. At times she was frightened at the clarity with which she sometimes knew—not suspected or expected but *knew*—that for instance a certain man would, if he employed him, rob her father (the man *was* employed and did rob), or that the fiancé of a fellow-student was a thoroughly bad man.

Her father treated her insights with a curious blend of

contempt and respect—he hated to believe there was anything in this nonsense, yet he would throw her a letter and ask her what she made of the writer. Alike with father and friend she felt torn between the claims of opposing charities: should she tell or not tell what she had "seen"? Which was worse, to take away a man's character or allow friend or father to suffer? At the Art School she soon refused to go on reading handwriting, but Dickie Orpen remembers her amazing insight into a character derived from glancing at an envelope.

"She read your mind," says another friend, "but her powers of this kind were a real trial to her. Once she came late to a women's luncheon and was told playfully that she must read a bit of handwriting as a punishment. Not knowing the writer was present, she said 'Oh, that's a secret drunkard.' Everybody laughed and Caryll was covered with embarrassment. It was only after the woman's death that the fact of her drinking became known."

"She often came to see me," another friend says, "in a horrible old brown dress. One day I was thinking, 'Why *must* she always wear that dreadful garment?' when Caryll answered my thoughts: 'So sorry you dislike this dress, but I haven't got anything else.' "

It was through the answer to their own needs that many of Caryll's friends became aware of her special powers. "If you were needing her," one woman said to me, "she *always* knew it. She would ring up or come round without being told."

"If I went to the telephone to ring Caryll," a man said, "she would be ringing me."

A girl in hospital wrote to her mother, "Caryll was on the chair beside my bed."

Caryll's mother had a Siamese cat to which she was devoted and which disappeared. She rang up Caryll two days later to tell her. That night Caryll saw the cat in a dream—shut up in a basement cupboard. She telephoned her mother. Mrs. Houselander, who lived in an apartment by herself, at once went down, and in a disused part of the basement found a cupboard and in the cupboard the cat.

Like many people with this gift, she often "saw" not only present things happening elsewhere and things which had not happened yet, but also past happenings. She might in a strange house see what she learned later had in fact taken place there. She told how once, staying in the country, she heard slow and dragging footsteps come upstairs and cross the floor of the room overhead. She went upstairs herself and saw a child coming into the room. The child sat down, then leaned forward against a dolls' house, pulling off her boots with a look of utter exhaustion. Caryll found that the room had been a nursery; the child, whose parents had not discovered that she was very ill with diabetes, had gone upstairs to change her boots, and leaning against the dolls' house had died there.

Once in an old church Caryll saw with horror what she learnt later must have been a Black Mass, a ceremony of which she knew nothing at the time. Other experiences will emerge in the course of this book. Some were apparently quite pointless, others valuable since Caryll had the skill to use them. A man from Czechoslovakia who knew her well remarked, as we discussed what has been called the sixth sense, "To my mind Caryll had seven senses. She had what you call commonsense too." Commonsense is not often the prerogative of the false visionary, and we shall see her commonsense at work as well as her insight when her mission to neurotics, misfits, and lunatics began.

3

Caryll took the whole field of extra-sensory perception with total simplicity, quite unselfconsciously. And this was supremely her attitude about what may or may not be akin to it—apparently similar experiences in the religious sphere. She would remark that she had met St. Jude in a Chelsea street "dressed in something like a seaman's jersey," that St. Michael had often appeared to her in shining armour. When she was a child he had (she said) sat on the edge of her bed, his helmet in his hand. She had tried to stroke the waving plumes and her hand had gone right through them.

Caryll did not, of course, think that St. Michael or the spirit of St. Jude was seen by her with bodily eyes. The details of appearance are a kind of rough translation into human language of an untranslatable reality—an imaginary picture of spirits who are as unimaginable as they are real. St. Michael, prince of the heavenly hosts, would be seen in armour, St. Jude as you might meet a fisherman who had just left his nets. She was often aware of such presences. "You always know," she said, "if it's one of the Holy Souls." She had never feared ghosts except one, a child, "so wicked and so young." She seemed as intimate with her guardian angel as was St. Frances of Rome and had many stories of his kind offices on her behalf.

One story she used to tell was certainly objective—and she was much puzzled by it when it happened. Having one morning missed Mass, she asked the sacristan if one of the priests could possibly come out and give her Communion. The sacristan absolutely refused to ask: Caryll, disappointed, stayed on a while to pray. The sacristan suddenly came out again and said, "Father is coming. Your brother came and asked."

Caryll said, "I have no brother," and the sacristan replied, "Well, he said he was your brother and he looked very like you."

One thinks of Raphael in the Old Testament calling the young Tobias "Brother," and though Caryll went home bewildered, she later became convinced this "brother" had been her guardian angel.

Yet there is validity in the instinct that makes the ordinary Catholic fight shy of such experiences, accepting them only in the lives of the canonized saints. It would be absurd, untheological, and deeply perilous to build upon them any claim to sanctity.

Caryll's own complete casualness about all this speaks for itself—for she was far from being casual about her sins, and the needs of her soul—for sacraments, for theology, for acts of charity. She would have accepted wholeheartedly Maritain's remarks in *The Degrees of Knowledge* that "the physical aspect of the inner life or its cloak of phenomena ('the weakness of ecstasy,' said St. Hildegarde) can stem from merely natural causes as well as from higher influences." Unless disciplined and controlled it can, he continues, be exposed "to lower influences, proceeding from one's physical temperament and the imagination; as well as to certain higher influences, still of the natural or preternatural, not the divine order."

Maritain does not rule out the idea that in these matters the soul, unknown to herself, may tend "towards a spiritual communication with angelic nature as such, which is the same in the good as well as the bad angels both contesting for their own ulterior purposes, for this immaterial *convivium* with the human being."

It is not surprising that, as Thomas Merton points out in *The Ascent to Truth*, St. John of the Cross "treats visions, revelations, and interior locutions as an unimportant bypath of the mystical life."

That Caryll was what is sometimes called a natural mystic there can be little doubt: that she saw

> ". . . earth crammed with heaven
> And every common bush afire with God."

Whether she had also that gift of God technically called mystical experience who can say? If she did she would have been the first to declare that the part of it similar to the extra-sensory perception whereby she "saw" past events, people's thoughts, distant friends, was of small importance.

But there are, as we have seen, some special problems in analysing the sources of Caryll's insights. She was an artist who saw in everything, from the wood she carved to the words she used, significance invisible to others. But she had, too, the keen imagination of the artist, she had a power of assimilating the experiences of others, making them the food of her own mental growth. She studied theology—and if her earliest "visions" of Christ in man taught her the doctrine of the Mystical Body, later experiences were certainly illuminated by that teaching. And she would have been the first to draw a sharp distinction between that great truth, illustrations of which she "saw," and "seeing" St. Michael in her childhood or St. Jude in the street. Even what Chesterton has called "the dumb certainties of experience" do translate themselves into vision for the artist: how much more the realities of the world of spirit.

The Catholic's difficulty in accepting what may be true visions arises from fear that supernatural reality may be cheapened or profaned by false. The sceptic's arises from the fact that he does not believe there *is* any supernatural reality to be profaned. Indeed he frequently does not believe even in man's immortal spirit. I was reading the other day the review of a movie, *The Hoodlum Priest*. The last scene, the reviewer said, was so powerful as to create "an illusion of immortality."

This is the fight also between spiritualists and sceptics; does spirit exist, and if it does will it survive the grave? Caryll had a curious experience with a war widow which she related to a priest friend. The young woman had no religion, had been to see Caryll and had also sought help at séances.

"At first the spirit or 'control' said Yes, her husband was there, happy, etc.; but on the second visit he said he was less happy, as she was visiting someone who made it difficult for

spirits to communicate with her, someone called C. H.! She
made up her mind it was me, and instead of keeping away
came to see me again; she said the spirits had told her nothing
but trifles, but the doctrine of purgatory was immense and
really helped."

It matters little whether, by temperament opaque, one
does *not,* by temperament transparent, one *does* see by a
sixth sense: it matters little whether there is a sixth sense at
all. The important thing is the throwing open of the eyes of
the spirit to God and His revelation in Christ Our Lord.

4

Perhaps Caryll was helped by the visionary side of her to
combat another side of her complex nature. She said of herself that she had "a strong lurch to evil." She did not find
faith or surrender to God easy; and I think we can trace in
her rhythms, which are the high point of her writing, the
repugnances and hesitations as well as the full self-giving, the
keynote in which was her identification with all mankind:

> Our fidelity to one
> Is to fall in love
> With the whole world.

Mysticism is often thought of as a solitary adventure which
the questing spirit expresses in terms familiar to him from
the religion in which he has been educated. But from St.
Paul's "I live, yet now not I but Christ liveth in me" to
Newman's "Cor ad cor loquitur" the Christian mystic at
least sees it in terms of a love affair in which God takes total
possession of a human soul and that soul responds with fullest
self-giving. And the Catholic Christian sees the transforma-
tion needed by every soul far less as a matter of giving by

personal effort, asceticism and self-denial, than as a receiving of an infinite gift from the Infinite.

This gift is made less often and far less profoundly by what may be called experiences in prayer than by the great pouring upon the soul of God's rivers of grace—the sacraments. Caryll writes sometimes of her prayers and her dreams, but the "essential chain," as a close friend of hers put it, the chain on which the beads of her life were threaded, was, from the hour of her conversion, daily Mass and Communion. Feelings in prayer would come and go: so much may this depend on the state of the body, the quality of the imagination. Dryness in prayer is a harsh fact—but this too can be physical, can mean little or nothing in that real world of the spirit seen only by God. What counts is the doing of the will of the God who loves us. In daily Mass Caryll found the daily miracle that this requires:

> For dread responsibility
> To live the common way,
> I need a miracle to be
> My portion every day.
> Christ's body to my timid soul
> To make my being whole.
>
> The cup, the host, the sacrifice,
> The mind that falls apart,
> Words spoken once and twice and thrice,
> Senseless from my distracted heart,
> Tongue tied, brain numb and morning chill,
> But Christ receives my will.

She goes through each part of the Mass, relating it to the taking up into Christ of the worshipper who through Christ comes above all in this hour to the Eternal Father:

Offertory   and   Consecration

I am the cold insipid water ready
to be poured into the chalice.
   Let me be put into the wine like
the drop of water at this Mass
   Let me be flooded through with the
strength, the colour, the splendour of
your Being, as the colourless water
is flooded with the crimson of the wine.
   At the words of consecration let
me be changed,
   changed by the miracle of your love
into yourself.
   In the chalice of your sacrifice, lift
me to Our Father.

Communion

He is still on earth in the host,
He is crucified in the Mass
And in my Communion,
rises again in me.

                ·   ·   ·

Whatever I have to suffer
However hardly I die to self,
He will rise in me.

However numbed I have been
By even the greatest sorrow,
The cruellest disappointment,
He will rise again in me.

These extracts are from an undated series of poems and
rhythms on the Mass written, I think, a few years later than
the ending of the Journal. There is also an illuminating
dialogue on Adoration, which shows Caryll remembering
things she had learnt as a child. In a little country church she

heard a priest preach on the Eucharist—and his teaching seemed somehow the more memorable because he was hideously ugly—resembling, said Caryll, "a florid pig." He died a few weeks later. "Between the sermon and his death I was one day talking to him. I was running someone down, saying beastly things of them. Suddenly I noticed that his eyes were shut. 'You are not listening,' I said. He replied 'I cannot—not to that; you see we are both present at Mass. Whilst you were trying to make me think ill of X, Christ Our Lord was offering Himself up to God to redeem them.' "

"But we are not at Mass," I said . . . and he said, "When your thoughts are hard or bitter or sad, let the sanctuary bell silence them. It is always ringing."

10

The "Phony War"

1939 WAS A YEAR of intense strain: as the summer drew towards its close war seemed almost inevitable. I have had the good fortune of receiving from Yvonne Bosch a packet of Caryll's letters dating from late August to early October 1939. She writes on August 26th of a

sort of quiet agony within oneself. . . . We may be spared still, and one understands so well now our dear Lord's prayer in Gethsemane, His fear, and His courage. But whatever happens in the future, it seems to me that in this which we are now experiencing He is saying "Fear not, it is I". . . .

I can't make my meaning clear, but I shall try to hang on to the thought all the time, in a mysterious way, everything that happens to us is not only His will, but Himself.

It was so lovely meeting you this morning, I came through that terrible black night as if it were a dark tunnel leading to a meadow all in flower—surely again that was Christ, "It is I."

I could have laughed out loud for joy when I saw you in the Oratory.

Everyone was waiting breathlessly. Iris was away and Caryll was troubled at not hearing from her, as she always wrote often and answered letters by return of post.

"During sixteen years she and I have always faced everything side by side, and though in temperament we are so unlike, the friendship and love between us is like a rock; it is a thing we both do not cease to thank God for.

"Still there is hope of peace, and I hope most eagerly and am now off to say a prayer to the martyr in the Cathedral."

Caryll does not tell in these letters her story when training for First Aid work, of the rather starched and stiff head nurse who addressed them, hospital fashion, by their second names. Caryll was "scrubbing up" in preparaton for a dressing when she asked, "Houselander, are you sterile?" Caryll could not resist answering, "Not as far as I know."

On August 31st she wrote, "Tonight hope of peace is slender indeed." She and Iris were summoned to the First Aid post, where they found great confusion:

. . . nothing ready at all. We had to begin by sweeping and. scrubbing the floor.

The thing that hurt me most in the whole business was the idea that the human race *could* be dragged into a thing of such violence, so utterly against the principles of the Sermon on the Mount, creating circumstances in which it seemed as if the simple beauty of life preached by Christ Our Lord were obliterated.

But now that great anguish has left me, it came to me like a blinding flash of light that Christ did not resist evil, that *He* allowed *Himself* to be violently done to death, that when He gave *Himself* to be crucified He knew that the exquisite delicacy and loveliness of the merest detail of the Christian life would survive the Passion; that indeed, far from being destroyed by it, it depended on it.

And so it is now; that which is holy, tender and beautiful, will not be swept away or destroyed by war; on the contrary, we can still say, "Ought not Christ to suffer these things and so enter into His glory?"

Three days later war was declared.

"Very little is ready," Caryll writes again; "our gas masks

(service ones) do not fit us, neither do our boots, and the rest of our equipment I could not find. However, we hope that all these things will sort themselves out."

They were working three days a week in twelve-hour shifts, changing after a few weeks into three consecutive nights— Caryll was allotted to gas decontamination, and says, "I am alarmed at even the degree of sheer physical energy [needed] to cope with it all, and *already* my wretched lung is sore from being in gas-proof rooms and gas masks—"

National service, she feels, is to be also "a service of humanity, and demands a heavy toll on each, and we ought to help men to carry into every place they go and all they do, the one idea of the deep, abiding love of Christ Our Lord, which far from being destroyed now, breaks out into flower, even in our weak, frightened hearts."

The First World War had come upon us suddenly; the approach of the second was a hideous nightmare which one hoped in vain to shake off. For the most part the actual outbreak was faced with courage, even cheerfulness. And then as the months went by a sort of dull depression settled on people's spirits. The early songs, "Roll out the Barrel," "Run rabbit, run" and the rest were more rarely heard in London restaurants. The sinking of ships brought severer rationing, much was said about the impregnable Maginot line, reporters were grumbling about their boredom, were using about the whole thing the word phony.

Some of us, as time went on, almost began to fancy that England itself might be no harder hit in this war than in the first. I don't think Caryll ever believed this: her premonitions had been too vivid to be forgotten, she was one of those who had held their breath waiting for Armageddon.

Curiously, although she records in her journal in 1928 the death of Smoky and speaks with immense confidence of meeting him again in heaven, it was not about him but about her "old family doctor" that she told Dickie the story of an appearance after death. It was in September 1939 just after the war had begun. Dickie was staying at Milborne Grove just after it happened. She found Caryll "radiant." She said it gave her courage to face the war and what it would bring.

She was waiting for the 96 bus in the Fulham Road (nearly opposite St. Stephen's Hospital) and couldn't help staring over and over again at a man who was one of the group of people waiting for the bus. In dress and manner he was most casual and relaxed, indeed bohemian. Yet he resembled to an extraordinary extent the family doctor to whom she had been devoted, but who was quite the opposite sort of person to the one at whom she was staring—very buttoned-up and decorous and prim and old-fashioned—she said he was a priest manqué and almost painfully shy, though a wonderful doctor.

To her horror (this was described with glorious Caryllish mime and absurdity) when she took her seat (one of those near the conductor's landing) the check-shirted bohemian clambered in and sat quite unnecessarily close to her. She said she behaved in the best tradition of outraged British spinsterhood, and moved as far away from him as she could—which was about two inches —when he gave her a jolly nudge with his elbow and an uproarious wink. She said, "Excuse me." But he laughed and laughed and said, "Oh, Caryll, you know perfectly well who I am. Don't be a goat. I've come back to check up on one or two of my patients and I want to talk to you about your health." He then talked on about health matters which ONLY this doctor could have known about, and asked pertinent questions about other members of the family—especially one who had a lesion on one lung. He was insistent that it was the *other* lung that must be watched carefully. He spoke of the war and what it would bring; and as the bus turned up Sydney Place he said, "I'll get off here. I won't vanish, people have got enough to contend with. Goodbye." And hopped off.

It was certainly a delicious farewell, and I can fancy Caryll laughing as well as radiant over her old friend's reason for refusing to vanish! Psychologists would tell us, I suppose, that in this appearance were revealed those elements in the man that he had been keeping under during his long professional life!

Whatever individuals may have thought, the government was preparing for an all-out attack on the country. Gas masks were served out—and you were obliged to carry them. In fact, they were never needed. What did later prove their worth in keeping enemy bombers high and preventing accurate aiming were the curiously reassuring huge siver-grey balloons shaped like pigs of which Hyde Park was full.

The *Grail Magazine* had been ready for press with a number on Modern Inventions. The day after war broke out Yvonne telephoned to Caryll to say it would have to be replaced by something else. Caryll answered, "I have already written it." What she had written was the first of the articles which later became part of *This War is the Passion*.

She writes frequently to Yvonne from the First Aid post. After a week or so things are getting organized, but she has made the terrifying discovery that "there are rats infesting the building—it makes my life there one long agony of terror. I am new and ignorant and have all the dirty jobs to do, sweeping, scrubbing, etc., and am often in the rattiest rooms about my lowly tasks!

"Inwardly I am incredibly happy. I did not know there could be such intimacy with Our Lord, such a true contemplation of Him as this life affords. I do not talk (!) and am shut up with Him in a kind of silence, and the fact that my work seems to produce one long ache in head and body only adds to the sense of Christ."

She likes the simplicity of the life, the total absence of class distinction, the plain food and the bare scrubbed boards from which it is eaten. (As time went on she felt that, not from snobbery but from variety of interests, they did fall into two separate groups.) Her fellow-workers are very nice, but "the atmosphere is incredibly unspiritual—it's almost frightening, no outward recognition of God at all.

"It makes me feel how necessary it is for Catholics to carry Christ there through their own Holy Communions."

In another letter she writes: "It seems to me that what matters is to create in this world a force of love strong enough to combat that of hate—and more particularly of fear. . . . I do so agree with you that the official hate propaganda is one of the greatest tragedies of war. And there ought to be a continual quiet resistance of it. There is not room for love and hate in one heart."

As for daily life, though Caryll sometimes compares her training to that of a novice, she feels that everyone is "suddenly plunged into a most gruelling discipline which far exceeds in severity any ever known in school or religious orders. *Everything* we want to do now we have to give up for more or less all the time."

Several times she expresses a conviction that no one should try to add anything to this heavy burden on themselves and on others. There is no room now for "orders, advice, or self-discipline. . . . More than ever before we ought to learn to become more deeply aware of beauty around us, when it is around us, and to appreciate the poetry and loveliness of the mind." She would like the Grail at Eastcote to "offer peace, a refuge where, in the presence of the Blessed Sacrament, people can get right away from war, can sleep, can see flowers and untroubled skies, and can so far as possible build up their nerves for what is to be suffered." She hopes Yvonne will look out specially for poorer people who have no other opportunity of getting out of London. She longs to bring back a spirit of "primitive poor Christianity for the post-war healing of the world"; she suggests the designing and printing of some beautiful black and white cards to be given to soldiers "with words on the back praying for peace, praying for *love* between all nations; these might come into the hands of the enemy too."

In this work of healing and preparing minds Caryll wanted to include above all the children who will after the war have to carry on. "I am already," she says, "involved in this with Father Bliss." And in the last letter before war was declared she had spoken casually of being rather extra-busy because she was trying to get at least a year's work done for Father Bliss, both articles and pictures, to make things easier for him in case she became a casualty. This meant, of course, the work for *two* papers—the children's *Messenger* and that for adults.

In her next letter she writes:

I have had some very very bad moments with a sheer physical desire to weep, but never, so far, *any* desire to get out of it or of what may come. At last, it seems to me, I have been allowed to taste the rim of the cup of Christ's passion—only the rim it is true, but even that goes very deep. Just the fact of having to go so *completely* against my own will in *everything* at the First Aid post seems to give me a sense of abnegation, which somehow seems to contain the very essence of love.

I'd no idea I would hate it so heartily—I mean the First Aid post. I knew I would dislike it, but I had not reckoned with my bodily weakness and understood how that, combined with mental aversion to the horrid, horrid "community" life, would make every hour like a kind of aching wound.

But the thing is that I go to it as to a lovers' meeting just because it's like that—often I have drawn the crucifix, and now I know I shall draw it on myself.

One reason for the intensity of Caryll's friendship with Yvonne she utters in this letter. She has found it hard to keep patience with the people who crowd to Milborne Grove on her free days. "It makes it hard for me," she says, "that most people who come, come to *get* peace from me, not to give it. Human contacts are so precious now, and I do so want strong people. I want also to receive the comfort of other people."

The nights on duty were broken by three hours' sleep in a

dormitory of twenty beds. Caryll discovered fleas in hers, so came in future armed with her own rug, which she would wrap around her completely and pull over her head. It became a place of self-revelation. "I do not attempt when in my rug to hide from myself that I now believe that love, human, personal love, is the root of all that is good." The religious life, she feels, cripples and distorts this "greatest grace."

She longs for "the strength and tenderness" of her friend's heart in which to rise "to the heart of Christ in His agony."

Besides the cards she had spoken of, Caryll wanted posters made of Our Lady and her Child: "Who could but be glad to be reminded silently by a picture that we have a Mother, that she can and will care for all mothers' sons?

"I myself, in my rug, thinking of you, so desire the big strong element of a mother."

A few days later Caryll has "emerged from [her] rug into such a happy day" with permission from the commandant to go to Communion in the morning. With our easier ways one shudders to think of a duty period from 3 A.M. to 8 fasting even from water, but Caryll describes it as "a long long glory of daybreak growing in my own heart because I should come to Him directly in the morning."

Despite the discovery of fleas in the bed, which led Caryll to cut her hair short so that she could wash it daily, things were, she said, growing better. Someone had put flowers all over the place, contrary to regulations, but they would be allowed to remain "so we can look at them all the time." Also the work has become easier and she is more used to the community life.

They had been discussing the next issue of the magazine, and Caryll writes in this letter that she has realized Yvonne does not want a number such as she had proposed, "concentrating wholly on the meaning of the war as the Passion of Christ.

"*Precisely* why I could not pick up, the fleas were too active, but at all events I thought you required something a little less intense." She proposed then a number on The Defences of the Mind—which, with "all this tremendous energy" poured into the defences of the body, were being neglected.

For this vast task she wants "to gather (not together in body but in soul) all, of all and any creeds, who are capable in any degree for this work and to do it with a will, but secretly."

The last of these letters, written on October 1st, before the Blitz struck England, is so revealing it must be quoted at some length. There is a kind of irony in the long hours of duty at the First Aid post waiting, waiting, for the casualties that never came. But the Blitz struck very suddenly, and time that had been too long was all too short for what needed doing by what was in fact a very small staff.

I was particularly glad that you can discover me, in my rug, as the helpless human creature that I really am.

I have had very little time for anything this week. I had one "shift" of eighteen consecutive hours on duty instead of twelve and in addition had to throw in an extra day's "duty" to make it possible for some others to have leave; also our two hours' leave during the day was cancelled this week; moreover, it is no longer allowed to read or write or anything, when we are "on duty" (except in the two hours which we did not get) . . . .

You ought not to fear my "genius and overwhelming ideas"— and I hope you won't for long. You know I am a very insufficient, frightened, helpless creature—I have no genius, only a little talent, and my only idea is to contemplate Christ in His life in people, for so long as I live among people on earth, and to do it with my whole being—hands, head, heart, etc.—not only with the mind.

It is very simple. Of the next life I have no imagination, it is something that I never think of. Here on earth Christ is almost visible, and because He is in us and with us, I agree with St. Catherine that "all the way to heaven *is* heaven."

But I must say that though my ideas were simple before the war, they are more simple still now. If I survive it, I am sure that I shall never again return to the compromise that pre-war life was. I have seen and heard and learnt too much already from the war.

I used to smart, to rage at the worldliness of so-called Christianity, and to come close on despair; now I see that certainly such so-called Christianity existed and does, even now, but it isn't the real thing. The real thing, however, exists. It is the hearts of simple people, and it depends not upon what school of thought one grew up in, or what creed one believes in, but on one's capacity for love and for humility.

I am sure as never before, that the Russian idea of Christ, humble, suffering, and crowned with thorns, is the only true one; that it is impossible to be a Christian unless the humility and poverty of Christ is taken literally and all that tends towards power, grandeur, success and so on, is avoided and despised.

So simple is the way, that in this fact alone there is joy; it is wonderful too to see how this flowering of Christ continues in the human heart and is indeed a seed sown by the Spirit wherever He wills to sow it. . . .

I have had a lot of opportunity of thinking of "the defences of the mind" from experience, observation, etc. One or two friends of mine, very dear ones too, broke down completely and seemed to be utterly shattered when war broke out; another lost her faith, and another all her money. Of these, two are finding healing, but only through prayer, through following a special, very simple method of prayer.

The average person of my acquaintance, who has been used to praying, finds it is necessary to learn to pray all over again. I never before heard so many people say that they are unable to concentrate at all—people who can do so normally.

I am trying to work out something in connection with this for you. But I must get [to] the Post. I see clearly so much to be arranged and I am very eager to talk with you—it would be well to arrange all we can before raids—these are fully expected when England has officially refused the insolent "Peace offers" of Hitler, not before. However, no one can know, and they may never come! I hope they don't, though for the moment Christ in His great mercy has so filled my consciousness with Him that I do not experience fear—I shall of course! But for all our sakes big battles, raids, etc., are to be avoided.

So changed is the world by Germany having simply handed over the power of Europe to Stalin that there will no longer be the possibility of *tepid* Christianity, but how it will end no one can guess.

It may be sooner than we think, but never before was there a moment in which it is so imperative to realize and keep the Inward Kingdom. This we must try to do, and you . . . must help me—the more I seem a baby in a rug to you, the more you will help me.

God be with you always, and all my love in Christ,

Caryll

11

The Blitz

THESE MONTHS WERE perhaps harder on the nerves, if
one really did realize what was coming, than the Blitz itself
when it came. Although there was so far nothing very much
to be done in the way of first aid, a small staff were working
for many hours day or night and almost longing for a casualty. Caryll had a rather wicked story of a warden who
walked in with a cut finger and had to be carried out after
all the zealous nurses had hurled themselves upon him.

Europe was under the Nazi heel for quite some while before the Blitz struck England, and refugees were pouring
over, especially from Belgium.

Rosamond Batchelor remembers how

in their spare time Caryll and Iris took on a little troupe of
Belgian refugee children who were housed in Eccleston Square,
and to whom they taught toy-making. They were children from
the slums of Brussels and Antwerp, who had been bombed and
machine-gunned on their flight along the Belgian roads—clever,
imaginative children, who brought extraordinary fantasy and
dexterity into the making of toys. When they had made enough,
Caryll and Iris staged a little exhibition of them at the house in
Eccleston Square, and sold them to bring in money for the chil-

dren. (I remember that I bought an enchanting Noah's Ark, with beautifully made, slightly fantastic, felt animals in all the colours of the rainbow.) Caryll gave a tea-party in the shed to these children—in fact, two tea-parties, as the shed would not hold all the children: one tiny boy, who was to be in the second group, found his way, all alone, on foot and without a word of English, to Milborne Grove from Victoria, to the first tea-party, as he felt he was being left out.

Then the raids started, and the Belgian children were sent to the country. An air-raid shelter was built in the garden at Milborne Grove, and on top of it Iris characteristically grew daffodils—a touch which always reminded me of Puvis de Chavanne's picture of Hope—a little girl sitting on a grave, holding a flower.

"They had," says Dickie, "ghastly nights in that measly shelter."

When the house in Milborne Grove was blasted Caryll and Iris were on night duty at the First Aid post in the Chelsea Women's Hospital. The first casualties came pouring in from the Church of Our Most Holy Redeemer, Chelsea, where the long line of people waiting to go to confession had suffered a direct hit. I have still in my prayer book the memory card for those killed, dated September 14th, 1940, with Christ Crucified depicted on one side and on the other: "Fear ye not them that kill the body and are not able to kill the soul" and "I am the Resurrection and the Life."

A stick of small bombs [says Iris] was dropped right across the Boltons—one of them fell in the garden of the house next door to us and blasted our doors and windows in, and made a general mess of the house. We returned in the early morning, our hearts sinking lower and lower as we saw the trail of damage leading right across our street. Poor old Jones was snugly sleeping in the air-raid shelter in the garden, and was happily unhurt, though very frightened.

It was then that I went to Nell Gwynn House and asked if we could have a one-room flat there straight away. We moved in the very same night, and slept on the floor on lie-lows, in thick dust, without light or curtains. We gradually made it more habitable, bringing things on our bicycles from Milborne Grove during our time off.

Our bicycles were our great stand-by, and we used to break the record down the Fulham Road during raids!

Rosamond remembers the flat in the days when it was

furnished with four mattresses, and a table, bought from the porter for 5/-, nothing else. Dickie's beautiful house (or rather, her mother's) in the South Bolton Gardens was partly demolished by a landmine: it was near us and sounded, I remember, like the crack of doom—as well it might, for it destroyed two roads of houses. Then the flat in which my mother and I were living in Redcliffe Square was blasted, and when my brother came round and found me with bronchitis in a house without any heating or lighting, he (and Caryll) persuaded us to take six months' lease in Nell Gwynn House, at the other end of the long corridor leading from the flat in which Caryll and Iris were camping out. Here another landmine fell on the flats opposite. ("Poor old Bobby, they do follow you about," I remember my brother saying to me after my third landmine.)

Dickie's mother was staying with her sister in the country, Dickie herself on duty at a hospital the night their house was destroyed.

I was [she writes] sent for on Sunday by the matron, who said, "Nurse, I'm afraid I have very grave news for you, the house has been hit. Your sister wants you to go at once, but you *must* telephone her first."

I naturally thought my sister's house was hit and my mother or my sister's children hurt—imagine my horror when I was told *no* telephone calls could go through, as the Weybridge exchange had been hit! It was only by three o'clock that I discovered—Oh, glory of relief!—that it was only the house in South Bolton Gardens that had been hit with no one in it. I was to go and salvage all I could before it was demolished.

I took the coach up to London through the growing gloom and was horrified to find that, far from being "cordoned off" and guarded by wardens, the garden was full of sightseers—one fox-furred lady beside me in the gloom said, "O poor deah Lady Orpen, I wondah did she perish?" I was distracted from a rude answer when I saw more and more people wandering about in the dining room, which resembled a rockery—one fashionable soul waving *my* christening mug in her hand.

Dickie strode in indignantly questioning their right to be there, and the sightseers melted away into what was now total blackness,

leaving me crunching about on the broken glass. Little wonder my footsteps took me down the well-loved road to Milborne Grove like a homing pigeon—. Oh horror! *that* looked uninhabited, only glass gone, but *no* one living there.

Then suddenly a tiny figure in the gloom and Caryll saying, " 'ullo, old dear, we was expecting you. Iris says come and camp in our de luxe air-raid shelter at Nell Gwynn," which I did— for all the three weeks' compassionate leave I was given to salvage among our ruins. They were kind and sweet and we giggled hilariously as the "preggers" (pregnant bombers) went rumbling over and the swooshers came down. Each morning Caryll and I would pick our way over the mattresses and toddle off to Mass. How well I remember the starlit mornings, the harsh smell of cordite and rubble a strange incense in our nostrils as we picked our way gingerly, Caryll's tiny figure with a child's beret perched very jauntily on her shining hair.

This flat of Iris's under normal conditions is a *very* tight fit for two, consisting of one medium-sized room, a kitchen and a bathroom. It is hard to imagine it when Caryll and Iris, her daughter Joan and Dickie were all sleeping there

—with such sleep as they could get. Dickie went out, she says, like a light, the minute she lay down, and she remembers the flat as a most luxurious air-raid shelter with that rarest of things in war-time, abundant hot water for a daily bath. But her hostesses slept less well. There was a night when Caryll was sitting up on her mattress reading poetry aloud to Iris. She was blown right across the room, glass from the broken windows, the curtains and the lamps, all following her. She and Iris, says Rosamond, "came round in their dressing-gowns to see if we were all right (Caryll carrying Roosey, her aged teddy-bear) and found a wounded cook lying on my bed, our curtains torn down, and my mother tranquilly admiring the beautiful colours of the flares falling in the street outside to guide the bombers. The whole night had an air of fantasy to me." And Caryll wrote to a friend, "There was Rosamond behaving beautifully as though at a polite tea-party."

Caryll herself felt very frightened during raids. But however terrified and however exhausted, she would pull herself together and execute a ludicrous dance in which she appeared like a clown—or a puppet whose bones are loose in their sockets and who moves on a string handled by a showman. Dickie felt the dance to be tragi-comedy of a high order, but Iris relaxed as she watched. "She was literally a stringed puppet and made the most ghastly 'ug' faces at the same time so that we had to giggle." Caryll's very presence helped Iris, and Dickie describes how she and Caryll were caught in a raid a long way from home and Caryll insisted on returning, "running down the middle of the Fulham Road with wardens imploring us to take shelter and shrapnel clattering down around us, panting out, 'Got to get home to Mum.' "

Several years later, Caryll wrote to an intimate friend:

During the war, I was simply terrified by air raids, and it was my lot to be in every one that happened in London, sometimes on the roofs of these flats, sometimes in the hospital, sometimes in Mobile First Aid in the street. I tried to build up my courage by reason and prayer, etc., etc. Then one day I realized quite suddenly: as long as I try not to be afraid I shall be worse, and I shall show it one day and break; what God is asking of me, to do for suffering humanity, is to *be* afraid, to accept it and put up with it.

But how, her friend asked, could this be done?

You asked me how I managed to accept fear in the raids. I've just remembered that I never answered you. Well—perfectly simply. Instead of kidding myself and trying to minimize the danger or to find some distraction from it, I said to myself: "For as long as this raid lasts—an hour—or eight hours—you are going to be terrified. So are lots of people who don't deserve it as you do, so you must just carry on and *be* terrified, that's all" —and at once the *strain* ceased. Oh yes, I was terrified: I've often had to resort to sheer force to hide the fact that my teeth were chattering, and been unable to speak, as my mouth was too dried up and stiff from funk. But at the time I felt that God had put His hand right down through all the well upon well of darkness and horror between Him and me and was holding the central point of my soul; and I knew that *however* afraid I was then, it would not, even could not, break me. I always volunteered (after this discovery) for *most* frightful things (if called on to do so only!) —like Mobile First Aid in the street, and fire watching on the roof of Nell Gwynn: and always knew God was there in a special way, to accept the offering of fear. It's only when we try *not* to experience our special suffering that it can really break us.

Mrs. Houselander had gone into the fire service. I doubt if she was ever frightened. Dickie's sketch of her in uniform perfectly illustrates the description she gave me, "Gert looked like a cross between Britannia and Boadicea." Willmott had taken a flat near Nell Gwynn House.

All windows had to be shaded at sunset so that no light could be seen from the street: special black curtains were used and air-raid wardens would ring or knock instantly if a gleam appeared. Violation of the blackout was a punishable offence. The phrase "night life of London" was taking on a new meaning. Much of it was lived underground. Vast air-raid shelters received the bombed-out victims and had become for many their only home. Caryll went down into several of these shelters with some of the Grail members selling a penny magazine, *P.M.*, especially written "for those who shelter." A questionnaire in an early number suggested that you mark yourself to decide whether you are a Shelter Blessing or a Shelter Pest. Both were to be found in plenty, and much depended on the answer for the comfort of those endless nights. In many shelters night prayers were said, and priests gave to thousands their blessing and a conditional absolution. All realized they might be dead before the morning, but they learnt to rest peacefully in the bunks piled one above another, some in stations of London's underground railway, others in storerooms where sacks of spices were still heaped, yet others in newly constructed shelters centrally heated for the winter nights.

Caryll noted the family corners made in these shelters, the pitiful little homes in which the mother must make the tea exactly right for her son rather than let him use the public canteen. Odd bits of salvage, a bird in a cage, memories of a bombed home, were used to build up the illusion of a nest, an abiding shelter in this world of destruction. The authorities tried to prevent this—if every sheltering family had done it, many Londoners would have been left in the streets. But the marshals in the shelters were amazingly kind. Overdriven as they were, out in the raids night after night, they were tender with the old and lonely and with the many semiconscious from shock for whom a familiar object was something to cling to.

What pictures Caryll saw night by night, fire-watching or exploring the shelters! There were First Aid posts, doctors, canteens, pianos and even concert parties; there were mothers

feeding their babies, whole families in bunk above bunk, one
man reading Walton's *Compleat Angler* ("Strange shades
of sunlit water and branches bending over streams and flies
and fish in this vast subterranean dormitory a mile long!") . . .

What an incredible collection of people sheltering night after
night deep under the streets of London. Tramps . . . babies who
were born here, bombs screaming from the skies; workmen,
mothers of families, poets and children . . . white man and
Negro, men and women of all the nations of Europe, young and
old, good and bad, Jew and Gentile, and all mysteriously sorting
themselves out so that generally like congregates with like.

After *This War is the Passion* appeared Caryll wrote to a
friend agreeing that she had put "the loud pedal on the
sterner side of religion," as it had been partly written for
members of a youth movement who "tend to the idea" that
a comfortable life "pretty oblivious of the world's sorrow is
consistent not only with salvation but with evangelizing the
world. I wanted to break down this complacency."

Here is the same note of criticism as in the dialogues. But
she certainly did not strike it much at this date. Her letters
are full of enthusiasm about the work in the shelters, the
growing of food on the tiny Grail farm at Pinner, the excel-
lent cider they made.

"Yvonne," she wrote when the Blitz was at its worst, "takes
it all with a kind of beautiful dignity that is very inspiring."

Caryll's own vocation as it developed was a very different
one from that of the Grail: it was chiefly personal—to neurotics hopeless of a cure, to those needing religion and hopeless of finding it, to the misfits in life, the despairing, the
spiritual "sea-horses." More and more after the war would
this vocation prove its worth, indeed its necessity, and its
almost terrible difficulty.

But the war had for the moment wrought some amazing

changes, and I think despite overwork, bad physical conditions and the anguish of seeing so much suffering around her Caryll, like many others, was uplifted by the sense of a great moment. All visitors to England felt and noted it: the whole country seemed to be hearing the words *Sursum Corda* and answering *Habemus ad Dominum*. These words from the Mass remind us that the war had in fact for the moment, in the limited framework of their own country, done for the English people what Christianity fully accepted and lived should do for all men at all times. It had put purpose into life, it had swept away the trivial, it had created a new sense of brotherhood that made class distinctions appear irrelevant.

The resistance was in England offered not, as in most of Europe, by certain groups but by the entire nation, and for the duration totally different people were directing their very varied tastes, powers, energies into one channel, making *e pluribus unum*—as we should all be doing in the multiform unity of Christ's Mystical Body.

"Don't imagine," Caryll wrote in the letter praising Yvonne and her work, "that we are depressed here: no, sometimes tired, always in very great need of your prayers, but often we can repeat Our Blessed Lord's words, 'It was for this hour that I came into the world.' "

Rosamond, still at the other end of Iris's passage, was seeing both her and Caryll almost daily: they had become neighbours at work also. Caryll, after about a year, left her First Aid post and went into the Censorship, where Rosamond had been from the first, and where Iris presently joined her. They were censoring English letters, Rosamond Polish. She writes:

Iris's memories of this period are hazy—perpetual exhaustion, snatching meals (*filthy* meals, she adds), dodging bombs, and, of course, the unforgettable tube journeys, when one could hardly find foot-room on the platforms, so crowded were they with bunks and sleeping figures. Caryll used to spend many of her lunch hours in the lovely old church in Ely Place, which was much frequented by the Censorship Catholics, and where one certainly had an extraordinary sense of peace and security. (Which communicated itself to non-Catholics as well: I remember asking a well-known choreographer where he had been during one colossal wallop in the lunch hour, and being told, "In the church at Ely Place, of course." But he was almost an honorary Catholic. He used to sit, at the table of Air Force advisers, reading the *Interior Castle,* and when I once commented on this, replied simply, "Well, it's the only castle we've got nowadays.")

I was working [Rosamond goes on] in the Uncommon Languages Department, a section of richly variegated humanity. Caryll and Iris were working next to the Air Force section, in which our "honorary Catholic," in the uniform of a Flight Lieutenant, was acting in an advisory capacity. He had such faith in Caryll's prayers that he used to appear round the corner of the cupboard separating the two sections, with his hands prayerfully folded, mouthing at her, *"A genoux!"* Caryll's boss, who presided at her table, disliked these interruptions, and once asked fretfully, "Who is this man who is always asking you to pray for him?"

The dramatic gestures and attitude came naturally to an actor, but the need for prayer was felt and uttered by everyone just then. A whole nation under fire was reacting by a strong realization that only God could save them. "We all appreciate," wrote Shane Leslie to a friend early in the Blitz, "and almost feel the hand of God moving around us like the old mystics."

"This Shane man is exceedingly interesting," wrote Caryll to her friend Henry Tayler; "oldish, you know. With side whiskers—I think that *you* would look simply glorious with side whiskers . . . He is also a Home Guard, and looks strange and yet so right in it. He is going to come and read poetry to us . . . would you like to come?"

Two correspondences of these war years bring them vividly before us. One is with Archie Campbell Murdoch, who with his wife Sheila was drawing near the Church, much helped by Caryll. She writes to him at immense length, in her lunch hour, in the night and the early hours of the morning, about philosophy and theology, about prayer, about books, about the war. The day of their reception into the Church is a joyful one, and Caryll bids to a war-time feast Iris and her other dearest friend Henry Tayler, whom she called "David"; his was the soul God had asked her to get for Him, and the second long war-time correspondence is with him.

"I very often offer Holy Communion for you," she writes in one letter, "often on lovely mornings with the whole world steeped in moonlight—I do hope you sometimes feel Christ's hands above you in blessing on those days."

They would plan for poetry readings at her flat or his, they gave each other books and gramophone records. Each happy moment snatched just now might be the last. "I got home all right, but it was not a very nice journey. I had to duck several times, and there seemed to be bursts from incendiary bombs in every direction, but I skuttled along and here I am."

Christmas 1940 had come and Henry had sent her a crib which she had set out on a "beautiful, softly coloured red silk handkerchief with orange candles on each side, and behind it like a little flowering tree some white freesias and a spray of jasmin. . . ." She goes on:

That experience when the bomb fell the other night was very queer. I knew of course that the raiders were right overhead, but thought I'd try to get home; then I saw the thing coming, it was a landmine, and they shot it in the air.

I thought, as one does, that it was coming at me, it seemed a certainty, but somehow just an ordinary thing to happen. Then suddenly the whole sky went a dull, cruel crimson. I thought, "I'd better get down on the ground," and the one thing that troubled me was that I was afraid of dropping some of your Christmas presents, which I was still carrying. It must have been only a few seconds, but seemed like years, as I was able to *think* so calmly and clearly about not one thing alone, but several, and also about several people—and not in turn, one after the other, but all together, as if each train of thought ran along in a parallel line beside the other—it was an absolute example of how different time is to what we generally imagine. Anyhow, down I got on my face, the proper place for a creature to be before God anyway, and suddenly I thought that the whole town was full of ringing bells—next ARP men and rescue workers just seemed to rise up miraculously from nowhere and simply refused to believe I was not dead, as I was in a veritable sea of plate glass, *all* the shop windows having fallen out all round me. They fell out from Sloane Sq. to the Town Hall, and you can imagine the blast when I tell you (and it's true) that though the mine actually fell on Ebury Bridge it broke windows in the Hyde Park Hotel! But actually I had not got even a fragment on me and did not get as much as a scratch. . . .

A few days later the Sheed & Ward office in Paternoster Row was totally destroyed. My husband had been sleeping there the previous night, so his escape was as wonderful as Caryll's. We did not know her yet but I, marooned in the States, had been reading her articles in the *Grail Magazine* and had begged him to be sure to see her when in England. *He* was able to get permits for travel, and was constantly back and forth. On this visit he planned a book with Caryll. Together they worked out what could be used that she had already written, what still needed writing and just what shape the book should take. In 1941 we published in the States *This War is the Passion*. A year later it was published in England.

In November 1941 Caryll had what she calls, with admirable understatement, "a slight blow, *all* my work on the way to America has been sunk." It seemed to her "absurd to

mind at all"—*things* should not count when so many people
were being killed—but she had "to begin again and do the
whole lot" (which included at least one set of Stations). She
was just changing over from the First Aid post to the Censorship, which might make this especially difficult. "But still one
must learn patience and to work hard."

A month later she writes from the Censorship:

There is one thing I can say about the work, namely I find it
more and more absorbing, and it seems to bring before my eyes
all the wounds and anxieties and courage and pathetic joys of
the people of the world. I am able to pray for each one, to offer
sacrifices when that seems to be called for, to commend them all
to God. I begin to imagine what it must be like to be a saint in
heaven and to see all the pitiful prayers of the world passing
through one's hands to God—I don't mean that I'm a saint, but
that as the stuff passes through my hands, I can pray for each
one, taking the hope or grief or anxiety of each and offering it to
God.

It never occurred to me that this sort of continual prayer for
people would arise out of this job; now I wonder it did not, for
it is inevitable.

Besides the unknown crowding around her, there were
her work companions, and one of these to whom she drew
very close was Christine Spender, sister of the poet, Stephen.

I first met Caryll Houselander [she writes] in the British
Censorship in the January of 1942. After our fortnight of training, we trainees were distributed among the "tables." Caryll
sat almost exactly opposite to me and, though she was the most
modest of people, invisible arc lights seemed to shine on her. At
first I thought she must come straight from an artist's studio—
and in this I was partly right, as I discovered later. But with
that flaming red hair, very white face, and garbed in a Morris-
like overall, she might just as well have stepped out of a mediaeval stained-glass window. Or have been an actress. Her hair was

cut straight with a fringe and hung nearly to her shoulders, and when she washed it, it shone. Her sight must have been bad, for she wore glasses with very thick lenses. But this somehow did not detract from the effect of the mediaeval saint. Some people might have called her quaint (in some ways she looked more like a mediaeval tumbler than a saint), but this word never occurred to me at that time, for she carried herself with a curious dignity and gravity.

Christine felt strongly attracted to Caryll from the first, and after a while they were thrown together, almost in solitude, being put to work in a basement room

all on our own, just censoring parcels. From a practical point of view I shall never know why we two were chosen out of so many to do this task, because we were both very slow at parcels, and on one occasion I managed to pack the secateurs we were supplied with inside a parcel and they were lost for ever! But Caryll had her own explanation of our being picked out. She told me some time afterwards that she had prayed to be given a sign if she were to "take me on." The sign was to be that we should be singled out together in some manner. She regarded our work together in the parcelling department as an answer to this prayer, and from that moment I was included in her circle and had much loving and prayerful counsel given to me. In the meantime we very much enjoyed our work together in the basement.

Not in itself interesting, it was their task to look for and report any censorable matter, but there was a pleasant atmosphere in the place and the messengers in the basement seemed to enjoy helping them to unpack the parcels and teaching them the proper kind of knot to use. "A green light filtered into the room, and we felt rather like two fish in a large aquarium. . . . As we got to know one another better we laughed more than we had done for a long time—we were after all living through grave times—and it was rather like dwelling in the innocence of childhood once more. Caryll was extremely witty herself and had a quiet little chuckle ready for any of my jokes."

Both were quite sad when after a week of this their boss upstairs urgently demanded their return, and

our men colleagues, the messengers, indicated that it was a pity we had to go just as we were all getting along so merrily.

During this week I sensed something of Caryll's implacable spirituality. I also discovered the equability—or so it seemed to me—which never gave way to irritability or bad temper. In the whole time I knew her I never saw her ruffled, though she did sometimes confide in me the things that pained or upset her.

Caryll's attitude to life interested Christine increasingly. She discovered that she made it a rule never to refuse a beggar, because thus she could follow the Gospel teaching. "Sometimes," she comments, "I wonder if she ever denied anybody what they asked." Christine noted with dismay how little Caryll ate, how few hours she slept. After the appearance of *This War is the Passion* she felt, like her other friends, great dismay over the flood of people who all "seemed to need help and to eat up endless time, for Caryll never ignored the needs of anybody. Her almost unwilling capacity for attracting disciples began to strike me. She never missed going to Mass and Holy Communion daily, however much effort it cost her and however far she was from a church. Yet I never once knew her late for work. Hers was a deep strength concealed by visible weakness."

To Henry, anxious about her exhaustion, Caryll wrote:

13.1.42 Lunch hour—at work
It's true I've been at the limit of my endurance. I think the cold makes everything more tiring. . . .

Don't worry—I will not get ill—I'm sure of it—ideas are pouring into my mind, everything that was puzzling through the years past becoming clear and illuminated, as if God just began to reveal all the secret beatitude that we ought to be aware of—and I am sure that I will be allowed the strength to write it, as it is meant for other people. It is not easy to write, just because it all seems so obvious. When I go to write I find I can't explain at all, it is like trying to teach drawing—one asks, "What on earth is there to learn?"

But daily life, as lived in war-time, gave small opportunity to the creative artist. Caryll and Iris had to start out early every morning for their work at the Censorship, Caryll having already made her way to Mass at either St. Mary's, Cadogan St., or the Oratory. They returned late in the evening. At night, when not on duty fire-watching, they needed their sleep badly. And somehow housekeeping must be accomplished: rations bought, clothes washed and mended, food cooked.

Fortunately they had Kate. This valiant woman cleaned their flat (and also that of Mr. Houselander), she took home garments to wash and iron, she stood endlessly in line at one food shop after another to collect the meagre rations and the unrationed extras—so often "sold out"—without which they could hardly have lived.

She had begun working for Iris at Milborne Grove and remembers her first sight of Caryll. "I thought she was a funny little thing. I said to Kathleen [the housemaid]: 'Who is that funny little thing?' Kathleen said: 'A writer. You'll like her, she's ever so nice and kind.' Kathleen thought the world of her. She came in and shook hands with me.

"Proper chain-smoker she was in those days. Used to take John [Kate's nephew] and teach him wood-carving in the shed.

"She used to say to me, 'Come upstairs and have a good chat.' I remember her saying after a bad night at the Post, 'We had a devil of a time last night, Kate.' She worked hard, never went to bed, I think. She was always working—never ate anything."

Every morning Iris left, in a small notebook, directions for Kate and exchanged news with her; every night Kate left her answers; and from these little notebooks we get quite a picture of the domestic side of London in the Blitz. What strikes one most, perhaps, is a surprising element in the proportions of things. The absence of fish seems at least as serious as the presence of bombs. A successful dish is hailed with enthusiasm, a predatory neighbour stealing some of the precious (strictly rationed) milk merits a page of the notebook. Here is a little of the dialogue:

Iris: Mince was a great success—except that the air raid came just as I was going to enjoy it.

Kate: I have cooked some Celery Could not get a cauliflower I don't know what you are Having for dinner I hope you will Find something we had a very near one on Saturday

Iris: There's some fish in the larder. . . .*If* you fancy any, do eat it for your lunch. I ate the whole pigeon myself!

Kate: Madam you just owe me 2/6 towards The pigeon. I hope The Stew will be alright.

The Boy left you 2½ pints on Sunday, another Lady saw Him put it in she ask Him if she Could Have an extra pint I should Think she had yours what do you Think

Iris: Four points left *in case* of biscuits. One whole book of soap left for cleaning soap and flakes. *Someone* must have taken the milk! Brutes!

Kate, especially when excited, tends to use many capitals but no punctuation: "The Laundry Has not Come Back yet and last week's is still There The Pudding has had nearly 2 hrs."

Laundry was indeed a serious problem, for clothes and materials were rationed as well as food. Coming from a house into a flat, Iris was fairly well off—but she had had overfull house in the flat rather long; there were still often three people, sometimes more, for sheets, towels, etc., and all these things wear out. So do clothes and shoes: "They said your shoes might be 2 or 3 weeks so Mr. Houselander is going to do them for you."

Mr. Houselander figures largely in the notebooks. He sends them stews, fish, a piece of cheese for cooking. Kate begs some onions from him, buys biscuits on his ration and then "begs" them for Caryll. Once the stew he sends had been kept too long, Kate reports it as "working" and "smelling the flat out." She has thrown it away. Iris adjures her not to tell him, and for the most part his cooking is recorded as delicious. His jugs and bowls pile up in the larder, and Iris apologizes for their weight when asking Kate to take them back to him.

Kate lived (and still lives) in Battersea. Both Chelsea and Battersea were heavily raided, and it was sometimes hard for her to get over the river to Nell Gwynn House. She would shop in both areas when anything ran out:

Kate: The Shopping was such a nuisance Lining up for everything I Had no Time for Cleaning But will do it Tomorrow. There is very Little Sugar in the Rhubarb So sorry I went 3 Times To The market And could not get any Fish

Iris: Hope these last two raids haven't been too near you? It *has* been horribly noisy.

Kate: Yes the Bombs were too near to be nice Last night However I am still alive I have made the cheese sauce. Could not get a larger cauliflower

Iris: Any chance of oranges?

Kate: I Keep asking for them

Iris: Hope it wasn't too bad round you last night?

Kate: No not Too near Balham Clapham I hope you did not want the Curry I Have eaten it for my Lunch I Felt so Hungary.

Sometimes Iris, sometimes Caryll gets leave, and when Iris is away Caryll continues the dialogue with Kate—who now has more time and can shop for the beloved Jones:

Caryll: The fish shop in the market always has nice fish every day now. So if you could go there it would probably save you in the long run—for Jones and me. I do not like herrings (Jones does) but I like their roes, and all roes [spelt rows: Caryll's spelling never improved]. I am also passionately devoted to Kippers, & I like mackerel. (But not with the heads on!)

Kate: Will you like some chops for the weekend on yr Ration Book I gave Jones some pieces of meat Today so he will have enough.

Caryll: I am very glad to hear of the kind porter's Spearhead advance against the beetles . . . a lot of very young ones are coming again. He must *not* use anything that would hurt Jones, and Jones had better go out & stay out all that day. Yes I would like chops as you suggest. . . . I don't understand how "points" etc. work.

(It was just as well Caryll had Jones to consider as well as herself, for when alone she once remarked, "I feel inclined to give up the struggle and eat blotting paper.")

Kate: What a Bad night I am like you all alone My Brother is on his Holidays. I Hope you weren't nervous

Caryll: Yes, that raid on Wednesday night was a proper scorcher! I hope he will run out of bombs soon! Glad you are O.K.

The housekeeping probably served as a counter-irritant to the bombs, and every little relief was hailed delightedly. Iris's lease in Milborne Grove had not run out, and the

house was getting a little builder's first aid. Kate runs errands
to it for Iris and brings back large quantities of bluebells
from the garden—noting that she has given some to Mr.
Houselander, as he had seen them when she went to him.

Iris leaves her a note no longer to do the blackout, as it is
now quite light when they get home. Each year one realizes
the coming of spring as some relief of their tension. Caryll is
writing just then to a friend, "I'm using the shed now, and
the blossom is thick on our little trees in the garden."

This was only April 1943, and there was a weary way to go
yet before the war should end. Sometimes raids were almost
continuous, and are noted day after day:

Kate: You have a surprize dinner
Iris: and a "surprise" raid.
Kate: Yes it was a surprize night But I went To Bed and Forgot
it was going on
Iris: Do hope you are alright. What a terrible night—could see
them dropping over Battersea way when on fire watch. Don't
know what to suggest for dinner.
Kate: Yes we Had a Bad Time Yesterday & Saturday I lost
some of my windows They were Too near to Be nice. I Hope the
Beans are alright I paid 2/- for Them But They bite a bit Tough
I am going to Mr. H. Tomorrow so will be a little Late in Case
you are Home Glad you are Safe I Have Been in The Cellar all
night
Iris: So sorry you had to be in the cellar all night! What did
your brother-in-law think of it? Will you eat the fish left over?
It is very nice.
Kate: My Brother-in-Law was very nervous he Had no Idea it
was Like That. Please give the 6d to Miss Houselander change
from Jones meat yesterday.
Iris: There is a sausage roll left if you want it. I do hope we
have a better week-end. Haven't slept in my bed all the week—
so won't change the sheets.
Kate: I have got all Rations on one book. I would rather have

a Bed to make Than Listen all night for Buss Bombs We Had one at the top of our Street I was shot out of my Bed it was ghastly all night digging Thank God we escaped but it has made me Feel a bit rocky

You are only allowed 1 lb of Jam and ½ lb sugar

I will quote no more of this record, which I found so fascinating, except Kate's almost final entry:

I have brought the two Frocks. If Victory Comes The weekend I shall not come on Monday

But before reaching this entry you must imagine life through more than three years of these little books with their prosaic details and their quiet tone of voice while London rocked.

Caryll's hopes for her work were encouraged by the immense success of *This War is the Passion.* The first rather large royalties she brought to Iris, done up like a cracker, saying, "This is for you." For the rest of her life, every time she received a cheque she would write to us saying that she was having a Mass said for everyone in the office. We could never fully convince her that the money was the just reward of her own hard work. To Henry Tayler she remarked, "Maisie and Frank are making a fortune for me without my doing a hand's turn."

The originality of Caryll's work came partly from its complete reality. Spiritual books are so often written in clichés by people remote from life. Caryll was living in the midst of human suffering at its intensest—she was aware of it all the time. Jacques Doneux saw her once coming from a visit to some crippled children, walking through the crowds at Waterloo Station as if in a trance. He went up to her and

realized she hadn't seen him. With the war he felt that what
he called "her old free and easy self" had gone. Rosamond
too felt that she was much gayer before the war—that from
the war chiefly grew her great stress on suffering. Iris agrees
but thinks that the change in her was chiefly the result of
overstrain and overwork. She had always worked hard but
never anything like this. "Night after night she would write
till the pen fell from her hand. She never held back, she
gave everything she had. Everyone felt *they* were *the* important person. Coming into the flat and finding someone who
would make a demand on her, she would stand stock still
as if she had been shot. It would be at least ten minutes before she could speak coherently."

In the autumn of 1942 they managed to get another flat for
Caryll. It was small and dark, looking onto a well; Caryll
said it was like a cross between a kitchen and a mortuary
chapel, and she named it the kitchmorgue. When Sheila
Campbell Murdock sent her a cleaning outfit Caryll wrote,
"I have more and more realized since I had the kitchmorgue
how real the prayer of contemplation is that consists out-
wardly in washing up, dusting and cooking; and to have these
mops and dusters and cloths to make even 'the outward and
visible sign' of it beautiful and to have them from you is a
delight."

However small and dark, a place to herself meant solitude,
to think, to write, to pray. But not as much as she had
hoped.

Censorship by day, fire-watching many a night, and in
addition Caryll was now writing and illustrating almost the
whole of the *Children's Messenger* every month, for Father
Bliss had grown so old that he could no longer do his job, yet
could not bear to give it up. Devoted to him as Caryll was
she plugged on—writing her own books, *when* I can hardly
tell, but somehow.

Even before the war she had had in addition to her

writing many people who had grown to depend on her advice. "I am a drain pipe," she once said; "God wants to pour words through me." But she also constantly spoke of herself as a neurotic, and I think we see from her correspondence how her own sufferings had taught her the art of healing. *This War is the Passion* helped thousands, only too many of whom now wanted personal contact and advice. Despite her other work Caryll never refused those whom she felt she could help, although it often left her drained. "When you have done something really healing," she wrote to a friend, "it happens so often that the only way you know it at first is by your own feeling of emptiness. Even Our Lord experienced this; when the woman who touched the hem of His garment was healed, He knew it by the sense of something having gone out of Him, an emptying '[power] has gone out of Me.' It is the same for His followers—we know the moment of healing, not yet evident, not by exaltation and triumph but by emptiness and a sense of failure! That demands huge faith, but you have it!"

By the "huge faith" required of us she meant the faith that *we* can throw ourselves totally on Christ. But even He needed to pray to His Father in a desert place apart; to commune with His special friends, His Apostles; to leave the crowd that thronged and pressed around Him for their healing—and from curiosity. As members of Christ's Mystical Body we owe to our fellows what help we can give them, but we do not owe to them neglect of our work, of our prayer, of others who may need us more. We do not owe our time to those who want merely to waste it. If Caryll had attempted to help everybody who came, she would have ended by helping nobody.

I would have been tempted to incredulity had fewer people borne witness to the persecution of Caryll by her disciples and admirers. If the knocker and bell produced no result, they simply went on knocking and ringing.

"Can you think of *any* way," she wrote to Henry, "in which one can convey charitably and in a few words that one is engaged and does not want to be disturbed?" It began while she was still with Iris. One week-end angels had guarded her. A girl knocked and knocked "for ages . . . it turned out she had got the number wrong and was hammering on an empty flat." And in another letter: "I am harassed by people as well as by bombs."

To Archie she writes: "Tell Sheila (who will laugh) someone is at the door, so I *am* going through the window to get to Rosamond, risking burglars."

Rosamond remembers well both the over-accessible ground floor flat and the move up higher after the war ended: "I used often to go round and see Caryll in the small, dark flat into which she moved from Iris's: it opened onto a well, and had a flat roof under it, from which one night a burglar climbed into her room: she woke up, terrified, to see him standing over her, but a moment later the valiant Jones, on whom he had trodden, sprang at him, clawing and snarling, and frightened him away."

The windows at the Censorship had been broken and boarded up, and presently Caryll's section was moved to the basement. The flat too was pitch dark.

Spring and summer made life a little easier: she could escape to Milborne Grove and write in the shed at the end of the garden. But there was never time enough. She grudged most those visitors who came only to pass the time, "in fact to waste and get rid of the most precious thing, of which one can't ever get enough to *use,* and there is only destruction in this frittering away of time."

To use time to the last drop in the service of those who needed it was not to waste it; and perhaps as a result of her book, a new field of work now opened before Caryll, when Dr. Strauss began early in 1942 to ask her to take on some of his boy patients.

Dr. Eric Strauss, a distinguished psychologist and neurologist, was President of the Psychiatry Section of the Royal Society of Medicine in 1953-4 and of the British Psychological Society in 1956-7. Almost up to his death in 1961 he was physician for psychological medicine at St. Bartholomew's and at the North Middlesex Hospital. He had studied both at Oxford and in Germany and always kept in vital contact with the many men, women, and above all children who were his patients.

The width and variety of Dr. Strauss' knowledge is indicated by the titles of his very successful books: *Psychiatry in the Modern World, Reason and Unreason in Psychological Medicine, Sexual Disorders in the Male* (with Kenneth Walker), *Recent Advances in Neurology* (with Sir Russell Brian). These last two books ran through many editions. It was certainly no small compliment to Caryll and no small proof of his own readiness to leave the beaten track when he felt that it was for the benefit of his patients that he should take a laywoman into collaboration for their healing. His child patients especially needed, he felt, something that Caryll had a genius in giving—not only love but the full realization that love had gone out to them and was surrounding them.

"Dr. Strauss is a genius," Caryll writes to Henry Tayler, "and sees how art and music can be and *must* be used as the expressions of love. . . . I wish you could find an interest in this child and help him musically. I realize all too well what a huge effort it is to add *anything* to lives as busy as ours must be now, but I do feel it would be a marvellous thing for you and your music as well as for the boy, if you could help, and the strength it would give to your soul would compensate you a thousand times for the effort it would cost."

On Good Friday she writes again:

I now have two patients of Dr. Strauss's coming to me, and great freedom allowed in the treatment of them. We've just got to work music into it. I know it is essential, and they will never be made complete human beings without it. You will be able to do great work through it. Don't imagine you haven't got the initiative, you convince yourself you can't "give"—but that's just nonsense, think of all you have given and do give to me! Nothing is so frightening or so baffling as a twisted human mind, but if you realize that Christ will work through you, the fear dissolves and you can help. The thing is to *ask* Christ to act through you and ask Him often and think often of how unsparingly Christ gave Himself to people in need: you won't want to limit the amount you will let Him use *you*, after a few such meditations.

Dr. Strauss was delighted with Caryll's work. She writes to Henry:

I am able to put into practice all my theories about psychology, and I have great hope that from our poor little shed and this one strange lovely boy, our wisdom school may really begin. Pedro has a mind like a beautiful valley almost hidden by a dark and shadowy twilight. In that twilight one hears the sound of tears and yet finds rare and isolated flowers growing, and these flowers have a positively sparkling brilliance.

Dr. Strauss quickly sent her the second boy, and Caryll became more and more absorbed in this new task:

I don't exaggerate, with these children I suffer myself, you can't help them if you don't. To give all my spare time to them seems silly, but you have to (I mean I have to)—and you have to share their sense of defeat, shame and so on, go with them step by step through the dark valleys and bring them out again to the light.

Henry agreed to the music lessons and even cancelled a week-end engagement so that his first pupil should not miss his first lesson. Caryll writes in overpowering gratitude for this sacrifice: but it is characteristic of her to treat it as an even greater thing than it was, and also to consider her friend as an equal partner in her new and arduous work:

. . . I feel that they are *our* children, and that makes it a thousand times more vital to help them to find their integrity and stand on their own feet and leave us—if I had children of the flesh I would want them to do that, and that's what I want these to do too. What then will remain to us as our children? Well, just what is twisted and awry in the soul of childhood today, *that* coming to us in one boy or girl after another, to go away whole, so that we can make our own the labour of helping that mind to a rebirth, and afterwards, as Christ said, "Rejoice that a man is born into the world."

The subject of these children haunts her. The demands of adults she responded to always with generosity but sometimes with dismay. Into "the mysterious dark places of these poor children's minds" she had the tenderest desire to penetrate. "They are most exacting," she writes, "and demand *everything* one has, but guilelessly." And again, "I think we can never understand little children. We can only serve them on our knees."

The chance for relaxation with her intimates was all too rare. She would say to Rosamond: "Come round for a *sub rosa*"—"the name," Rosamond says, "that she gave to our uninhibited conversations."

Once or twice [Rosamond writes] there was a poetry reading by Father Bliss: and once, at Christmas time, I was invited to a play planned in my honour by Caryll, Iris and Henry. It was to be an exact reconstruction of a play acted at Caryll's convent school, a play in which a pious young Catholic girl goes to a

ball and dances with "a Protestant gentleman" (acted by one of
the girls wearing trousers, with her dress over them), for which
injudicious act she comes to ruin and is cast out by her father.
Caryll was to play the Protestant gentleman: but alas, I had
bronchitis on the night, and the play was put off and never
staged at all.

Caryll took me to another play—a Passion Play, put on at
Westminster Cathedral Hall. I was impressed by it: she wasn't:
and when I protested, "Well, it's very dignified," she replied,
very truly, "But the Passion wasn't dignified—shockingly undig-
nified." And afterwards she said to me, "I'm afraid it didn't move
me at all. The only thing that ever moves me at the theatre or
cinema is the death of an old dog."

In *This War is the Passion* Caryll talks of how hard it is
to meditate on Our Lord's sufferings, especially when suffering oneself. "The mind becomes bleak." The war was, she
realized, Christ suffering still in His Mystical Body of which
we are all members. This suffering must not be wasted. Our
Lord must become to us not a picture out of a book, not an
unreality, but the most profound reality of our lives. And
after this terrible hour in which *we* live His Passion shall
we be ready for His Resurrection in ourselves and in the
world? What is happening *now* to our minds, what will
happen when the stress and strain let up? War may awaken
noble reactions, but it is essentially brutalizing. And the
regimenting it has involved may keep us adolescents all our
lives, able only to move with the crowd, unless *now* we
begin to prepare for our own personal apostolate.

After the war what will have happened to the mind under the
tin hat? . . . Now is the time to prepare defences for the mind.
. . . *The first is prayer.* . . . Prayer alone can teach us to concentrate again . . . make our minds ready for other essential
things . . . for the contemplation (not merely observation) of
beauty.

Say the word God and let it pervade you. . . . His hands are around you, they shelter your life as a flame is sheltered in the storm.

There are people who have no need in prayer to use words at all:

The muted music of the human, suffering Christ touches a responsive chord in their own being. . . . They have no words even for Christ. Perhaps they do not understand the music themselves. It would not sound in their voice as it sounds in their souls.

Our Lord came and found His apostles asleep—well, once or twice He has found me asleep on night duty, but here is a literal chance of just praying by staying awake to atone for sin.

In wartime we sometimes cannot go to daily Mass. But

there is never a moment when the Host is not being offered up for us: we can without a missal join in any Mass going on, and be really present to Christ on some secret altar.

The prayer of the Church is the single voice of the one Christ in us all, therefore our own voice. [Men must become] aware of His life in them. Then each breath is a prayer, each beat of the heart, and the rhythm of the creature flows naturally into that of the Creator—but I am describing heaven.

Next to prayer she sees as the chief Defence of the Mind a right attitude towards suffering. This war is indeed the Passion, and "There is no way of learning the Passion of Christ except through the adventure of our own heart."

The challenge of suffering has sometimes been faced by the agnostic, while "we shut our eyes to such things as poverty, pain or death and fled from the agonies of the spirit."

But while we should beat our breasts, it should be with

full awareness that ours is the harder task. If the agnostic does his best to make men happy and fails,

his attempt has at all events set him free; where he cannot heal he can pass by, where he cannot end poverty he can forsake it. His duty is to alleviate sorrow not to share it.

But just where the non-Christian's responsibility ends, that of the Christian begins. He, like the other, has the duty of sharing in the world's effort to break down human misery, but where he fails to heal he must share it, he can never with a clean heart pass it by.

[Christ's followers] must set their pace to the footsteps of a crippled world and step by step enter into the more delicate sufferings of mind and spirit. . . . For every thousand women who can now dress a wound on the flesh, there is only one—if as many—who can begin the healing of a wound in the mind. It requires much more education to attend to a broken heart than it does to attend to a broken leg. . . . We will find out over and over again that, if only this person can be brought to reveal his unhappiness, his nastiness will heal up.

To the Christian, suffering is not a problem to be explored by the human mind, but a mystery to be experienced by the human heart.

We have to stretch Christ in us, then, to fit the size of this war, the cross overshadowing the whole world . . . the arms of Christ stretched on the cross are the widest reach there is, the only one that encircles the whole world.

To Archie Campbell Murdoch, who had experienced on his way to the Church the trouble of mind that makes scandals past and present a real stumbling block, she wrote a comment on her theme:

The way I look upon the abuses and so on which inevitably crop up in the visible Church is that they are necessary, because they are the Passion. You see the Church *is Christ,* and therefore Christ's Passion *must* go on in the Church. Tragic, even frightening though it is, we know Christ better with the kiss of Judas on His face.

But, how to stand what could be the bleak misery of that, and to know the glory in it as well as the tragedy? There is a problem, and if you don't solve it, it breaks you.

The ecumenical longings so widely felt today had begun to stir in many during the anguish of the war years. The enormous menace of godless totalitarianism was drawing together in Europe Christians even of races opposed in the fighting, and of all denominations. When the Sword of the Spirit was started in England it was intended by Cardinal Hinsley as a movement in which all Christians could co-operate—and the response he received was enthusiastic.

It was in this atmosphere—largely lost, alas, in the post-war years—that Caryll as author of *This War is the Passion* was invited in 1944 by the Anglican Bishop of Southampton to speak at Oxford. It was, I think, the only time she left London during the war. She prepared, as she told her audience, with much prayer and with a profound sense that *she* could have little to say of *real* value. The talk took place after dinner, and Iris, who had come to Oxford with her, paced the streets in nervous apprehension while it was going on. They were all, Caryll said afterwards, charming and courteous and put her at once at her ease. Among her books is one inscribed "Miss Caryll Houselander, gratefully from the Winchester Diocesan Clergy School, Wadham College Oxford. July 1944."

Her immensely full notes—more by far, I should think, than she could have used in one lecture—show her deeply concerned with what her own experience had taught of the generation growing up to face the post-war period: a generation undisciplined, uneasy, loathing exhortation and feeling they had had more than their share of hardship and restraint. To this generation these clergy were pastors, and

Caryll could only give them her own recipe for dealing, not with the young alone, but with all humanity—to bring Christ to them by discovering Christ in them.

On this visit she made friends, too, with the Prioress of the Carmelite Convent: the prayer of her contemplative friends meant an immense amount to Caryll, and she had a long and intimate correspondence with this nun—broken tragically, and to Caryll quite inexplicably, by the publication a few years later of *Guilt*.

But this book belongs to a later chapter.

12

After the War

"I OFTEN THINK," Caryll wrote to Archie Campbell Murdoch when he came into the Church, "of Our Lord saying to St. Peter, 'Satan has desired to have you that he might sift you like wheat, but I have prayed for you that your faith shall not fail.' Every Mass is Christ praying for us that our faith shall not fail. I think the time may come after the war when we shall realize more than ever how much we need that prayer of Christ."

And in another letter: "Don't you think that Catholics ought to make public (and of course secret) reparation for the atom bomb massacre? I do. Shall we arrange a sort of barefooted Tyburn walk? I am in dead earnest about it."

This was not the prevailing atmosphere, and Caryll came more and more to realize that her appeal in *This War is the Passion* for building the defences of the mind could only succeed if opportunities increased for developing and exercising it in religion, philosophy, and those intensely valuable approaches to religion, art and music. She had wanted my husband's co-operation but wailed to Henry Tayler about how "utterly impossible" it was to fix a date with him, "as he could never tell me *when* he was coming, but, like the Bridegroom of the Gospel, always came 'at the hour you know not.' I had lots of interesting talk with him which concerned you very much."

Caryll's letters to both these friends of hers are full of post-war plans. The correspondence with Archie is even more interesting and, because he was seldom in London, more voluminous than that with Henry. She had a scheme for a bookshop which should also be a great deal more. There would be lunch-hour gramophone recitals of good music; a very small entrance fee for this would pay the rent of the shop—if enough people came. There would be poetry readings. Above all, books were to be reviewed and discussed. Realizing as the idea developed that none of them had the training needed, she suggested adding to their poetry readings a specialization by each one in a different field of literature, or at least the study of different books. Let them begin by reviews and discussions among themselves until they were ready to do this in public.

In her vivid imagination the scheme became ever vaster, more varied and more absorbing.

"Of course as we shall all be working *for* the shop on our off days, toy-making, music research, reading, carving, book-writing, etc., we shall be *actually* working for it *all* the time anyway, only we need not all be *there* all the time."

The approach of peace felt like an hour for new beginnings. Work at the Censorship would soon be over, and we all know how the end of a job in sight brings a vision of glorious empty days: a thousand schemes spring up in the imagination which a long life could hardly implement. Experience rapidly cuts them down to size, but when growing they also glow in all the colours of the rainbow.

Caryll, as Iris notes, was in no state to undertake anything fresh. Even when the Censorship did come to an end she had more than enough to do and was suffering badly from overwork and lack of sleep. Indeed Iris was sometimes near despair trying to hold Caryll back and save herself from being swept into her friend's most extravagant schemes.

The bookshop was only one of the many projects that sprang up during the post-war years in Caryll's vivid imagination. She could not think of a human need without longing to meet it, and it took her a long time to realize that there were limits, growing always narrower, to her own strength and that she could not hope to rouse her friends, even had they the abilities with which she credited them, to the degree of self-devotion her ideas demanded. At one moment it was to be a Home for murderesses, their "life" sentence finished. Caryll hoped by crafts and social therapy to help them to reintegrate into human society. At another time it was a plan for a Children's Home, with Rosamond in charge, Charles Scott-Paton assisting and Iris doing the cooking and housekeeping. Iris was persuaded to go with her to inspect a large and beautiful house reputedly haunted, which Caryll thought would be suitable. "Whether," Rosamond comments, "any of *us* was suitable was another matter."

Prudence might have suggested to Caryll that she was at least thinking beyond her strength. But she was already acting beyond it anyhow, and she once said, "Holy people insist that Prudence is the 'queen of the virtues.' I doubt it, subject of course to correction, but if Prudence does hold that position, then I would prefer to discover a charwoman among the virtues and consort with her." Despite Censorship, fire-watching and neurotic children she finished two more books and began a third before the war ended. While planning the bookshop, she added that her own chief work *must* be to write: "I shall want to put in some money . . . and I want to help on the Apostolic side, but that is *all*. I want to earn my own living as a writer and not have my energies eaten up by business."

To Christine Spender Caryll spoke violently of the *necessity* that was upon her to write. If she did not write she was ill; it was a form of "constipation." And in a letter she says: "The suggestion that I would be happier if I dropped my work for a bit is like telling me I would be healthier if

I stopped breathing for a time! . . . My writing is both my life and my living, you know, quite literally and in that order."

Caryll was one of the rare writers who could, in fact, make a good living with her pen, but the order in which she put her life and her living was exact. Also to Christine, urging her too to go on writing, she says, "I read, and I fully believe this, that creative artists of any kind can only renew their energy by using it in creative work, their art; that if they do not, it does not simply go into whatever they use (or do) instead of their proper work but flickers out altogether; consequently, after some months' frustration of their art, they cease to have any energy. This is certainly what happened to me."

After a meeting with Christine she wrote again: "You say I look better; as a matter of fact one single day of solid writing, without fear of interruption, makes me feel as fit as a flea, and once I can ease my guilt about not seeing people and just write, I feel well, and as far as a person can and yet be human, happy. But the very moment I overstep the mark, open the door to the merciless inrush of people, try to answer their demands and so on, I really do very nearly collapse—in fact I did so twice."

She had discovered the answer earlier, but though she could tell it to Christine she could not enforce it on others or on herself.

"I am certain that for me the real *Communion* with people is in writing, and this does not only apply to strangers but to my intimate friends; I have realized that when they keep me from writing they are actually destroying all hope of Communion between us."

Her second book, *The Reed of God*, seemed to prove her point by the immense correspondence it drew forth. Monsignor Ronald Knox wrote what he said was the only fan letter he had ever written, "Only it is not really a 'fan.' " Caryll wrote to Archie, "It's an incredibly humble and moving little note which must have been inspired by perfectly *enormous* kindness and graciousness and makes me feel less than a farthing."

But it heartened her greatly. Caryll was unsure enough of herself, certain though she was of her vocation, to welcome words of praise and be deeply grateful for them. By great ill-luck the huge mass of her fan letters was destroyed, but this was the most widely read of her books—and is still so today, especially by converts who so often begin by finding devotion to Our Lady a difficulty. The Catholic child, as soon as he can walk, "walks to Our Lady's altar. Every trifling thing is told to her and every great sorrow; she is sharer of all earth's joys and griefs.

"She is not wearied with our littleness, her smile comes down to us like a benediction through the sea of flickering candles, and she blesses our wild flowers withering at her feet."

Even the devotion of the Catholic child may be distorted by the foolish admonitions of the pious. Caryll had been told, by someone she deeply respected, never to do anything that Our Lady would not do, or "the angels would blush." As she could not imagine Our Lady doing any of the things in which she delighted—such as blacking her face, sucking two bull's-eyes at once or turning somersaults—she faced "a blank future shackled with respectability."

She not only could not imagine Our Lady doing the things she loved to do—she could not imagine Our Lady doing anything that she could try to do. The answers she found to this problem became the theme of her book. We could not without presumption imagine ourselves called to imitate the preaching of St. Paul, the writings of St. Thomas, the Foundations of St. Teresa of Avila. But we are called to the imitation of Mary, because we are all called to her vocation—to become Christ-bearers.

Advent and the loss of Jesus in Jerusalem are Caryll's two principal "contemplations." In each of them she develops the doctrine which dominated all her thinking, that of the Mystical Body. It is as members of Christ's Body that we are identified with Him and become other Christs. In Advent we must give ourselves as the earth to the seed that Christ may grow in us. "We must begin by making acts of faith in the presence of Christ in our own souls." But we must always be seeking Him too in the souls of others with faith that He is there.

What of those who have driven Him away by sin? "We should never come to a sinner without the reverence we would take to the Holy Sepulchre."

The sinner has chosen to drive away the divine presence, but many, striving to love and serve, experience at times a keen sense of having lost it. It was not Mary, Caryll reminds us, who lost Our Lord, but Our Lord who went away—and now with us too He has withdrawn the sense of His presence that He may be about His Father's business—perhaps because we have sinned but perhaps only because he wishes us to seek Him, like the lame boy when the other children danced after the Pied Piper—he "still heard the music in his heart and still followed."

We too may be lame, may be slow, but "the path is picked out by the impress of the Child's feet in the dust, and our seeking is, in itself, finding, a continual endorsement of the promise—Seek and ye shall find."

A variety of reactions also proved that speech through writing was a communion only with those with whom she could communicate. To a priest who had loved the book and asked for an article on Our Lady's Motherhood for his magazine, Caryll wrote begging him if there was any heresy in what she had written to "root it out. Truth is always more beautiful, and finally more fruitful, than the mistakes one sometimes makes in pursuit of it, and of course I am no theologian."

She went on, "I have learnt one thing from *The Reed of*

God—namely, that any word spoken about Our Lady has an amazing effect; it either pleases out of all proportion or arouses furious resentment. I know several people who really hate my book, one of them someone who is devoted to me!

"I suppose it is because of the extraordinary power of Our Lady herself: hidden behind our faulty words is this amazing challenge of absolute integrity! It makes me very careful what I say about her."

It was not really what she said about Our Lady that upset a good many people so much as what she was saying about us all, her unremitting attack on unreality in life and in religion —the unreality that worships Christ in church but refuses to see Him in mankind, the unreality that takes refuge in organizations and committees, thinks of humanity instead of men, and fondly dreams that sociology and reformed economic conditions can take the place of religion.

As an unreal worshipper she confesses:

I brought my flower and flame to the crucifix on the wall;
But for the Word incarnate not one white star of them all,
To Christ the living and dying, crucified in mankind,
Blunt nail in the quick flesh, sharp thorn in the sensitive mind.

My candles have burnt out at the carved, archaic feet,
While I passed the poor man by with broken boots in the street.
I have said to the worn face of the polished dark-worn wood,
"Lord, Lord!" I was mute to Love's substance in flesh and blood.

But for those "unconsciously ashamed of religion," who claim service for their device, she says, "The saints are a rebuke and challenge hardly to be suffered, for their way is always the impractical way of the Sermon on the Mount: poverty, humility, the folly of the Cross. And yet, when the years move on and we look back, we find that it is not the social reformer or the economist or even the church leader who has done tremendous things for the human race, but the silly saints in their rags and tatters, with their empty pockets and their impossible dreams."

This book was quickly followed by *The Flowering Tree* —a collection of Caryll's rhythms including "Philip Speaks." It was sad that Dr. Mackail was no longer there to circulate the book as he had the poem—which he had had printed privately as a booklet and broadcast among his friends. Lawrence Binyon replied hoping for further poems from Caryll: "I think 'Philip Speaks' is a beautiful poem," he wrote. "So many poems of the modern school seem to show a determination to avoid old forms without the capacity to create a new form; but here I feel that something has been found." Dorothy Sayers too thought it beautiful and said, "I shall treasure it all my life." John Masefield read it through "with very much surprise and pleasure," and only waited to express his gratitude until he had "read it twice with some interval between the readings." Canon Raven, then Master of Christ's College, Cambridge, recovering from a heart attack, the culmination of four years of "emptying out," wrote that this "discovery of Christ" had lifted from him "a load of 'dry dust'—depression, futility and (I'm afraid) self-pity."

These and many more tributes had been sent on to Caryll by Dr. Mackail—but no number of tributes will induce the public to buy poetry as they buy prose. *The Flowering Tree,* although it was acclaimed by a few as the best thing Caryll had yet done, only sold about half as well as the other two books.

"It is the thing that means *most of all* to me," she wrote to a friend. "It is always a *very* great joy when it does find an echo in another mind—and that happens very rarely."

Caryll too felt that she had "found" something through her rhythms. Not a new way of writing poetry but a discovery about the universe which made the use of rhythmic speech a path to peace and a means of contemplation. She had long used rhythm thus herself and had urged its use on others. The making of the book was a matter of choosing and sometimes improving the best out of a large number of rhythms written over the last ten years. Caryll altered her rhythms more than she did her prose, on which she made hardly any corrections.

We were corresponding regularly at this time, and she sent me a long letter about her chief idea "that we are really part, as it were, of a vast Rhythm and that when we become more recollected we become more and more conscious of it." Also, if we thus cultivate recollection, "those thoughts expressed within us rhythmically are heard by our minds in everything around us, even in the traffic in the street."

On the many people who asked her advice, she always urged the peace of rhythmic prayer—"some measure that would keep the harmony and balance of music around one's thoughts and emotions, in order that one should not be shattered or disturbed by things around one." The interruptions of her own life were incessant, but she discovered as she went on that they could be "caught up and woven into the Rhythm.

But apart from being *heard* in the mind, I think a Rhythm, and perhaps more especially a prayer one, has to be one which can be *seen*. Things which look very affected, like putting one word in a line now and then, are done on purpose. . . . It is really on the same lines as writing music with different note values, chords and such, and with counterpoint. I am not at all musical, though I am exceedingly fond of *certain* musicians, but I can take the keenest pleasure in *looking* at musical scores. That is all a bit beside the point, but I have long wanted to point out to you that Rhythm is not in my mind simply a freer way of writing verse, but it is a part of a plan for contemplation to be spread in the world.

I wish I could find the letter Caryll wrote me after D Day. Perhaps it perished in the fire in our New York office which followed the blitzing of the London one. We have moved house three times since, so the search is complicated and thus far fruitless. The impression was of a very different atmosphere from that of the yelling mobs on Armistice Day 1918—but they perhaps were performing in Piccadilly. Caryll painted a vivid picture of family groups sitting on the grass in the parks who talked to her of their thankfulness that slaughter and torture, broken nights and broken glass, were over, and life could be lived normally again. Tranquillity was the key-note of the letter. But Caryll's own hopes rested on God alone, and her optimism was tempered by fear that the need for God might be forgotten amid the relief.

She wrote in an unpublished rhythm dated August 10th, 1945:

> We offer to you,
> Swordless Lord,
> those who have perished
> by the sword.
>
> We offer our harvest festival,
> the barren earth,
> the yield of blood,
> sown in the potter's field.
>
> At least, not a lie
> in your presence, Lord.
> We offer ourselves
> and the waste of our conquering,
> we who have lived
> and died
> by the sword.

It was not her writing alone that put an end to Caryll's dream of the bookshop: she had even thought of her books as an element in its success, and she would have poured her royalties into that as she did into everything she cared about. But of her two chief allies, Henry had a double mind on the whole subject, and Archie just after the war wrote to her of an idea gradually shaping in his mind of opening a school for backward boys.

Caryll responded enthusiastically: "I think it is a really superb idea and that it is intended by God for you . . . everything has led up to it as if all your actions, buying the house and so on were (as I feel sure they are) part of a pre-ordained plan." She goes on to attack vigorously the idea that "only unpaid work is real charity (love). This is a snobbish idea which grew fat under the Victorian worldliness and is not the Catholic idea." Everyone ought to work, and "their whole-time job should be their holiest and most charitable self-giving. If they are not able to find a work that fulfils that ideal, they are crippled all their life long."

As she would have been crippled without her writing. But Caryll's friends noted with interest the contrast between her strong feelings on this point ("The idea of working for nothing *always* ends up either in incompetence and failure or in at least slight patronage") and her own continual pouring out of her own work as a gift. Her main point is incontrovertible: "To say that charity is *only* what is not paid for and not a means of living is the same as saying that the only people who can fill their lives with charity are the rich, the few exceptions to be pitied who need not earn their living, that . . . the huge majority who do have to work can only really glorify God in their spare time, when in all likelihood they are tired out and have only a fifth best to offer."

As to the bookshop, "It was a great dream and one side of it will, I am sure, come about one day," but it is clearly not for now and he will be wise to "go all out on the little backward boys."

The Flowering Tree was published the year the war ended, and it looked for the moment as though life would become a little easier for Caryll. The kitchmorgue had been truly debilitating but, by what appeared almost a miracle, a tenant on the top floor suggested an exchange, because her mother hated lifts!

"Various memories of Caryll," says Rosamond, "in her high flat at Nell Gwynn House came back to me—the flat itself, with its wonderful dark sparkling view over London at night, and Caryll opening the door to me in her autumn-leaf-patterned overall with its broad leather belt. She loved the thronging, hive-like life of the flats. One of her projects was to run a kind of good-neighbour service—free, needless to say—for the flat-dwellers: she and Iris were to put up a notice in the hall offering to cook, shop or otherwise help those temporarily bedridden or in some way incapacitated."

It is always interesting to meet for the first time someone known intimately by correspondence. My husband had prepared me for Caryll's appearance—as it had seemed to me in an exaggerated fashion. Yet as I stood waiting outside the door of her flat and she came up behind me laden with parcels I was conscious of a genuine shock. The dead-white face, the thick glasses, the fringe of red hair, a touch somehow of the grotesque—it was so surprising as to take one's breath away. But we had hardly exchanged a word when we felt (both of us, I could swear) the perfect ease of long intimacy, and began a conversation to be picked up at any moment thereafter. It was not until much later that I found she had used the word grotesque about herself.

It was an exquisite little flat, shiningly clean, always flower-decked, books everywhere, a Russian ikon with a lamp in front of it, a put-u-up covered by Caryll herself in an attractive off-white material, a comfortable chair for the visitor and some sort of stool or low seat for Caryll herself. In such matters she probably did still seek discomfort; she certainly never sought comfort. She adored entertaining her friends, but she was not wholly skilled at it. Molly Paley has told me how, coming up for a day with Caryll, she would arrive about half-past twelve. "Caryll would put a pot on the stove; about one-thirty she would put on another, but we were lucky if we had lunch by two-thirty." Charles Scott-Paton had a strong impression that Caryll had often tended an oil stove just before preparing lunch—he would entreat her to let him come just for a talk—perhaps a drink—and not make these preparations for a meal which, I gather, he hardly even pretended to enjoy! Other friends have happier memories of immense and enjoyable meals, but always eaten by themselves, urged on by Caryll while she nibbled a bit of toast or played with the food on her plate.

My own memory is of teas with sandwiches we neither of us ate, followed by sherry that we both of us drank. Caryll was all in favour of drink; Charles avers that during the war she and Iris would make fearful concoctions out of a modicum of gin and some terrible cheap wine which was all they could get. And in normal times, "If she only had 35/- in the house she would spend it on a bottle of gin for her visitor."

In a letter to one friend she speaks of entertaining a whole group of convert Jews at tea. The first arrived at two and the last did not leave till eight-fifteen. Strongly drawn toward the Jewish people, Caryll once told a friend, "I'm trying to work the Jews into the Mystical Body." She found the long afternoon fascinating.

Startling in contrast was her attitude to what is technically known as a party. "The thought of one in the afternoon or evening," Rosamond remembers, "would almost benumb her throughout the day." Caryll told Christine Spender that this dated from childhood—that she remembered throwing herself into a cold bath in the hope of getting pneumonia and escaping a party—also how, when staying with "hearty" people who forced her to go riding with them, she could not sleep and became really ill. I only remember her at one party, and I could hardly believe it was Caryll: stiff, unsmiling, almost unable to speak, looking as though she wished the earth would open and swallow her. I did not, as did Iris and Rosamond, have the experience of seeing the swing from a silent to a garrulous Caryll, who went to confession the day after a party and spent the afternoon writing letters trying to unsay the uncharitable remarks she had made.

To Archie, who had feared she condemned parties as "mundane and unfruitful," she wrote greatly distressed that she should have appeared to despise the "lovely glowing kindness and skill in hospitality" of his wife and himself which "could never be other than beautiful and fruitful. If I give the impression of despising such things, I am very guilty—and it comes from a mistake. (A) I avoid parties because I am so conscious of being grotesque, ill-dressed, awkward and talking too much, that it is a torture to me to go anywhere, and this is always followed by several days of remorse. Another word for my reaction is vanity, and I've been unable to overcome this, although I've tried since I was four!—and tried at the cost of more than one nervous collapse."

(B) was the need for concentrating on her writing, the choice between "flogging one's mind and will to go on and write, and to say NO to nearly all else—or of letting the writing go." But to Christine Spender, enthusiastically praising *The Little Locksmith,* she speaks of the perfect expression in this book of her own feelings: "I must feel that I look as deformed as she really did, for though reading her makes me ashamed of it, I am *as* self-conscious about my looks—not looks only, but presence—perhaps even more so. She did realize that her true self was in her soul and how radiant and wonderful *that* was, but I feel that my soul is even worse than my body and every personal revelation an added indecency! But there is comfort and hope and strength in every line of that book."

To Archie also, who had voiced the meed of praise that all

her friends so strongly felt they owed her, she wrote: "Don't think any good of me, because I am quite truly dirt and prefer to forget my dirthood as often as I can; if I have to be reminded of it even by kind words which must be contradicted, I have to make myself wretched—'vanity of vanities, saith the preacher, all is vanity.'"

Caryll rejoiced in her new flat, but one drawback had not occurred to her. With her success as a writer the unending siege of callers became even more serious—and now there was no escaping through the window as there had been on the ground floor. Part of the difficulty in resisting this siege came from her own over-sensitive conscience. Despite a realization that "communication" was best achieved through her books, despite the fact that she was obliged to write for a living, she found it terribly hard to snub any who felt they needed her. "The people who most blame others," she wryly observed of the besiegers, "are often the worst offenders."

Iris remembers standing in the bathroom with Caryll, both holding their breath and listening to the unending knocking. And if the knocking stopped it might be merely that the caller had decided to wait a while in silence. People who hardly knew Caryll would knock and knock, go away and return, or simply stay in the passage. She told Henry Tayler, "Somebody was bloody well camping outside my door." Iris finally installed a peephole so that Caryll could see who the visitor was.

Any real need called forth from her the utmost energy of sympathy, and her closest friends had often to bewail her inability to find the time for them, so busy was she with the people with genuine spiritual needs who came to her unsent or were sent to her by doctors. These, too, the timewasters were robbing—but it was not always easy to discriminate.

On Good Friday 1947 Caryll wrote to a friend, "After

Easter I shall have to go to hospital to be operated on for hernia, the result of perpetual gastric chills in the cold [weather] and a life-long faulty sort of middle. This is not at all dangerous but very humiliating to my exceptionally vain nature, but as it means lying in bed for two or three or four weeks I will have a lot of time to write to you, and will."

It is startling in the extreme to find her not long after this operation planning with Archie Campbell Murdoch to teach art to his pupils. He had in the end not opened a new school but taken over an existing one at Frensham. This would mean a weekly expedition, leaving London early in the morning, teaching all day and getting back to London late in the evening. She did this from the autumn of 1947 till March 1949. A series of letters shows, even more than with the bookshop, the intense imaginative powers which she poured out on anything she undertook, the vastness of her dreams but also the practicality of her detailed applications. We are reminded of the fact that in England the end of the war meant by no means the end of shortages. Everything, including art materials, was in short supply. Everything was expensive and the school was poor. Caryll budgeted accordingly, but she let her hopes loose upon the future. A school of fifty backward boys was the human material in which she believed enough to aim at immense results. In a letter to Archie dated September 14th, 1947, she is back in her own youth thinking of the happy days at her Art School. The boys should, she suggests, form a club. She and her friends had once called themselves The Cheerful Idiots—the boys' club could be "The Frensham Savages or some such name." The members will do practical jobs for, e.g., school plays, "designing dresses and scenery, making masks, wigs, devils' tails, haloes, etc." They will also start a toy industry.

A Polish soldier, in whom I was interested at this time, had some skill as a binder. Caryll thought this would be a splendid additional craft, and I promised, if the school employed him, to provide the needful equipment and to send my own books for rebinding and persuade my friends to do so too. I was highly amused to discover from the Campbell Murdoch correspondence that my modest offer grew in Caryll's imagination to my taking over all the school's financial problems. Archie need have no further worry since I, though "utterly tactless to put it mildly," was "a darling, full of energy, drive and goodwill"!! It is another example of Caryll's conviction that if one sympathized with any good work, one was also prepared to spend upon it the same limitless energy as herself.

Dr. Strauss remembered Frensham well as "the only school that had a circus." This had been started by Archie's predecessor and was remarkably successful. It proved that originality of approach could create something of real value for these boys and helped to swell Caryll's hopes. Both she and Iris went to see the circus and were much impressed by it. Caryll declared that the circus pony was allowed in the class room during lessons: clearly an unusual school.

Boys can, Caryll says, be taught to draw "by playing at cave-men, with such materials as cave men might have, i.e. white chalk, red chalk and charcoal" and draw messages "on the wall of the cave" (represented by brown paper). They will learn that "art is, first of all, *saying something*. The next term they can make a Christmas crib."

In the Lent term they can study the Last Supper, reading it aloud with each taking a part, then write down "all that was used—cup, bread, lamb, etc." Look next at diagrams of everything used at Mass, see its relation to the Last Supper and Passion—and the most talented among them can learn to make a portable altar, painting a crucifix, carving simple wooden candlesticks. During this term let the lesson occasionally stop early, some really good records of Mass music be played and the boys be taught "the way in which a number of arts are brought together for worship (also for ballet, theatre, etc.)." The whole school could be taught something of the theory of art, all could learn applied art in some form, "crafts, toy-making, lino-cuts, things for a school play, etc.," and by forming a sketching club the few real artists could be discovered who must receive special encouragement.

And then, giving her imagination free rein, she begins to foresee how great a work this school might initiate:

I have been thinking how wonderful it would be if you could keep up the acting tradition by forming a school company of mystery players on medieval lines, who, apart from a Christmas and Lent play, would get a repertoire of stark simple little mystery plays and go round in the summer term to act them in the open air, in villages where there is no Mass. If funds allowed they might hire (even borrow) a local wagon for stage, have a few very light and simple properties they could carry, and give the show to the village folk. I am sure the time has come when the evangelizing of the *countryside* will be the great apostolate. Glance at history—the rise of industrialism draining the country, all the stress on the town, neglect of agriculture, neglect of villages generally; but now the need for food has turned the light full on the country and recruits for the land are multiplying. Is it not the right moment to bring the Mass back to all the little villages? I think your mystery players would be a very real apostolate. . . . .

(Later Caryll felt that this would be yet another suitable form of apostolate for a group, led by Charles Scott-Paton, to include herself and many of their friends!)

The boys were divided into four groups according to age and ability. Caryll gave a lesson to each group on her weekly day. "I'm down at the boys' school at Frensham," she wrote to a friend that autumn, "teaching all Tuesday from dark to dark." She decided to begin with toy-making—the first toys to be made for a circus which could of course be created from the life. "If we start at once on the circus, we shall have something to show sooner, and it will be much easier for them to learn the other aspects of art if they have some concrete thing they can actually see, that they have done first."

They should all have practice between lessons, and she won the co-operation of the school carpenter. Half of each class on her own days should be working in his work room, half in the class room, "and I can go between them."

The club was changed into a "guild" as in mediaeval days, "with a period of probation. Entry into it to be determined by quality of work (including care of tools) and co-operative spirit, the original members to vote on the probationers." Caryll promises prizes for the best original sketch and for the "best toy-makers from every point of view."

The circus is to be followed by the Christmas crib. The figures would doubtless be drawn, painted and cut out as she herself had cut them out for Grossé's year after year.

Caryll had written to Archie, when he first planned the school, of these "Christ-children" he would be helping in the realization of their Christhood. They were not neurotics like the boys sent her by Dr. Strauss, but most of them were in some way ill-adjusted, many as a result of extraordinary war experiences. One boy had been driver of a tank, another after the murder of his parents had lived alone in the Malayan jungle. I was seeing a good deal of Caryll at this time, and we discussed her theory that the shape of modern life also and the demands of their parents had often turned normal boys into misfits. Some were potentially brilliant but hopeless examination subjects. Others backward at books had great aptitude for crafts or even for painting and music, but had little chance of earning a living at either. Others again had been held back by fearful or over-possessive mothers from any experience of life.

Which was worse psychologically, "smother" love or the lack of love's expression? With all her belief in total abnegation and her dislike for compromise, Caryll could not bear one form that this attitude has sometimes taken. She had no use for a saint who, with whatever suffering to herself, whatever love was in her heart, could step over her son to enter a cloister or become a nun when she still had young children dependent on her love. What effect, she once asked, in view of modern psychological knowledge, might Abraham's preparations to sacrifice him have had on Isaac in afterlife?

Caryll planned to see in the holidays those boys whose homes were near her flat. "They were so eager to come," she writes, asking for addresses she had mislaid, "for an afternoon's carving and TEA." There is an interesting correspondence with the mother of one boy who was learning wood-carving.

"I really am interested in Tony," she wrote. "He is a fine, beautifully unspoilt boy, and a great joy to teach. I think he will prove a fine craftsman." She is hoping to get tools for him so that he can carve in his spare time as well as in class, and she is grateful for suitable bits of wood sent by his father for the class. Tony's mother asks Caryll to carve a statue of St. Anthony to be given to him as a confirmation present. Caryll (of course) refused money for this commission, which she joyfully undertook. "The payment that I would really like for doing it is a few pieces of wood to use myself—odd pieces of any nice wood suitable either for carving or fretwork."

For Tony she proposed to carve "a statue of St. Anthony to have a base with a design of fishes carved in relief on it. You know he preached to fishes, and they put their heads out of the water to listen." (Here came a pleasant drawing of the fish.)

Tony's mother wanted to meet Caryll, and all was arranged for her to go to tea at their house. And then occurred

what constantly did occur with Caryll. She was always mis-
laying addresses, muddling dates, but above all losing her
way. She always resisted up to the last moment any suggestion
that the way was lost. (Iris has again and again been taken
up blind alleys, Caryll swearing that they were nearly there.)
And then would follow one of those paroxysms of apology
and self-condemnation which she so urgently entreated others
to avoid.

Her letter when she failed to turn up this time is worth
quoting both for the comfort of those who lose their way and
for its light on Caryll herself:

I do not know how to apologize for the fearful rudeness of
failing to come to you this afternoon. The dreadful thing is I
was actually there. What happened is this. First of all, I took
a wrong bus (I did not start from home, and believed the bus
to be the best one for you). Before realizing my mistake, I had
gone a long way out of the way, and then lost time getting back
on to the right road and eventually on to the right bus. By the
time I really did arrive in the vicinity, I was already embarrass-
ingly late—then I could not immediately find the road.

Having at last found it, I made my final and most idiotic
mistake. I thought your number to be 54; I had most carefully
copied down 54 in my diary beside the appointment.

You doubtless know the length of your own road and that 54
is at the far end of it from where I started. When at last I got
to it, I hesitated about going on, owing to the time; then to
crown all I found you did not live there. It is a house full of
flats, and I knocked on every one of them in turn—of course in
vain.

Now I was hot with shame and self-hatred, and began knocking wildly on other doors, but alas, not on the right one. Once
I came to a house called "Mary Magdalene," which sounded so
Catholic that for a moment my heart beat high: I thought that
perhaps in an excess of piety you had named your house so! but
it proved only to be the Vicarage.

I wandered like a lost dog up and down, hoping to see a

glimpse of Tony in some window: then a new, horrible idea came to me. I felt sure that I must have addressed my letter to No. 54, since I was so convinced that you lived there. So you might not have had it and presumed (for I am sure you are most kind) that for some reason I had not had *your* letter, and that I was not coming.

Now, I thought, what could be more horrible and confusing for you than to have me turn up, unexpectedly, and at half-past five instead of 3:45—just when you would be likely to be putting your smaller children to bed, or about to prepare your husband's dinner, or both!

I decided that it would be best for me to slink away like a mangy dog with its tail between its legs, rather than continue knocking on all the doors in the road until, far too late and possibly unexpected, and certainly an appalling nuisance, I found the right one.

When at last she reached home after this pilgrimage she discovered the correct number in her address book!

Lonely, and especially refugee, children Caryll rather especially cherished.

"One day," Rosamond relates, "a small Polish boy said suddenly, in the middle of a class: 'Miss Houselander, may I tell you something?' and when Caryll gave him permission, he said simply, 'My father was shot in front of me.' "

Years later she wrote to a friend about the school:

I have seen many wonderful things happening there in children's souls. There they have every kind of child (boys); some have been in the Polish army when eleven years old, others in concentration camps in Siberia carrying logs of wood all day, when nine years old. There is another Pole, who escaped from Russian captivity; as a small boy, he was taken to Siberia and all through the journey from Poland carried a baby under his coat, against his body to keep it warm, and thus saved it from perishing with cold when they crossed the frontier into Siberia. After, he and several others escaped and got to Italy and from there to England with the same baby!

Another boy from Czechoslovakia turns up later in Caryll's correspondence, as a young man for whom she is anxious to find a wife. She must be a "cosy girl with no nerves at all . . . a nice plump solid girl who will look after him and bear child after child." He is still nervy after his terrible experiences, but such a marriage may make him into a normal and happily integrated person.

Caryll's longing to give children a normal and happy upbringing was intensified by every experience she had of the scars left by early suffering. She took a keen interest in one boy from a poor home whose people could not afford even the very moderate school fees. Caryll insisted on paying them. Her godson David Billaux sent gifts of clothing about which she becomes ecstatic. Indeed a large part of Caryll's letters is taken up with litanies of thanks—to Henry, Archie and other friends for books, for flowers, for records, for Tio Pepe Sherry. No one could thank more gracefully; she always made you feel that the gift you had chosen was the most perfect, the ideal choice. She discussed the book, arranged the flowers, savoured the sherry in her letter. In this letter you almost see the clothes on the boy. She herself certainly gave no small thing in giving her time—for she refused any payment except her fares. And Archie's cheques for these were received like her publisher's cheques for royalties, as if themselves a gift!

But her health was becoming more and more unequal to the strain. In the summer term of 1948 she misses a class owing to "a violent chill in the innards of so immobilizing a nature and so biblical in type (see the penitential psalms)" that she could not leave the house. A little later she is prostrated by earache and toothache and then again by "a rather desparate [sic] gastric attack."

Finally on the feast of St. Joseph 1949 comes a very sad letter to "deliver a blow (it was to me, anyway)"; she must give up her teaching. The doctor has told her that she has a really bad "internal condition . . . a congenital but really radical weakness . . . resulting in a sort of internal general post. I won't weary you with the sordid details." She mentions her operation of two years earlier and that her doctor is threatening her with another: "the alternative is *no exertion,* a fairly sedentary life and so on." Another undated letter speaks of "a small spot of lung trouble." Dr. Paley had rightly foreseen that Caryll would always have "rotten health."

She writes a great deal about possible arrangements for the future, but the most fascinating thing about this letter must for a headmaster have been the amazingly detailed knowledge it showed of each boy—his potential as an artist; those who could carve, those who could paint, the rare boy of high talent, the considerable number of competent craftsmen—and enough of each one's character to be quite a guide in the handling of him for whoever should succeed her.

Two months later she writes of her sadness over coming no more. "It is a real sort of nostalgia: I always knew that I loved the school and everything that it stood for." Her consolation is that good craftsmen, certain to be better teachers than she, have taken her place "who can give far more time and energy to the job . . . the improvement will be immediate and wonderful. . . . I am by nature a person to start things, to sow seeds as it were; it requires others to see them through."

This spring of 1949 had brought another and more shattering blow to Caryll. Christine Spender has described how when they were together at the Censorship a kitten that she loved got enteritis and had to be destroyed. Going downstairs with tears streaming down her face she met Caryll. As she sobbed, "I loved him so," she felt that most people would in war-time have thought such feelings for an animal out of place. But Caryll said, "Love is never wasted. It is Our Lady's birthday today. Perhaps Our Lady has taken your little white cat for her birthday present." "Somehow," says Christine, "the idea calmed me and I was able to go back to work once more."

Later Caryll wrote to her of a dream. "I went up the slope of a mountain, a snowy mountain, and there on top, made of shining snow, with tiny wings springing from tufts of swansdown on his shoulders, was your kitten dancing. He had ice-blue eyes."

Caryll's sympathy with Christine had been what the word really signifies—a suffering with, for she loved her own cat Jones with the kind of love that many could only give to a human friend. A chapter in *This War is the Passion* compares his attitude to her with what ours should be to God: total trust and love. Jones had been terrified by an unpleasant black cat "definitely marked by the underworld," but "no sooner had he jumped on my lap than he relaxed, he went limp, not with fear, but happily, deliciously limp, and indicated by various signs known to me that he wanted his ears scratched—that done, he went to sleep. I ought to be able to treat God as my cat treats me, only, whereas my cat is deluded about my omnipotence, I am right about God's."

One was very much aware of Jones's presence in the little flat—a peaceful presence: he was not the sort of cat that makes demands on the visitor. Caryll once told me she had wanted a really plebeian cat, a perfectly ordinary tabby, and this is what Jones looked, but when he attacked the burglar or tried to get Caryll to stop working he manifested a character by no means ordinary.

He often figures in her letters of midnight and later: "Jones, who is on the table, keeps whisking his tail across the paper, making it very difficult for me to write". . . . "It is very late, and Jones keeps sitting on my letter, pushing the pen, etc., so I think I must stop."

Jones was growing old—in one of her war-time letters Caryll reckons his years as equivalent to 91 in terms of human longevity. He was, however, playing with a ball and wanted to show her that he had years of energy in him still. In 1949 he was almost twenty, which by the same comparison of life-spans meant that he was in human terms more than a centenarian. To Christine, who would best understand her feelings, Caryll wrote of his illness—an attack of jaundice caused by a growth on the spleen. The vet was hesitating whether to "put him to sleep"—but the decision must be Caryll's.

I am just breaking inwardly; my cowardly nature can't stand it—I feel that we ought *not* to wait till he is obviously suffering, yet I just failed to be able to insist or argue, and now am in a state of terrible indecision. When he does get another attack, she said she will come and put him to sleep here. This is my own request; I could not bear to carry him out of his home and see him go off among strangers, afraid and feeling abandoned—to die. And yet now, having made this arrangement for her to come here, I feel unable to face seeing it, and holding him while he dies. The fearful uncertainty about *when* it is to happen adds torment to it; you see it's like living in a condemned cell with him.

If only it could have been done right away—. But God forgive me for going on like this, when so many poor human beings have had to stand and watch their own little children dragged into lethal chambers and gassed. I was thinking of them last night and offered up what I am suffering over my cat, for them!

But today I am shattered, can hardly concentrate, and my nerve *really* gone. However, I am praying, and will lay the burden on God—who is always ready to take the burdens of us poor sinners.

I am trying to make penances and ask for them to be accepted, instead of him having to suffer. It seems so much more just for a human who has had years of joy from his innocent little life, to suffer, than for him to do so, because men sin.

The darling old fellow is sitting on my table purring now.

I wonder whether anyone before or since has done penance to relieve the sufferings of a cat. But for Caryll the hardest penance came in the final decision that she must let him go. In the end she could not make up her mind to let it be done at the flat. Iris brought a basket and persuaded Caryll to let her take Jones to the vet. "His death was," Caryll wrote, "a terrible grief. I was nursing him day and night. The decision was the hardest I have ever taken. He was nearly twenty years old, and we have always been together since he was orphaned at a week old! I fed him on drops of milk at the end of a paintbrush then, and so kept him alive. It is like having torn out part of myself. But I feel we owe it to animals for the intense joy their innocent little lives give to us, to spare them useless suffering, to be willing to pay the price in our own grief—so the darling old chap is no more."

13

Caryll, Iris and Clare

OTHER THINGS HAPPENED during the period of Caryll's
teaching at Frensham, including the publication of two more
books and the beginning of a third. *The Comforting of
Christ* was not wholly new: it was an enlarged edition of
This War is the Passion adapted to the new conditions
brought by the peace. In some respects, especially in relation
to mental suffering, these conditions were less new than a
relapse into a disease temporarily suspended. The war had
put purpose into empty lives: now that purpose seemed at
an end. No, Caryll said, there is more to do than ever: "If
we do not work to keep the little homes and loves and lives
of our people, our victory will mean nothing." She was
herself keenly aware both of mental suffering—"the mind
of Christ bleeding under the crown of thorns"—and of the
physical sufferings of homeless Poles, of refugee children, of
the maimed, the broken and the sick. We "must not think
of a ward full of 'cancers' or of decrepits . . . of people as
'casualties,' 'cases' and 'operations' but as Christs. . . . There
is another more general way of teaching oneself to face
up to the world's suffering. Instead of forgetting, remember."
And again:

"The risen Christ said, 'Do not touch Me!' He has a mys-

terious life of illimitable joy, secret to everyone but His
Heavenly Father. But, paradoxically, He told us to touch
His wounds. 'See My hands and feet, that it is I Myself:
handle and see.' It means this—

"We cannot see Christ in His glory, but we can see Him
and touch Him in man's suffering."

People had been lifted out of fears, only too natural and
reasonable, for "the duration." They had thought more of
others' sufferings than of their own danger. Now the vague
fears of the near-neurotic had returned to many. Instead of
her Jones, frightened by an alley cat, Caryll now describes
a tiny boy whose nurse scolds him for being afraid of being
left alone in a hotel bedroom. " 'You're just a silly little boy
to be afraid when there is nothing to be afraid of.' When she
had left him, I heard his pitiful voice calling after her, 'I
am afraid of the nothing—nothing—nothing.' "

But, just before peace came, another child had calmed
a whole church full of people waiting tensely for a bomb
to fall by running out into the aisle and looking up laughing
at a statue of Our Lady:

"Someone had pushed a flower into the hand of the
Divine Infant in his Mother's arms and now it was quivering
from the vibration of the bomb.

"To the little boy it seemed that the crowned Christ-child
leaned down and waved to him with a scarlet flower."

Caryll is still talking on her favourite topic, the indwelling
of Christ in His Mystical Body, but there is increasingly a
fresh slant in her work. She was getting onto a tremendous
subject, which she began to deal with in the second of the
books published in 1947, *The Dry Wood,* but which reached
its high point in yet another which she began that same year.

"The older I grow," she told a friend, "the more unwilling
—and afraid—am I to preach. That's why I prefer writing
fiction: it's more like a big gesture of sympathy—like taking
hold of another sinner's hand and pressing it lovingly as we

walk together. . . . When I write 'spiritual' books now, it's for the reason that I know that many people will read them who won't read fiction. . . . And I also want to give sympathy to a lot of those; but, believe me, the last one I wrote . . . not yet published, I did literally write in tears."

This book was *The Passion of the Infant Christ,* but Caryll's solitary work of fiction (as distinct from short stories) was on the same theme, although handled very differently. She felt about it as about a child "whom one knows to have hereditary disease, and yet one must love it."

The story of Willie Jewell in *The Dry Wood* is the story of innocent suffering, and the whole book centres on this: the holy old priest (based, Caryll told a friend, on the Jesuit Father Considine) upon whose prayers in heaven his flock count for the cure of this child; the scandalized reactions of the worldly monsignor; the conversion of Timothy Green; the return of Carmel Fernandez to her home and her father's reception of her; Solly Lee carrying his magnificent red flowers to Willie's coffin and praying for God's mercy; and above all the last chapter, "Mass for the People of the Parish" —all these are centring on one thing which was increasingly central in Caryll's thinking.

"Willie was about to do something completely, which no one but a child could do completely. He was going to die Christ's death. He was innocence, and he was going to pay the price of sin. He was going to suffer the passion of Christ. . . . His hands were gripping the bed-clothes now, as if they had been made alive to die.

" 'He is holding on to the nails,' thought Rose O'Shane. 'He is holding on to the blessed nails lovingly.' "

The Mass for the people is Christ on the cross. The world cries out to him, "Come down from the Cross, and save yourself and us." But it was by staying there that he would save us.

His fingers closed on the nails. He would not come down from the cross. He would not dethrone the children; He would not discrown the poor; He would not break faith with sinners or fail the failing; He would not forsake the young men coming up to die His death. . . . His heart broke open and the river of the world's life flowed out of it. A crimson flood sweeping His heart and brain and flowing out into the tips of His fingers, swept through His Mystical Body.

This was Caryll's favourite meditation—we fallen men and women brought suffering into the world, caused suffering to Christ. But now our suffering can itself become redemptive because Christ suffers *in* us—the members of His Mystical Body. And the one sinless being on earth is the young child who suffers and at whose sufferings the world takes scandal against God. Believing as we do that an eternity of unimaginable happiness awaits that child, the mystery is still stark of why he should have first to suffer here: we cannot pretend to understand it any more than any other mystery; but in Willie Jewell Caryll depicted a child *accepting,* whose death becomes one with Christ's and wins joy, peace and triumph for others. Of the exploring of this deep mystery she wrote to a friend:

My book is a spiritual book. It is on the subject of "redemptive childhood," which I believe to be the special kind of holiness in our century. It was inspired by Clare*—at least, in a way it was, but on the first night of the war, and my first night in a First Aid post (an unnecessarily macabre one in a rat-infested basement), this book, or some strange presentiment of it, came into my mind. It was as if the Holy Innocents of Bethlehem whom Herod murdered were flocking around our heads, singing shrilly with joy, and the phrase "Passio Infantis Christi" kept echoing in my mind. . . .

I had started another book when Clare came, but on the first

---

* See below, pp. 227 ff.

night she was in my room the same experience repeated itself—
I put aside the book I was writing and did "Passio Infantis
Christi" instead.

It may have been on that very night at the First Aid post
that Caryll had an experience which she relates in another
letter and which certainly strengthened her sense of the mysterious power God gives to His little ones. It confirmed also
her belief that one can really get to know people by praying
for them . . . "and of course quite certainly one can by praying *to* people in heaven." She goes on:

During the war, one night we were in the midst of a long
and exhausting air-raid. Our London barrage had been going
on for hours, German planes coming over, in batches of over
a hundred at a time, in relays all night, and the barrage, which
meant a non-stop, ear-splitting thunder of gun-fire going all the
time. I was in a hospital helping give first aid to the wounded,
and got sent to a ward where there were patients who had been
operated on that day, and so could not be moved to the parts
of the hospital considered a little more safe (i.e., the basement,
where our post was). I was told to go to the ward and keep those
poor patients (who could not move an inch) from being afraid.
On the way upstairs I realized that my mind was quite empty
and that there was not one thought in it with which to reas-
sure anyone; and in any case I had no doubt the hospital would
fall on us in a few minutes!

Suddenly I became acutely and *unquestionably* conscious of
the personality of a little child of three at my side—the child of
a friend whom I never knew, but of whom I had heard constantly from this friend, and to whom I had often prayed. It
seemed that this tiny child directed me from heaven, filled my
mind with things to say, and with things that were effective
and did the trick! A day or two later I had a letter from the
dead child's father, saying: "I heard the barrage even from
here" (he was in a suburb outside London), "and when I
realized what was going on, I went on my knees and prayed

to Mary [the child] to stay with you all that night, and it was the anniversary of the night she died". . . .

It was in the day-to-day experience of sharing with her friend Iris Wyndham the care of a baby that Caryll learnt the deeper wisdom of the book that she was now writing. The book and the baby were in the background to her teaching at Frensham and all her other activities. In the same letter in which she told Christine Spender that she was going to teach at the school, she also told her that Iris's daughter Joan, who had married Maurice Rowdon, still an undergraduate at Oxford, was about to have a baby. She had only a single room with no conveniences, and wanted her mother to take charge of the baby from birth until she could make arrangements to take it herself. "She will come," Caryll said, "on Sundays; she lives in Oxford. The baby will be in Iris's flat by day and in mine by night. P.S. All my spare moments, if any, have to be devoted to learning 'Mothercraft.' "

Iris tells me Caryll was at first angry with her for agreeing to take the child. Iris had intended to do the whole thing herself, but it was obvious that Caryll would do her utmost to help her friend once the decision was taken. I well remember with what doubts and hesitations she viewed it: neither she nor Iris knew anything about the handling of babies. Joan, as a child, had had a nannie, and besides that there had been the maid inherited from her mother. Having been, like Iris, brought up in this world of plenty, I remember vividly my terror of bathing a tiny baby: my nannie's day out was a fearful ordeal. Caryll had helped occasionally with her sister's and other small children—but certainly never with a new-born infant. Their two flats were, respectively, on the ground floor and the ninth floor at Nell Gwynn. Each consisted of a bed-sitting room, a kitchen and a bathroom.

And Caryll had in her own life been so much more up against difficulties, her imagination was so much more vivid than most people's, she saw in a flash every conceivable problem that might arise. To her friends the danger loomed large that the writing which was both "her life and her livelihood" *could* not go on. Christine Spender had been one of those most bitterly opposed to the plan, and it was only seeing what this experience meant to Caryll that eventually reconciled her. To Rosamond, almost the only one in agreement with her, Caryll said, "How can I go on writing the sort of books that I do write if I turn away when a need like this comes to my door?"

It was older children that Caryll had been teaching and curing, whose minds she had been finding so great a thrill in exploring. But she had also god-children to whom she was devoted. David Billaux was one, and Dickie's daughter Elizabeth. She took the office with intense seriousness. To Henry Tayler, asked to be godfather of the new baby, she wrote of a pamphlet by Fr. Martindale which had taught her to understand how much this should mean:

That which lit up my mind at the time and has remained as an inspiration ever since was the realization that being a god-parent means much more than taking a promise; it means representing, *being,* that perfectly innocent child before God; it means that, jaded and shopsoiled though we are, we are ourselves as it were made new in the shining water of Baptism, the flame that is given in the ceremony for a symbol of Faith is relit in our hearts and *we* receive the white garment of Chastity, not as ourselves but as the little child. I have made it a practice to go to Confession and Communion every so often *as* my infant godchild, until she comes to the age of reason, to go on *being her,* until in the sacramental active life she has the use of reason and can be herself. This is like carrying a sinless child in one's heart always, and when one feels the burden of one's own beastliness heavy upon one, or is depressed or conscious of being old and disillusioned and very sere and yellow indeed, one always returns to the thought that one is not only oneself by oneself, but also a little new, untouched, untried, unspoilt child, whom God has given to one in trust. This is the beautiful inward life of being a godfather, and then there is the sterner side—until she is not only at the age of reason but independence, *you are her reason* and the flowering sword of her defence.

The baby came to them at three weeks old, and soon Iris's radiators were festooned with drying diapers, and a small pram which served as a crib was installed in Caryll's room. She tried to learn a little at a school for expectant mothers— but the school refused to take her, on the ground that she was *not* a mother, actual or expectant. Iris, counselled by a baby clinic, prepared the bottles with scrupulous care, giving the exact amount prescribed. It was only after much yelling that the baby succeeded in getting the doctor called in—she said that hunger was the only thing wrong.

In the letter to Henry about his office as godfather Caryll described how Clare's day began:

The only prayer I've said for her (as being her prayer) up to date, and this she "says," by arm gestures every morning at six o'clock, is the little child's prayer made by the poet Herrick, which is:

> Here a little child I stand
> Heaving up my either hand,
> Cold as paddocks though they be,
> Yet I heave them up to Thee.

Having agreed unwillingly to the plan, Caryll was throwing herself into its execution with all the energy of her character. Indeed there was about Caryll in action an element for which the best word I can find is exorbitance. She not only did all she had undertaken but she seemed always to think up ways of adding to her own burden. She would

throw in unnecessary extras to help or comfort a friend—
offering, for instance, to visit a schoolgirl daughter who already abounded in aunts, hurrying to meet a mislaid traveller
who could really have been left to her own resources; accom-
panying a friend to a difficult interview which she might
very well have been braced to face for herself. My daughter
used to say that the worst of Caryll was that if you were feeling sorry for yourself the intensity of her sympathy made you
much worse. Preventing her from spending her energies in
one's service was as difficult as paying her for a job or refusing the money she would pour out when she had any. And
she always seemed to pile onto a difficult task the last ounce
of discomfort for herself.

Now she did not give up her writing, but instead of getting
Clare accustomed to a shaded light in her bedroom she
would work on her current book for hours on end in the
bathroom. Later on when Clare was no longer living with
them she often came on visits. Caryll had full charge of her
at the flat when Joan brought her while Iris was at the cottage
in the country. Her love for the child grew and grew, but
for both her and Iris great effort was involved in these first
months. When Clare was a month old Caryll wrote to Henry:

Actually, about the work involved in the Baby, the gloomsters
are right, it *never* stops . . . poor Iris is just wearing out—the Baby
is adorable, though, and that is a mercy. We both feel such an
enormous love for her already and I am getting over my baby
terror and repulsion. She is so completely a *person*, an individual, that this fact rules out all general applications to mere
"baby." But as for fatigue! Well, I went to the Sheeds on
Christmas Eve and Frank said how fit, etc., I look, and Maisie
said that after all the baby works out all right, and I was very
careful not to disillusion them. In point of fact, I feel giddy
and mental with fatigue, and so, I am certain, does poor old
Iris.

Small wonder she felt "giddy and mental" if one considers the life into which Clare had entered:

Well, here I am [she wrote to Christine on April 26th, 1948] like a diver who has been below the surface for so long that he can hardly breathe above water.

I finished my book yesterday . . . one simply has to do a book at white heat, that is, not admitting anything that can take one's *mind* completely off it for an hour, and insisting upon at the very *least* half the day, every day, without a break. I stuck out for the whole of every morning and tried for the afternoon too, and in any case worked from 10 o'c. every night until 3 o'c. the next morning.

I am starting a new book tomorrow.

This must have been *Guilt*, put aside some months previously—and it fits and supplements remarkably *The Passion of the Infant Christ*. But it must have needed strong will-power to write from ten to three night after night in a tiny bathroom!

We must all *become* as little children, Caryll insisted. And the condition for this is courage. "Courage not only to take the necessary steps to return to childhood after we have grown up, but courage to grow. up in the first place." The perpetual adolescent is childish but not childlike. He is "afraid of life . . . of making decisions, of taking risks; afraid of falling in love, of making a home, of having children; afraid of sickness, of growing old and of dying."

The spiritually impotent man is dangerous, for he tries to compensate by material success—he is more dangerous than an atom bomb or bacteriological warfare. "For no man who does not plunge himself into the magnitude of the littleness of Christ is safe to exercise power."

Thérèse of Lisieux is the great exemplar of redemptive childhood. "No one has ever realized the value of little things as she did; for no one has ever realized more that the Christ-

Child suffered in her and that the Christ-Child can suffer nothing that is not in the redeeming Passion of Infinite Love.

"It is this sentimental, passionate little nun, St. Thérèse of Lisieux, who in her own life has defined the sanctity of today, the answer to the Herods of today: it is the sanctity of spiritual childhood."

Caryll saw a danger in confusing the "terrifying prospect" of Thérèse's "hourly, even momentary little sacrifices," so hidden, so far beyond *"our* human nature," with what she called the ludicrous system of double entry practised by some religious people—"debit and credit," "merit" and so on. Detachment, a nun friend once told me, could easily become selfishness—I will remain indifferent to that person or thing, because I may be called upon to lose it. God, Caryll said, showed us by His approach to us how we should approach Him: "It is a way not of detachment but of attachment; not a way of indifference but of love." And so, far from Thérèse's "little way" being a method of double entry or a constant strain in pursuit of perfection, "it is the repeated relief of giving spontaneous expression to love that is too great to be endured without it."

And here, as she contemplated Christ in Clare, new lights came to Caryll on an ancient theme of hers: Christ a *reality*.

"I have seen," she writes, "the hands of a foster-mother chapped and bleeding from being continually dipped in hard water in frosty weather and have thought to myself that the stigmata are not, after all, reserved for a few rare mystics."

Those hands were her friend's. She had grown up taking care of their beauty, but had forgotten this task in a new and greater one.

"The perfection of surrender to God is Mary with the Infant Christ.

"There is nothing more mysterious than infancy; nothing so small and yet so imperious. The Infancy of Christ has opened a way to us by which we can surrender self to Him absolutely, without putting too much pressure on our weak human nature."

She would have all mothers join in this contemplation through the "new timing of our lives, a more holy ordering of our time . . . no longer to be ruled by our impulses and caprice, but by the rhythm of the little child. We must learn to sleep lightly, aware of the moonlight and the stars, conscious even in our deepest sleep of a whimper from the infant and ready to respond to it. We must learn the saving habit of rising with, or a little before, dawn."

Many mothers will smile a little broadly at this. A healthy baby does not call for this exaggerated guardianship. But the conclusion is wholly true. If in each service of a baby we counted the cost, we "could not list what must be done and given and given up." Every day would be "a period of trial made up from ceaseless small tortures."

But in our contemplation through our love of an infant we learn "the giving up of self which is Holy Poverty. As long as we have something else to give, we always cling to self; but the infant lays his minute hand on that and rejects everything else."

The splendour of our task may be measured in terms of the Holy Innocents—killed because Herod feared "that any one of them might be Christ.

"Any child might be Christ! The fear of Herod is the fear of every tyrant, the hope of every Christian, and the most significant fact in the modern world."

Caryll wrote to a close friend of "the sheer joy" of Clare. "The whole thing has been an experience that has taught me more about God than anything that has ever happened; now I think I can say, without blasphemy or presumption, that I have a faint idea of what Our Blessed Lady felt." The child had grown deep into both their lives when Caryll wrote, shortly after her first birthday:

I have come down to the cottage because Iris has gone to
help Joan to take Clare, and I could not endure to think of
poor Iris coming back late, exhausted and broken-hearted, to
a cold empty cottage—so I came down today, after she had
gone, to light the fire, prepare the dinner, and have it cosy
and glowing a welcome when she comes. I am getting anxious, as
it is eight o'clock and no sign of her. It is strange alone here, the
wind is howling like a stormy sea and nothing but dark vast
fields, swept by the wind all round me.

Iris had put aside all the money she earned at the Censorship to buy this cottage. It is near Terrick, lovely with its
low ceilings, black and white rooms, and above all the glowing garden that surrounds it. But when she bought it in 1946
the garden had ceased to exist: it is the work of her patience
and skill, reclaimed from the surrounding field. Only one
taxi driver in the neighbourhood will consent to drive up to
the cottage—there is no road through the field, and there are
times when access is literally impossible. A sea of mud
surrounds it in winter, even though from a distance this looks
like a green and pleasant field.

Originally a shepherd's cottage, tied to the Elizabethan
farm at the end of the field, it then consisted of two rooms,
one up and one down, the only staircase a ladder through
the ceiling. Alison Williamson, who still lives at the farm,
remembers the arrival of the last shepherd to live in it, whom
she herself had hired: he and his wife climbed out of the van
which had brought them, and after them eight (hitherto un-
mentioned) children. And there they all lived. There was a
double line of magnificent walnut trees leading up to the
cottage across the field (many of these have now fallen, or
been felled to make way for the pylons), and a twisted old
damson tree on the front lawn. Iris moved in in January,
during a snowstorm, helped by Jacques Doneux's sister. To
reclaim the garden she had an assistant called Tony, possess-

ing the real gypsy's eye for wild things—he could find twenty nests in a hedge where Iris could find one, and could lay his hand on a hare in her form. Caryll and Tony also got on very well together, and he still speaks of her with regret: she gave him one of her books, with which he was delighted: and they had long talks on religion.

"I must end now," Caryll concludes one letter, "as there are endless country chores to see to—life in town, by the bye, is much less tiring."

"In the morning," she says in another, "I have to struggle through the field, in the midst of which we are situated, to get to Mass, or rather to get me to the road that gets me to the bus that gets me to Mass six miles away [actually 4½]; and the poor old cows think I am a milkmaid and follow me in a line, the first one breathing heavily in my ear"!

But she wrote in an unpublished rhythm:

On the Road to Mass

To Christ
I give glory—
born in the white Host
this winter's morning.

I crown Christ
with a diadem
of white thorn
in the rime.

I adorn
His garment's hem
with diamonds
on grass and stem.

To Christ I give glory,
born in the white Host
this winter's morning.

The cottage was supposed only to be a summer place, but as Iris grew fonder and fonder of it she tended to stay longer. They both kept their flats at Nell Gwynn, and Caryll divided her time between the two, trying especially to fill in in the months when Iris had fewer visitors. She had mixed feelings about the cottage; she kept her passion for London, she continued to feel worn out by country life, yet the picture as it builds up from letters and rhythms is one of beauty and charm. She loved nature—especially flowers—but very differently from those who make gardens. Her hands were creative with wood, Iris has green fingers. Caryll writes:

The incessant efforts of the people here to draw one's attention to this or that detail of nature is a positive distraction: one has so intensely the sense of all nature, taken as a whole—sky, earth, blossom, stars and sun and moon and rain and dew, all together—being a thin veil on the eternal light, or a faint pulse of everlasting light. In London, one flower brings the whole wonder and mystery of this shining veil into one's room, but in the country it seems to me one wants to receive it whole, as one receives Communion, and it is difficult not to become irritated by being asked to see it in terms of gardening or the interesting habits of ants—however, from the point of view of gardeners and Fabre fans, it is otherwise!

I decided to make an index of subjects in one of Caryll's longest correspondences: the two leading words in it are Clare and flowers. For this very lovely child did not disappear out of Caryll's life for very long at a time, and never out of her thoughts. In one of the largest bundles of letters she is sometimes on the same page with the flowers which this special friend, Lois Boardman, so often sent. Flowers became, I think, linked in Caryll's mind with Clare. They were, she felt, "a living miracle of water and light." "I surrounded our little baby with your snowdrops," she writes, "the biggest and whitest I have ever seen, and she looked and stared at them and smiled . . . I want her always to have flowers near her in my flat, the joy of those snowdrops being by her was inconceivable." They were Caryll's own favourite flower: "some theologians say that angels are allowed to disguise themselves in animals, flowers, rain drops, snowflakes and so on. It seems to me that snowdrops make one think this true."

Primroses "look as if they are made of light . . . not only did they light the room, they made it smell like a country wood"; cowslips are "living yellow light . . . what a peculiarly lovely, delicate green their stems are—what an astonishing *variety* of greens God does use." Flowers sent her at Easter "did literally bring the Resurrection into my room." Some have been arranged around Clare's photo, and they will be "smiling a welcome." Later in the year sweet peas "were like little clouds of shining butterflies."

But the flowers are almost eclipsed by Caryll's delight in the clothes and toys made for Clare by this friend and her daughter Brigid. One dress "really looks as if it is made out of a blue cloud." There are "perfectly lovely" fair isle jerseys in intricate patterns, dolls most exquisitely dressed and even a doll's bed. As she gets bigger, letters of gratitude from Clare herself are enclosed. We learn too that she loves to have pretty things to wear, to change her clothes many times a day, to dress up as a princess. A year or two later "she always asks me to get her 'smart' clothes and asks everyone anxiously, when she has something new, whether it is smart."

Reading Caryll's letters builds up in the mind not only a picture of her but also of the largely forgotten and exceedingly uncomfortable world we were living in for so many years after the war. "Here," she writes to an American friend, Lucile Hasley, as late as 1948, "if you want to buy a loaf of bread even, you have to queue for it; meat or fish that isn't high has a queue miles long: as to bananas I no longer try." When Clare was staying with her she had sometimes to take her along, and this in wet weather needed "all the supernatural help there is." Alone she could largely neglect that side of life, but not with "the necessity to eat so pronounced in infants."

I remember at this time bringing back from Brussels a branch of bananas some fifteen pounds in weight and being gazed at in London by many envious eyes; I remember too buying sherry and discovering it to be heavily watered. The meat and cheese rations were still minute.

Naturally enough the Sprats had started again, and Caryll wrote thanking a friend for a donation:

"There is new increasing and quite heartbreaking need for the work that the Loaves and Fishes do and everyone, owing to the appalling taxation and cost of living here, is less able to help. There is a tremendous lot of 'Sprat work' being done, but against huge difficulties, so your gift brings me a big shaft of light and hope."

Myself enlisted by Caryll in this very unorganized organization, I was told how a visit to a theatre or cinema, a "slap-up meal" or a bottle of wine given to the depressed and discouraged came most definitely within our scope. Life was drab for everybody just then, and for people with tiny fixed incomes or inadequate earning powers it seemed grim indeed.

The faults of character which sometimes created people's difficulties were far less repellent to Caryll than those faults which make for success in this world. She said once of an acquaintance supposed to be a very good Catholic that it was hard to judge as she had none of the temptations that beset most of us. Her only temptation was to be arrogant— "which," said Caryll firmly, "she *is*."

Arrogance, worldliness, selfishness were the only real bars to her sympathy. "I am all on the side of love," she said once, "even illicit love." Rosamond tried to enlist her admiration for someone she knew, "who was—almost incredible combination—beautiful, saintly and intellectual." Caryll said,

"I'm sorry, I can't take any interest in people like that. I'm always far too conscious of being the bruised reed rather than the lofty pine."

The censoriousness of the "good" was the sin she most deeply hated, and she felt that Our Lord's parable of the Pharisee and the Publican and His words to sinful women were not meditated on enough. To a much harassed friend she wrote ironically:

"It is true that in heaven you will not have to wash up, and neither will you be criticized, because there, God be praised, there will be a large proportion of harlots and sinners (we have Christ's word for it)—which will mean that there will be tolerance, charity and happiness. But don't go yet, wait 'til you are wickeder and better able to enjoy the refreshing company of the harlots and sinners."

I have put the word "good" in quotation marks because the root of Caryll's thinking on all this was that *none* of us is good, but self-deceit is easier for those whose sins are less apparent. She wrote in *Guilt* that while both rich and poor sin by pride, "Pride is a painful sin to the poor, a pleasurable one to the rich; the pride that is roused by a snub hurts, the pride that is inflated by flattery soothes."

Caryll's views were in fact unusually balanced, but it was a balance reached through the violent statement of positions usually held to be incompatible. About this time she put two of these opposites together in her correspondence with Lucile Hasley.

Lucile had, like myself, come to know Caryll through her writing. Caryll also had read and admired articles of hers and a little later wrote the Introduction to her first book. They began to correspond. The habit—more American than English—of asking questions as a way of getting to know a person suited Caryll. She was indeed once startled by a questionnaire sent by an American nun which asked, "What is the most intimate experience you have ever had?" But she did not mind what is called giving herself away—indeed she could well have made a Chestertonian play upon the word, for she *gave herself* to every correspondent and was overjoyed when they were willing to give themselves in return. Mrs. Hasley was more interested in ideas than many of Caryll's correspondents, and we owe to her a statement, of real value because of its realism, of how Caryll felt about the tendency of Catholics to fall into groups determined by class, type or other minor matters:

Regarding the conflict between the "Catholic Worker type" and the "Keep to the Middle of the Road"—what strikes me is that there ought not really to *be* any conflict, and that it is caused by a whole lot of mistakes which are generally accepted without question. First of all, take the Catholic Worker type. You get papers from them, in which practically every article is a very vital grouse about injustice, and a few boosting up the worker as such, and they are usually illustrated either by a wood or linocut of Our Lord or St. Joseph driving a huge nail into a splitting plank with a wooden mallet which would be ruined by the action. (Being a carver—in wood—by trade, this picture worries me.) But what is lacking in these papers is any articles that seem likely to make Christ more real to the worker himself in his own life, as if the only consideration is his just grievance and the duty, shared by him with all men, to try to remedy it. What is absent is the suggestion of his being in unity with Our Lord in *suffering* injustice, or any real understanding of work itself, the integrity of the artist at work, which should be every worker's ideal, or the honour he has in practising and suffering as Christ did, or the glory of being poor, and so on. Also it seems to be presumed that the rich man (a) doesn't work at all, (b) doesn't suffer any injustice at all. I could start pages on the superficial side of this—but don't want to get away from the heart of it, namely that in the Mystical Body we are all one, and we do all experience the Passion in a thousand secret ways, and we share—if we want to or not—in each other's lives and responsibilities. When I read snob-stuff from "Catholic

Action" people of the "Flame" type,* and when I see it practised, it turns my blood to poison; but I think the tendency to
segregate *every* type and class, at least in the mind, leads to a
vast number of individuals completely misunderstanding themselves and their own glory. If every one was concentrating on
being a "Christ" in and through his own circumstances as they
are, then I think that inevitably all the injustices *would* be
righted.

Delighted that Caryll's biography was going forward, Lucile wrote to me:

I still get stray letters from unknown people thanking me for
having introduced her to them. Also, I'm not at all surprised
that she was more complex and had more of a "history" than
you expected. For one thing, *The Rocking-Horse Catholic* indicated many undeveloped areas. . . .
My impression of her (or intuition) is that she was almost
savage in both her reactions to people and things and in her
convictions; that she had a strong sense of guilt (personal and
universal) ; that she was possibly starved for love, and that she
had great humility as re: her writing. (She never minded editorial correcting and was grateful for small peanuts.) Also, of
course, she was very much a poet and artist—delighting in the
beauty of simple things (i.e., candles, bread, etc.) —and doted
on children. But you know all this . . . and I never even met her.

"Blood turned to poison" was indeed suggestive of what all
her friends knew Caryll's reactions could be. She used to
make me think of Browning's lines:

> Dante who loved well because he hated,
> Hated wickedness that hinders loving.

In *The Passion of the Infant Christ* she points out the

* This is an allusion to an imaginary youth organization depicted
by Caryll in *The Dry Wood.*

devil's disadvantage in his agelong fight with Christ—*he* cannot become incarnate, *he* has no mystical body. But while he cannot take our flesh, he cannot only tempt us to "snivelling sins of the flesh," he can actually seize by possession a human individual. I have known her to declare someone possessed—and then she would suffer agonies of remorse for what she had said. It was not for her to judge. And it was herself she judged most fiercely.

Lucile had noted a gentleness in her writing, but Caryll's long candid letter goes on:

> If I appear gentle—alas, I am not: I asked my dearest friend, with whom I live—she should know—and she said "I don't think so." But *any* holding back there is at all in me is based on cowardice. I am a frightened, abject creature (a) because in youth I was broken right across (psychologically!), early and irrevocably, so started pretty well defeated; and (b) because I really am a sinner and suffer a continual guilt (remorse which measures my vanity) and fear, not alone of being seen just as I am by those I love, but even of facing myself and seeing—. So I do not dare to judge, though in private life I do even that, and am often sore and bleeding from the shame of the rash judgments I have made myself and my indiscretions regarding them.

Lucile's phrase "possibly starved for love" seems to me to go very deep. She certainly had been during much of her life. The overwhelming romantic love poured out on Sidney Reilly represented something in Caryll that she always had to take into acount. Her letters show her giving and receiving an immense amount of affection from friends both men and women—but I, at least, have the impression that Caryll would very much have liked to be married. The closest of friends cannot give what comes as the normal result, often little appreciated because so normal, of a loving husband and children. Despite her critical faculty she tended, one also sees in the letters, to overestimate what any human being can give another. Many of her friends asked more than they could offer—especially those tormented by neuroses who were seeking her help. What I have called her exorbitance was partly a pouring out of the great powers of love she had. I expect most of us disappointed her—and drove her back on God. But the coming of Clare into her life added, as Rosamond has well put it, "a new dimension," giving to her a fulfilment she could not have dreamed.

14

Caryll's Correspondence

As we have seen, it was not Caryll's books only that burdened her with the weariness of endless hours of writing. She begins one letter to a friend with almost a sigh of relief at doing something else after writing *Guilt* for eight hours on end, and she reproaches herself for weakness in not going on with the book. But often the letters themselves were the burden, for they were a response of compassion in almost every case to a real human need. Each one of them is intensely personal, dealing with the problems, sympathizing with the trials, of her correspondent. "I have been simply overwhelmed with people, always in some urgent and desperate need, and never one that can just be 'solved'—indeed what human problem ever can be?"

This realization may well have been what drew people to her, rather than to the guide with the too-ready textbook answer. That, and the rule she had set herself many years earlier and from which she never swerved—to choose always the thing to do into which she could put the most love.

Then too she approached her friends and their difficulties with reverence and a profound humility. To a young friend she writes: "I have prayed now to be allowed not to give you wrong advice, for you are much holier than I am, and certainly much wiser and more thoughtful than I was at your age, and I am not in any way qualified to guide you, so take everything I say always simply as the words of a friend, to be weighed for what they are worth and disregarded if they seem not to be helpful."

"I have so often prayed," she writes to another friend, "for you and your husband and boys, especially for little Michael, so often and in so many different places, the Hospital Ward, the Cathedral of Chartres, the London streets."

And in another letter she gives the advice, if one can find no words, just to repeat a name to God again and again, "Knowing *He* knew all that was behind that name, and keeping it, so to speak in His ears all day." Or say again and again the words "Lord, into Thy hands" and then "I confide X, or myself—and perhaps it can help to meditate on what you mean by 'into Thy hands'—hands of infinite tenderness, infinite love, absolute power. . . .

"It is amazing to think that in heaven, when everything is understood, we shall keep on saying to one another, 'How astonishing that we should ever have doubted the mercy in it all,' 'Who *on earth* would have guessed what was *really* happening?'—and so on."

To a young woman, unhappily married and feeling a divorce to be the only solution, she wrote:

Of course, you would be bound to a life of celibacy, and if you, being weak, should slip off the carpet, you ought to realize it's a sin, and one that can't be rationalized because it's good for your nerves—or so you imagine—any more than it would be *right* (and not merely nice) for a repressed old maid like myself to alternate between bouts of fervour and bouts of too much gin, to relieve nervous tension! Sometimes, in this land of heroes, the aridity both for fervour and for gin is equal! . . .

I will write to you again, a more considered letter. But don't let me lead you astray. Remember, my dear, I give advice that is rather more human and sympathetic than orthodox, and I not only temper the wind to the shorn lamb but also to the neurotic sheep, whose need seems greater. But the root reason is that I *dare* not give unctuous and rigid counsel to anyone, because I am so profoundly and always conscious of being a sinner myself, not in imagination but in reality and with a ghastly accumulation of irrefutable proof. Consequently I *dare* not say to people, "You must do this or that because it is right," knowing full well that if I were in their shoes I would do something very much *more* wrong than they would.

Now God bless you and support you, and above all deliver you from this dilemma. Tell Him He *must:* point out to Him that though you want to do His will, you are a weak human creature, and every step of the way is on sharp stones: but He is all-powerful and can do whatever He likes, with no effort at all, and so let Him help you now!

An even harder case was where human love had to be denied its expression or God's laws broken. An unknown reader of her books wrote, having struggled for long but finally given way.

Overwhelmed with compassion Caryll writes:

Have you absolutely assured yourself of the validity of your husband's former marriage? [She suggests consulting a wise and sympathetic priest and then goes on]: I can only say this; you have wrestled for a long time with an agonizing problem; you have in the course of that struggle shown your true love of God by terrible sacrifices done for Him; your husband too *tried* to do an almost superhuman thing out of love for *your* love of God, so that however sad you may feel now (in one way), you can assure yourself that those moments in which the love of God in you rose to such heroism are always present to God; He will always see you in those great moments of love for Him, and He will never allow someone who has given Him those moments of love to be lost.

I only beg of you one thing, namely, do not cease ever to trust in God's love and mercy for you. I am afraid you will not be happy, fundamentally, and I am afraid that, starved of the Sacraments as you will be, you may come upon times when you will be tempted to let the Kingdom of God slip away from you; you may even be tempted to despair one day. Well, when and if that happens, do remember that with God there is no past and future, and your moments of utter *love for Him* are always present to Him, and He will never let you perish.

No, you don't seem "dreadfully weak" to me; I only wonder how you managed to ever be so dreadfully strong—I could not have done what you did, for a week!

You are so right to go to Mass and pray, and so brave in the way you face facts and do not try to twist things, in spite of such very awful provocation, I am sure you will be given grace in abundance and the whole thing will come right.

I am bound to say that I think few things more cruel for a child than to see her parents separated; I know by experience, for mine separated when I was nine, so I am glad your little girl is spared. But I shall pray hard and often that God will help you and either remove the stumbling-block or make you saints, so that you can live together, but in abstinence. But of course I know that that is nearly impossible.

The tragedy is that sexual love is such a right and holy thing in itself, which makes it harder than ever to deny it in a case like yours.

I'm afraid this is a poor letter. I wish I had the power to counsel and comfort you well, but I can only pray for you and that I most surely will do, and do you also pray for me—and please if it is ever *any* help to you to write to me, do so. I've destroyed your letter.

To a friend in a state of profound discouragement she writes: "I am so much a sinner that I understand well how the slightest discouragement from outside oneself, added to the chronic close-on-despair inside, can crush one altogether. . . . One doesn't want a preacher, or even a shining example, but someone who will share the burden, even if they know they can't carry their own."

She felt that people far advanced in holiness sometimes seemed to fail in sympathy because they saw the future reward of suffering more clearly than the present anguish. But, too, she wanted to send her friends on beyond herself for strength and comfort:

There are few indeed who, having arrived at a really deep sense of the reality of divine things, the inner meaning of suffering and the wonder of the joy just round the corner, still realize *wholly* the misery one feels when one is far off still from such *realization,* however much one believes in it. They are so profoundly conscious of the hidden good for us that they do not always remember what it *feels* like at the stage when, though we hang on like grim death to the good, it doesn't seem worth it. We have to take the advice of priests as we take the advice of doctors when they recommend drastic and painful treatment, knowing it is the painful way followed by happy life, or compromise followed by death.

But whom, then, *can* we go to for comfort?—because we need comfort, sympathy, love, as well as wisdom and practical help and cure: in fact, we need not only help, but that someone should be as concentrated on us as we are on ourselves, supporting us, loving us, feeling deeply for us, every second of the day and night. Well, Our Lord is the only one who can answer that need. If you go often to visit the Blessed Sacrament and pray in the presence of the Blessed Sacrament, tell Our Lord in your own words, or your own tears, or your own numbness, that you can hardly suffer it. Ask Him to help you: you can be perfectly certain that He will.

She asks her friends to pray for her and for each other: "It is a most blessed thing in you," she writes, "that instead of becoming *obsessed* by your own soul as so many do, your worries are about others, and you put the beautiful holiness of charity and love before the excessive preoccupation with personal perfection. . . ."

Asked to advise those seeking psychological help and healing, she always counselled against great sweeping resolutions. One correspondent had weakened herself by refusing to eat, but was now trying to build up normal health once more. Caryll wrote:

You are simply trying to overcome your fears by doing violence to yourself and you are not strong enough to stand that violence. . . . You must start by small, gentle acts of will; nurse your will, give it small tasks but let it be set in the right direction.

Useless to say, "Now I will be perfectly normal and fit and I will want to be." But useful and creative to say, "I will drink this glass of milk, and so be a tiny bit stronger this morning."

Very *gradually* you will build up enough strength of mind and body by these *little* acts of will to *really* want to get well. But it *must* be gradual. . . .

Let every meal be a prayer, every hour of sleep, every denial of an impulse to overdo things you feel a compulsion to—and believe me you will at one and the same time cure yourself, and cure the suffering of the world.

You see, *God's* Will for you is to serve Him, in His way, as He chooses *now*. It is only a want of humility to think of extreme vocations, like being a nun or a nurse, while you try to by-pass your present obvious vocation. . . . *Today* you have to use what you have today, and do not look beyond it. You have your suffering of mind and body, you have that hardest of all things, the building up of your will by doing what you don't, and at present *can't*, feel you want to.

She realizes that an earnest spiritual life can well coexist with neuroses, the desire for perfection may be genuine, however misdirected:

I believe the only solution is to concentrate absolutely on God, especially on Christ in your soul—not even looking to see how *you* are getting on, only looking to see if He is getting stronger in you. I learnt a lot in that way from Clare. If you

concentrate on the spark of Christ-life in your soul—the Infant
Christ in you—as one has to concentrate on keeping the little
flame of life burning in a frail little infant—I think you would
find that day after day *everything* is given to Christ quite naturally and easily, and you hardly noticing it.

One of the reasons for looking away from self, for avoid-
ing preoccupation with our own perfection, is that *we* do
not know wherein that lies: "I often think that the ideal of
our perfection that we set up, and often go through torture to
achieve, may not be God's idea of how He wants us to be at
all. That may be something quite different that we never
would have thought of, and what seems like a failure to us
may really be something bringing us closer to His will for us."
We should "keep making short little interior acts of love,
asking God to fashion us in His own design; then He
certainly will, and sooner or later we certainly will be just
what He wants us to be. . . . But I can only tell you my own
way, yours may be different, and if it is, it is certainly the best
way for you."

To a still more intimate friend she explains her "own way"
more fully:

The only resolution I have ever found works, is "Whenever
I want to think of myself, I will think of God . . . just some
short, sharp answer, so to speak, to my thought of self, in God.
For example:
"I am lonely, misunderstood, etc."
"The loneliness of Christ, at His trial; the misunderstanding
even of His closest friends."
Or:
"I have made a fool of myself."
"Christ was mocked—He felt it; He put the mocking *first* in
foretelling His Passion—'The Son of Man shall be mocked,'
etc.—made a fool of before all He loved."
Or:
"I can't go on unhelped."

"Christ couldn't. He couldn't carry the cross without help; He was grateful for human sympathy. . . ."

Other examples as they suggest themselves—just pictures that flash through the mind. This practice becomes a habit, and it is the habit which has saved me from despair.

From another letter we learn how early she had begun this practice:

. . . I realized when I got your first letter and its enclosures that your friend is in a very pitiable state of mind. If one could get such people to put into practice a simple rule which I invented for myself at school to attempt to cure my own awful self-obsession, they might be, if not wholly cured of the misery of self-pity, at least cured sufficiently to have *some* times of happiness in their lives. The rule is just this: "To think of God every time I want to think of myself."

Of course, I have never for a single day achieved this perfectly; usually there are hundreds of failures daily, but even when "self-think-on" takes the form of the humiliation and remorse that follows on our failures and sins, there is more comfort in thinking of God's love and forgiveness—how good *He* is—than in dwelling on the hurt vanity and misery of what one is like oneself. The mere effort to think of a suitable thought about God to counteract the one about self, helps to break through the self-obsession. One even becomes *interested* in God. . . .

For all Christians there is, as members of His Mystical Body, the one general vocation of being Christ in the world. In regard to special forms this vocation may take, Caryll writes:

If, apart from this work of *being Christ* in your own world, you have in fact some specific vocation, to do some particular thing for Him, this will, in His own time, be made known to you, either by an irresistible inner compulsion or else by so obvious a chain of circumstances that they *can* only be regarded as a finger pointing clearly in one direction. Even one's psychological difficulties and deficiencies of personality are, as soon as one's will is wholly abandoned to God (and He has always known if at a certain point it *will* be), means of almost compelling one to walk in one's true vocation. Most so-called nervous breakdowns are only the collapses of a personality trying to be other than that which they must be to fulfil God's plan for them. A real contemplative breaks down if they try to excel in action, and one intended for an active vocation breaks down if they attempt to be a pure contemplative, and in both cases, the certain cure is to see God's guiding finger and walk wholeheartedly in the way it points.

"Perhaps God is shaping the child," she wrote to an anxious mother, "for the work *He* wants her to do, and when she is ready for it, He will show her clearly what it is. All my life I have had the greatest belief in the saying (I think of Walt Whitman?), 'When the builders are ready the architect will be at hand.' "

Young people have vast ambitions, and the commonest feeling of the neurotic is that of frustration: what could he not have done if life had been kinder, people more understanding? But Caryll points out that even Our Lord Himself, who was God, had allowed Himself to be, in His human nature, limited and frustrated.

No doubt, one who loved men as He did would have longed to heal *all* their sicknesses, to enlighten *all* their minds, to transform the world by miracle upon miracle of love, but God did not will that for Him. On the contrary, He willed that He should be, humanly speaking, a failure, should be nailed to the cross and suffer there in helplessness. Indeed, the moment when His love was consummated, in which the crisis of His redeeming power was reached, was when the hands that could heal with a touch were nailed back out of reach!

"I was—yes—*compelled,* as by my angel," she writes to one in great anxiety, "to pray for you and your family almost all the time . . . your name was woven all through the Midnight Mass like a litany."

And, to the same: "Sometimes I wonder how on earth you can endure all that you have to. You must be redeeming half the sins of the world."

"Don't forget you are carrying Christ's cross, and never, never forget how *slowly Christ* had to go up the hill carrying His cross."

They could not but realize, each one of them, that Caryll in spirit carried each one's cross, suffered with each, prayed always for each of her friends unceasingly. She had first learnt in her French convent to "offer up" this or that action, self-denial or suffering—an idea only comprehensible in the light of the doctrine that we are all members of the living Christ. Caryll tended to see the doctrine of Christ's Mystical Body not only in relation to the world's redemption but in terms of Our Lord's whole human life. He had healed, consoled and taught through His human nature as well as dying on the cross in it. Now He will, if we choose, heal, console, teach through us who, as His Mystical Body, still do His human work on earth.

"Because you do really love God," she writes to one friend, "your suffering, bitter though it is, is healing the world's sorrow. Don't think of it in terms of what is unbearable to you, but when a specially bad hour ends, even in sheer weariness, think, 'That is a drink of water to someone dying of thirst,' or, 'That is a bar of chocolate for a hungry child.' It's mysterious, but true."

Excusing herself for delay in writing to one correspondent, Caryll mentions a few of the letters which "it seems a real sin against charity and, what matters more, plainly inhuman" not to answer. An enclosed nun psychologically ill and allowed to explain her trouble to Caryll only. Someone she

had never met, who knew no Catholics and whose approach
to the Church had resulted in ostracism on the part of an
entire family, hitherto most devoted; none of them had
spoken to her for a month. A kind-hearted friend who had
run over and killed a child and felt himself going out of his
mind with remorse over the accident. Another friend, her
soldier husband's leave indefinitely cancelled, coping with
her own and her baby's influenza, burst pipes and a flooded
flat, "suffering utter loneliness and depression." A friend
whose sister in a sanatorium was dying of TB, and an Irish
priest far advanced in the same disease "from whom I have
now three very pathetic letters." A young friend off on her
"honeymoon" with another friend's husband.

Running in and out of all these letters are plaints about
the perpetual problem of time. Lucile Hasley, among the
series of questions through which they were to become better
acquainted, had asked Caryll how she dealt with correspondence. She replied:

Well, it simply defeats me. I get letters from America, Canada,
Australia, India, Africa, Holland, Germany, France, Switzerland,
Hungary, Portugal, Spain—mostly from people in real trouble of
soul or body. Sheer fan mail I seldom answer, though I feel
guilty, for I am really grateful to those who are kind enough to
write it. But I try to answer the people who really do want
help—and I just am never through. I have reduced myself to
four hours' sleep in twenty-four, and still it is never done. To
add to this dilemma, I work (under doctors) for neurotic and
borderline people and in a mental hospital, and they, each one
of them, expect my whole attention: they too write letters almost daily, and are fearfully offended if they are not answered. . . .

By the bye, there was one more question you wanted a reply
to: how I earn my living—just writing. The other things mentioned are all unpaid. I have had to give up all other paid
jobs, except writing, so as to have time to do it in, and it's now

harder than ever to get the time! I have done lots of other jobs, but I don't now—excepting (also not for pay now, though I used to do it for my living) wood-carving. I only want to carve crucifixes, and now and again a statue of Our Lady or a saint— but it's hard to find time, though there is no work on earth which in my mind is more soothing and healing than carving wood.

The catalogue of people to be written to ended with three priests, "who probably," Caryll wryly comments, "won't get written to at all."

The measure of the need determined the order of writing —and its amount: some of the letters are of a colossal length. But the proportion of clergy in this list points up something we all realized—very many priests felt the value, as did so many doctors, of her help in curing and healing.

An odd little incident occurred one day when Caryll herself was in one of her not infrequent states of exhaustion and depression. In the confessional the priest said to her, "What will help you will be a book by Caryll Houselander called *This War is the Passion*. You probably won't understand all of it, but read such-and-such pages."

"What did you do?" my husband asked her.

"Read them, of course," she answered. "I always do what I'm told in confession."

She took her weekly confession very seriously and found it sometimes very hard. As we saw, she had as a child suffered terribly from scruples—and she said later that all the severe pain of soul and body that she had suffered in her subsequent life did not equal the misery of the psychological illness of her childhood. To a convert friend whom she had sent to a priest she wrote:

I only hope you will go on seeing him, as I *know* he has a real gift for psychological healing—just knowing him and seeing him, really *very* seldom, has done wonders for me myself.

Funny he offered you "Hope" as a working idea, because only
about a week ago, as the result of a real act of contrition, I
suddenly realized what hope is, and that I had *never* known before. I had always acted and reacted as if Faith could do
everything and all my sins would just vanish in due course if
I prayed and took practical steps to avoid the occasions of sin,
and I was very discouraged to find that on the contrary they always got worse! Then, like a flash of light, I realized that *Hope*
is a sort of splint on my broken spiritual limbs, which can keep
me going and reasonably happy—also more humble—all the
time—and it really has been my great support ever since.

I think you will only do yourself good by confiding in Fr. X.:
he is a real "other Christ."

But invaluable as spiritual advice could be, she observes
to another convert—from High Anglicanism—that she will
find a difference between the Catholic and the Anglican idea
of confession. She had, as an Anglican, "usually perhaps
without realizing it, used it more from the point of view of
personal relief and spiritual direction, than from the point
of view which is the really sacramental one, direct contact
with Christ."

Confession was a great trial and effort to two sorts of
people who loomed large among Caryll's friends—converts
and neurotics, so she gave a good deal of advice on the subject. The book she begged them all to read was Fr. Alfred
Wilson's *Pardon and Peace*. Very often, on this subject, as
on many others, she is sweeping away rubbish that had
gathered in a certain type of spiritual reading and making
the Church's ancient path more visible. She reminds her
correspondents that only mortal sin need be confessed. In
these letters she is dealing with venial sin and the dread afflic-
tion of scruples. To a friend tormented by scruples she advised: "Go to Communion even when you think you're in
mortal sin—because you won't be." She lists the conditions
that make a sin mortal: such sins are not easily forgotten. All

the same, "Do not," she advises, *"try not to feel guilty.*
Accept the feeling of guilt as just and offer it in reparation for
all sin." But let the examination of conscience be brief, only
two minutes.

Confess *only* what comes to mind in that two minutes.
Never repeat or go back upon a confession . . . Once you've
made the confession—finis—ahead, closer love of God—all the
rest *behind* you. Don't turn back from God to sort out an
abandoned dung heap. . . .
Remember Confession, like Communion, is *first of all* a contact, a loving embrace with Our Lord. All He asks is that you
should want to be sorry, because you want to come back closer
than ever to Him. It does not depend on an exact recitation of
sins but a loving will to come closer to Him.

To another friend she said, "Try to think of Him as a
child. You couldn't be afraid of a child."
God does not want to "trip us up . . . rubbing His hands
and saying, 'Ha ha she forgot something! I'll jump on her for
that.'" Trying to magnify imperfections

to be on the safe side . . . would blind you to God's loving
desire to forgive you and take you close to His heart. Only one
thing makes you safe, putting your trust in God.
But the devil loves to distract from God's love and mercy
by worry about sin. The only cure for this worry is to concentrate not on self-perfection but on the love and tenderness of
God. The best prayer is the *Veni Creator.* . . .

The advice of the eyes fixed on God she gave constantly:

The devil knows that the soul whose heart is fixed on God
is lost to hell, so he must drag the gaze back from God to
self. . . . Even ignore your own soul: Keep your mind on God,
on His love. For prayer imagine (only it is not imagining, but

true) that at every second of the day about four Masses are being said, and that you, your life, yourself as you are, now in this second, are your offering for the Mass, and offer yourself as you are in union with Our Lord's offering at Mass.

No need to wait for the chance of quiet or solitude to do a more prayer-ful act. Give all this busy life to God in the Mass:

the act of taking So-and-so's temperature—all—just as it is, to God. Leave it to God to transform all this into Himself. . . . It's all you've got, and He gave it to you. We are like children whose father has given them a sixpence to buy a birthday present for himself. The father knows the child can't bring him a present costing a pound: he can only give back what he has been given and whatever little scruffy object he produces; the father loves it, for it is his child's offering of all he *can* offer—and that is only his own gift back again, but back again made more lovable to him by an exchange of their love.

An idea that appealed immensely to Caryll she used when counselling a friend approaching the Church and finding what seemed insuperable difficulties in the way. Caryll writes with deep sympathy for those left behind who cannot see the reason for the step. She strongly urges that prayer be continued steadily. The danger of this friend, on the verge of conversion, was to feel that she could no longer pray in Anglican churches; still she had not yet, partly because of family problems, begun to go to Mass. She had, Caryll reminds her, received grace, through many a spiritual communion in the Church of England; let her continue to make them. "If you stop praying between the two Churches, so to speak, then indeed you will flounder—and the bewildering temptation to do so is very real. . . .

"If you can, you will find it a great help to go to Mass, making your spiritual Communion there." Soon anyhow she will be obliged to go, and it might be as well to begin going at the same time that she makes the announcement of intending to join the Church—"the one bout of anger covers that too!—rather like when a convicted burglar owns up to a dozen or so other burglaries, in order that one sentence may cover them all!"

Her friend felt she still lacked the courage and grace to go on—and this brings us to a view on which Caryll always acted—for instance, years ago starting the Sprats and since then constantly in matters more purely spiritual.

You have prayed [she said] and have not yet, as you think, had the complete answer. This is usually because you have not given Our Lord something He asks for in order to answer you. For example, when He worked miracles, He asked for some trifle, which one would suppose useless, as for example the loaves and fishes for the feeding of five thousand. And again, for the Mass, He asks the offering of the simple substance of bread and wine for the miracle of the Consecration. You say, "He hasn't worked the miracle," "He hasn't given me the courage I need." Well, the answer usually is: "You have not given Him anything to work the miracle with. Of course, He *can* do some miracles without, but usually He asks us to give something, and if the miracle you ask is personal transubstantiation—that *you* may be changed into Him—then clearly, unless you offer *yourself*, all of yourself, He can't do it—for what has He got to change?

Perhaps this slight glance at a struggling soul striving to help others may best be ended with some scattered thoughts about prayer.

As First Aid for all kinds of fear and anxiety I can recommend ejaculations. Just say again and again, "Sacred Heart of Jesus, I put *all* my trust in you"—and mean it, put Our Lord on His honour. It is quite marvellous how this carries one through. Our Lord likes to be told that you trust Him, and will *not* fail you.

[In anxiety and temptation] Drown the devil's voice with the name of Jesus: even when people are talking to you, say it inwardly again and again, until you seem to be breathing it. Don't trust your thoughts of Him: trust Him.

Another thing that is very healing and lovely in practice is to just say the name of Jesus, or God, inwardly with each breath you draw in when going off to sleep. You can't realize what peace this brings until you have tried and persevered in it for a time. If you get the habit, the result is wonderful.

During a time of acute anxiety, "I finally decided that I must give up stating the case in my prayers, and telling God what I thought He ought to do, and instead just kneel down before God, and put [it] before Him simply by saying [a] name."

In another letter she adds:

. . . like the old peasant who had a bad foot, but since he did not know which was best for him, to be cured, to be lame, to be in pain or out of pain, he just went to church and said, "Lord —foot."

When one becomes overwhelmed by one's personal troubles, plus weariness, probably plus the loneliness of having no one near at hand to whom one can talk, and who will understand if one does, it becomes very difficult indeed to say or to mean "one's own" prayers; but in the psalms one does find every possible human experience, and even to read them seems to be putting oneself in touch with someone who has experienced *all* our own feelings.

Prayer *should* be a deep inner rest, something which calms you and increases your *trust* (the more it *does* increase your trust, the more it gives you inner peace and rest).

In a busy and harassed life, this *could* not be the result of prayer, if the most important thing were how many words you can get said in a day! Lots of deeply holy and prayerful people *can't* say *one,* even at Mass. Prayer, as the Catechism tells us, is "raising the heart and mind to God"—there need be no words, but only an inexpressible adherence to God, an attitude of mind and heart, a simple wordless desire to be one with Him. This makes it inevitable that one recognizes His Will for one at the moment in every circumstance, and knows that every act, however trivial, done in this spirit, is done for His glory and *is* prayer.

Personally I find the best way is that used by the Russian starets (holy man) and also by St. Ignatius, simply saying (not necessarily with the lips) the name of Jesus, or the word God, as often as you can, until it is woven all through the day, and this prayer can be further simplified by simply *breathing* it (the name of Jesus, or God, or whatever you like)—that is, "saying" or "thinking" it in your mind with every breath you draw in.

Much of Caryll's vast correspondence has, alas, been lost or destroyed. The letters her friends have entrusted to me, for there are still many hundreds, have helped greatly to the writing of her biography. They have done something else which makes me hope one day to publish a selection from them—they have explained more than anything else could what one friend meant when he called her circle *Caryllinati.* It will be remembered that St. Catherine of Siena's followers were called *Caterinati*—with the suggestion that they were half bewitched by this strange woman. Their answer was that she did indeed bewitch them with a supernatural witchery, throwing God's spell over their lives.

15

Guilt

I HAD THE GREAT good fortune of a short talk with Dr. Strauss about Caryll just before he died. He was in the hospital, and what struck one instantly was at once the beauty, the peace and the suffering exhaustion of his face. I hardly liked to weary him, but he instantly spoke with deep affection of "that divine eccentric."

"Don't you think," he asked me, "she had mystical experience?"

We went on to talk of all that was unusual in her insights and perceptions even outside the religious sphere, and we discussed a little the immense question of the relation between religious vision and *psi*—and of the "borderline," as he called it, between the two. He had noted, as I had, how "matter of fact" was Caryll's attitude about her experiences. He commented on her appearance: "she looked like a ghost"; on her asceticism: "she didn't eat enough to keep a bird alive"; on her great insight into people and on that quality in her which made her, as he put it, "not vulnerable to the world."

I asked him about the work Caryll had done for him. He had been so delighted with her treatment of the boys that he began immediately after the war to send her adult patients "for social therapy."

"Had she any training?" I asked.

"No," he said, "it was just natural genius."

"Forgive my dense ignorance," I said, "but what exactly is 'social therapy'?"

"With Caryll," he answered, "it meant that she loved them back to life."

Another doctor, a woman and a great friend of my own, also asked her to help with patients whose troubles were mental as well as physical. There was one she told me about —a girl whom Caryll gradually coaxed into leaving the house where she had imprisoned herself and resuming normal life. Caryll felt keenly, and repeatedly told her friends and her patients, that they and she alike must rely on prayer. To one she writes:

I do feel very deeply for you. It certainly seems that prayer is the only help—that and taking each trial separately, trying not to look miles ahead with the overwhelming picture of years of succeeding crises to weigh you down. Prayer does bring such amazing answers that it is reasonable to hope that every separate crisis may be the last and happiness may come very suddenly, when you least expect it.

. . . Do you find help from the rosary? I find just holding on to it, even, helps. Of course, some say that is mere superstition, but it isn't if it symbolizes holding on to God, as it does for me. I have been visiting a girl once a week for a doctor: the girl was a baffling nerve case. She used to have about three attacks a day resembling acute attacks of St. Vitus' dance, and followed by palpitations of so violent a nature that the doctors marvelled that her heart could stand up to it. . . . She had been previously two years in hospital and has seen every specialist, but no one could diagnose her case and she just went on getting worse. She had no religion, and her only reaction to God—a very vague idea to her—was fear and aversion.

I gave her a rosary and told her to try to say *something* with it in her hand—her own prayer—or say nothing, but *mean* to hold on to God. From the hour she took the rosary into her hand she has been better, and is now almost cured. . . . I do not attribute this cure wholly to the rosary—at least, not directly, as the doctor tried a new cure, based on a guess of her own and as a desperate chance, and I think she had found the right clue; but I think her finding it is all part of the answer to the girl's first prayer with the rosary. . . . Her mind has flowered too, literally changed from a narrow, self-obsessed mind to a big, objective, clever and loving one.

The doctor herself attributed much of the cure to Caryll's own powers—and to her steady, patient visits. Helping to release a person imprisoned in a shell of misery that could be broken: this Caryll felt was worth all the blood, sweat and tears that she could give. It was worth anything except the abandonment of her writing, because this might have an abiding result long after she and her patients were dead— and also because once she gave it up she too would sink into the morass of nerves, anxieties, scruples that spelt neurosis. Of this danger she was always keenly aware. Never has any spiritual adviser more sincerely said, more profoundly felt, a oneness with those she was advising.

Caryll had made the important discovery that because we are all sinners the gulf between the technically well-balanced and the neurotic is less wide than is often assumed. "In neurotic and even psychotic states," she wrote in *Guilt*, "we see the people called normal, including ourselves, under the magnifying glass." We all suffer at times from anxiety and fear—*unreasonable* anxieties, unfounded fears. We all meet on the ground of a weakness that only some have realized. No man is strong unless he is rooted and founded in God: Caryll met her patients as fellow-sinners as well as fellow-neurotics, but always with an invincible confidence that God had chosen the weak things of the world to confound the strong.

Writing to the mother of a neurotic daughter, she says:

"Give [her] my love and remind her that this poor sinner on earth (shaking with nerves and depression) is praying for her—but not alone, in the company of all the angels and saints and the Holy Souls, all the multitude who are surrounding her with their Christ-love.

"It is always such a relief to me to hand over my aching conscience to *them* when I say the Confiteor."

And to the same correspondent: "I always ask my angel to speak to the guardian angels of the people I want to reach quickly."

For this friend Caryll had another day felt "compelled to pray," and again and again in the lengthy correspondences that have been sent to me (this one alone totals 244 pages of typescript) she speaks of praying for the family, anxieties, difficulties of each one. "She focussed her whole mind," says Dickie Orpen, "on each of her friends."

It was largely, I believe, Caryll's sense of guilt and the psychological breaking in her youth that gave her such power to help others.

Of recent years we have learnt that there are fields in which none can help unless first they have needed help. Alcoholics Anonymous have more cures to their credit than all the rescuers who tried to rescue from outside. Divorcees Anonymous have prevented divorces when the wisest marriage counsellors could not. The best swimmer cannot rescue the drowning man unless he is in the water with him. He may be pulled under, he is taking a risk, but he must be there.

A home for neurotics well known to Caryll and constantly recommended by her works on this principle: all but one of the staff came there first as patients. From the depth of their own experience they can reach the troubled mind. A wise old priest who was their chaplain said once, talking of the marvellous success of their work, "They must have been themselves wounded before they can heal others. It's perilous but it's essential."

The fact was—and increasingly *is*—that the multitude of borderline cases was enormous for whom there was no place —not cases for shock treatment, not certainly for certification, yet needing the sort of care this Home could give only to a handful. I once asked one of the nurses what was her principal work, and she answered, "Listening." And Caryll said once she would like to open an office in London where people could come solely to pour out their troubles. "If there were more good listeners," she said, "there would not be nearly so many neurotics."

But she realized the danger. Introducing a patient of hers to a priest she greatly admired, she wrote cautioning her about not broadcasting his name without good cause: "I know how terrible it is for anyone who becomes a legend . . . if they are so pitiless as they are to me, who have neither his life-giving power as a priest, nor his wisdom as a man, and can really do nothing for them—what hope would he have of survival if his fame as what he is spreads?—and of course it will."

Caryll was writing *Guilt,* in which she powerfully diagnoses the ego-neurosis which may end up in real mental disease or may be cured by the sufferer himself if guidance be given him. And meanwhile she too was listening, to speech and to letters, an amazing number of which she answered. A refugee whom she befriended and who often visited her remembers her "writing, writing, writing."

Caryll did have something which her priest friend probably had not—the wounds of her own past. And she was willing to show them. Indeed she would often say almost eagerly that they had never been healed—that she was *still* a neurotic. Had she to write to anyone with an anxiety neurosis or a fear neurosis, she would explain her understanding of what they felt because she too had felt it, could feel it still.

Sometimes I am frankly puzzled by all this—was she to some extent Chesterton's Father Brown who could put himself in the shoes of the sinner, Chesterton's Gabriel Gale who understood lunatics because he felt he might have been one—or indeed Chesterton himself in his boyhood who could imagine committing the wildest, when he never had committed the mildest, crime? There is no question that Caryll's imaginative sympathy had a very wide sweep, and I would not put it past her to have thought herself inextricably into someone else's problems. But at lowest she must be taken as a witness in any examination of her case.

How seriously should one take her oft-repeated assertion that she understood neurotics not merely because she once had been one but because she still was one? There did certainly seem in her feeling about parties the living remains of an old neurosis, but when she talked of her profound understanding of other forms of this disease, of fear neuroses and starvation neuroses, I confess to having felt a little sceptical.

On the chief bit of evidence she produced I knew something of her physical experiences. Iris says that by and large, when she was catering for them both, Caryll ate normally. Dickie remembers her in the Milborne Grove days carrying home newly baked rolls for breakfast and eating them with enjoyment. But food never meant very much to her: during the war she had given away most of her rations, and when she had her own flat she cooked only for visitors and ate less and less. But there was something else. At what point exactly I don't know, but at some time a little before the war Caryll quite suddenly stopped smoking which, cut down after her conversion, had gradually become again an overpowering habit. She smoked as she worked, she smoked from morning to night, she woke in the night and smoked.

Giving up smoking and cutting down on food may well have both been elements in a fresh outbreak of asceticism on Caryll's part—and eating very little for a long time does really mean that you come to be unable to eat normally.

One must listen to Caryll's own evidence in this matter,

but also weigh it with that of others. When she said she *could* only write when she was hungry, was this unconscious (or even conscious) camouflage or was it really the expression of a compulsion?

I was sorry I had not asked Dr. Strauss what he thought about it, but I did ask her own physician, Dr. Heyman at Nell Gwynn, first why he thought she ate so little and next whether he thought she was a neurotic. She was not, he said, "interested in food. She would peck at it if you put it before her, otherwise she would forget it."

Neurotic, he said, was the last word he would use about Caryll. "She was hypersensitive, and had a great flair for helping and understanding people through her sensitiveness." He thought her "fey" but remarkably well-balanced.

Anyone with Celtic blood knows something of what "fey" may mean—and how it can coexist with the hardest-headed sanity. But the sanest mind may reel when subjected to the continual pressure of surrounding unbalance. Anyone dealing constantly with neurotics and psychotics has occasional doubts of his own sanity—and will occasionally react with some form of violence. Caryll was unvaryingly gentle *with* her patients, and if Dr. Heyman is right she saved herself on the steep slope, maintaining an always slightly precarious balance, by an occasional vehemence of speech about them that masked her fundamental charity and was largely a nervous reaction against neurosis.

"She would help people," he went on, "in the most unassuming ways, so that they often did not realize she had done them a favour. They began by being slightly amused, gradually grew fond of her, and ended with deep admiration for her great nobility of character."

Whatever was happening inside her, Caryll displayed an iron strength of will, working with a sick and feeble body longer hours than a strong man finds possible, keeping afloat somehow in the flood of suffering humanity that surged around her. She attributed this wholly to letting herself go—as the swimmer abandoning himself to the water floats while he who struggles drowns, so she abandoned herself to the ocean of God's love and was upheld thereby.

The siege of the flat went on, and the door was barred occasionally against gossips and time-wasters. (It always amuses me to remember one of these, a religious, who had, we surmised, worn his brethren to the point where they fled from the sound of him.) With real neurotics Caryll was endlessly patient. "Remember," she wrote to the relative of one who was by her vagaries reducing her family to despair, "neurotics are the salt of the earth."

People finding their way into the Church, people half out of it, the unhappily married, parents with problem children, children with problem parents, neurotics who recognized their state, neurotics trying to evade it; finally, lunatics at St. Bernard's Hospital, better know as Hanwell, where Caryll records an early visit as one of the great experiences of her life:

I had an incredible day at the Lunatic Asylum yesterday. Met several Queens—Female ones—one the "Queen of the Whole Earth" whose hand I was allowed to kiss and who conferred many titles upon me! Half, more than half, the lunatics are practically sane, except on one point, and some even go out to work every day. I've seldom—if ever—been present at anything so moving as the prayers in the tiny Catholic chapel in the evening, organized entirely by the patients, the prayers of their own choosing and said aloud; and what a mystery and what an example—an ex-Trappist monk, a young girl, an old lady bent double nearly, but in spite of it and of being insane, beautiful, and a handful of others, all people who had started out in life intent on a high vocation, and given it indeed utter abnegation, put away in a lunatic asylum. And this is the point—*they* reached out in their prayers to the whole world. As I knelt among them listening at first and in the end joining in unconsciously with them, I grew more and more amazed at their petitions:

> "For Russia"
> "For the suffering people of Europe"
> "For the starving people of India"
> "For the sick"
> "For prisoners"
> "For the conversion of the world"
> "For purity of heart in the world"
> "For purity of heart here."

And then, to me the most moving petition of all, "That we here in this little chapel dedicated to Your Divine Heart may have perfect abandonment to Your dear Will."

Think of *my* grumbling petitions!

After all the petitions and many more, there followed interminable litanies, and I must say I began to get a bit anxious because it seemed the prayers were going on for ever; I began to wonder if I was once more taken in, and it was but another form of obsession! But no, it was simply an almost unbelievable showing of the heart of the Mystical Body of Christ literally bleeding before God with the wounds of the world!

And all round this kind of buried little chapel (it seemed to be the catacombs, it was in the basement) —the world of the lunatic asylum was a visible close-up of what *is* happening in the world, but with all the masks and bandages off. A lunatic, one of the "displaced people," raving without cease; another (this made my blood run cold!), a martyred mother raving about her daughter in a padded cell. As to those who find immorality necessary to rid themselves of their biological inhibitions, I would advise them *not* to read books for sensitive neuropaths, but just to call at the asylum and see just what depravity looks like and feels like, face to face, when the guilt feeling has finally been liquidated!

I could go on for hours—but I must not, but it has opened

my eyes to the very heart—almost to the answer—of the problem of evil—as to the matrons and nurses—well, you just see
Christ on earth!

If you want to go there I will take you one day—I shall go
there pretty often.

Miss Gunn, who was then Matron of St. Bernard's, recognized as Dr. Strauss had done Caryll's insight and power to
help patients. She remembers this first visit vividly, and many
subsequent ones. There were two Queens, she says, the
Queen of the World being a very domineering character.
Caryll genuflected to her beautifully and kissed her hand,
but was received with the utmost haughtiness. The other,
lesser Queen went through the ceremonial with the utmost
graciousness, and then suddenly, as though a ray of reality
touched her, she said to Caryll, "It's very kind of you, my
dear."

A puerperal case had just come in, utterly distraught and
violent. She was in a padded room and Caryll went in quite
unafraid and knelt beside her. She said, "What a lovely
comfortable padded room you have. And it's nearly as large
as mine."

For quite a while Caryll kept her tranquil. Then she broke
out again. When Caryll next visited the hospital the patient
was drugged and had made up her face. Caryll did not recognize her—but she instantly knew Caryll, and after her dis-
charge she corresponded with her. Miss Gunn too began to
use her for social therapy—and especially for carrying on
the correspondence so often helpful to ex-patients. "She had
a quality of persistence in replying to letters," Miss Gunn
says. "One patient wrote her more than sixty pages at a sitting. She replied—as always." Experience at St. Bernard was
wide and varied. Caryll saw shock treatment there—and it
horrified her. "In those days," says Miss Gunn, "it looked

exactly like an epileptic fit. Today it's gentler, more like a tremor."

Caryll also attended a ball at the hospital. "One man fell in love with her and danced with her all the evening. She was exhausted. It was surprising how well she danced."

I don't know whether this was the patient described to me by Caryll who was certified after he had coshed several old ladies and who told her he had learnt from the life of the Little Flower how you could sanctify indifferent actions "such as swinging a stick" by offering them up!

Caryll often gave one comic sketches from the hospital, but laughter and tears were close together and she never ceased to feel the tragedies she was witnessing. "You met very interesting people," Miss Gunn says of the hospital, "much more than if they had an arm or a leg off."

Caryll would certainly have agreed. Miss Gunn believes that, valuable as her services were to some of the patients, her primary aim was to try to learn more. She had something very important to say, she wanted more and more evidence of the validity of her theories. Perhaps it was lucky that Caryll's writing *was* her livelihood as well as her life, or it might well have been stifled under the pile of work for the lame, the halt, the spiritually blind, to say nothing of those possessed.

Into *Guilt,* the most important of her books, was pouring all the experience she was gaining, much of which is reflected in her letters, all her own profoundest meditations and the fruit of fairly wide reading.

Although Monsignor Knox's "fan letter" to Caryll has, alas, disappeared, she told my husband the chief thing in it. He wanted her, he said, to open a school of spirituality for those who write spiritual books. Had she done so she might very well have begun it from her experiences at Hanwell, and the incredible revelation of that underground chapel. For the very heart of what she had to teach was revealed there—we must indeed try to help the lunatic and the neurotic towards a cure, but we need not wait for that cure for them to become living and active members of Christ's Mystical Body. Just as one immobilized on a bed of sickness can offer his illness itself as both prayer and heavy penance, *so can the mentally sick.* They may be far closer to God than the mentally healthy, their prayers can not only stretch but *reach* to the ends of the earth. And, as she has indicated, she saw in the asylum a smaller world but one in which good and evil stood out startlingly under the magnifying glass of mental derangement.

I despair of cataloguing in a few pages all the mental and spiritual treasure to be found in this, Caryll's richest book, but I shall try to indicate a little of its profusion, for it has been for me the school desired by Monsignor Knox. Little as I should ever dare to write directly spiritual books, I have learnt from it a little understanding of that integrity which sainthood only can bring, and of how sinner and neurotic alike can search for and find the road towards it.

Nobody would deny the almost universal *feeling* of guilt even if they deny the fact of sin and call the feeling neurosis —fancying that a psychiatrist can rid them of it "as a dentist might extract an aching tooth." In fact, guilt is no unreality: each one of us has sinned, and the neurosis usually lies in a "searching of conscience to find not what *is* there but what is not." Our real sins we fear to look at, and there often results the strange phenomenon of "a man whose self-love compels him to love a self that is not real." Thankful to grasp at the idea that his sense of guilt is mere morbidity, "he prefers to shrink to the limitations and spiritual frustrations offered by Freud, for they offer him an escape from being guilty; in fact they even offer him an escape from the responsibility of being human, for a soulless man is not a human being. . . .

"From ceasing to know what he is *like* man has ceased to know what he is."

He had before Freud came along cut out from religion the confessional which taught him to face sin, an infallible moral teaching which taught him what sin was and "the sweet and terrible mercy of purifying fire" that is called Purgatory. He learnt instead in many sects to project his feeling of real guilt onto pleasure instead of sin, a game of cards on Sunday, dancing, reading fiction, going to the theatre, "everything that is either gay or beautiful, especially that quality which has the lovely little lilting name 'levity.' " In this unreality "religion blossomed in the peace that this world gives," and man's "vague uneasiness about God" was overshadowed by the distorted ideas of Him "indelibly impressed on nearly everyone by the escapist religions—the sentimental, sweet God who would surely not have created the tiger, and the dour, vengeful God who would surely not have created the sparrows."

The sense of guilt is there whether you have any or no religion, and men will try every mechanism of escape, from fastening on what is not instead of what is wrong in themselves to projecting onto others their own evil side, which meanwhile "waxes stronger and stronger out of sight. The beast is preparing for the battle in secret."

"We are safe only when we are consciously at war within ourselves."

Hitler, in the opinion of the great psychologist Jung, "was the most prodigious personification of all human inferiorities. . . . He represented the shadow, the inferior part of everybody's personality, in an overwhelming degree." And Caryll strikes the note of warning that she would reiterate again at the end of the book: the war criminals were, "with very few exceptions, sane, normal people, people like you and me."

This remark helps to explain something that distressed many of Caryll's admirers—I think because they did not understand what she was driving at.

It is certainly surprising to come suddenly on a portrait of
Peter Kurten, the multiple murderer, in the very middle of
the chapter called "Christ and Guilt," at a point where he has
no possible relevance. The printer or binder may be responsible for this kind of thing, but it added further bewilderment to those puzzled by the collection of "Illustrations" at
the end of the book which was obviously intended by Caryll
herself to be arranged just as it was, i.e. with saints, criminals
and degenerates all cheek by jowl.

Why did she do this?

She had at first intended to make an appendix of these
studies, but both my husband and I found them so interesting that we advised making them into a section of the book
itself. But it would probably have been wiser if she had introduced them with rather more explanation.

Irma Grese and Thérèse Martin were both timid, gentle
little girls: the one turned into a monster of cruelty, the
other into a great saint. Arthur Rimbaud and Benedict
Joseph Labre were both of them dirty and ragged: apparently
equally by their own choice—but one was a degenerate, the
other a lover of God and man embracing a strange and painful vocation. The stuff of human nature may be the very
same in two people—but given into God's hands by one to
be shaped into sanctity—and handed over to the devil by
the other.

These cases were suggestive rather than fully analysed—
but Caryll, wanting to startle the complacent, managed to
startle people who were not so much complacent as unaware.

She saw the humour of the situation and wrote to my
husband of a Catholic bookseller who

fell on my neck [spelled kneck!] when I went into his shop
lately and said someone had been in there with an American
copy of Guilt, and that as soon as it comes out here he would
like to arrange a "window" of all my books, with my photograph

in the middle. He said that as *Guilt* is illustrated by photographs, wouldn't it be a good idea to put the ones in it round mine, sort of radiating from the central star? I said, "A splendid idea"—knowing they are mostly criminals, murderers, etc.— and went away chuckling at the idea of seeing myself "radiating" Leopold and Loeb, the Dusseldorf murderer—and so on. I would have to get my photograph taken for this, and I feel I ought to have it done with the "Grail smile," especially if there is a photograph of Irma Grese, that great group leader, in the book!

Do you approve the idea?

P.S. I've still not seen *Guilt,* but still hope.

P.P.S. Sub Rosa and under privilege—I think *The———*[a periodical] is absolute poison! They will never help anything religious.

To return to the main line of the book: in a group people are prone to lose individuality and with it sense of responsibility: they can too easily project the evil within themselves on others and try to destroy them instead of fighting it. The group mind is one danger, but individually by recourse to psychiatry, by confession to friends in search of reassurance for themselves, men try another road also in an effort to get rid, not of guilt itself but of the feeling of guilt.

Caryll was far from despising the "experimental science" of psychiatry. It may do great good in "the treatment of mental, nervous, functional disorders." It "has a humble and yet magnificent service to offer in simplifying man's response to grace," when he suffers from that psychological illness which "can be the means to sanctity as much as any other illness" but can also be "demoralizing and destructive to the soul."

The sacrament of penance does not depend on the skill of the priest as psychiatry on that of the doctor; it is not something that will succeed in one case, fail in another. "It is never an experiment; it is always a miracle." It will "*always* do very much more for the incurable neurotic than remove his mental suffering. It will, while forgiving whatever sin he has really committed, change the suffering of his mind into the suffering of Christ's mind, infusing into it the redeeming power of *His* suffering."

Learning to look not at the ugliness of our sin but at God's forgiving love, "our very sorrow for sin will become joy in the contemplation of God."

"The key to human nature is Christ. He is the pattern in which man was originally made, and by becoming one with Him, man can be restored to that pattern and become whole."

"The beginning of human happiness, and even of human sanity, is to begin to know God."

"Adam was the first sinful man, and he tried to repudiate guilt; Christ was the first sinless man, and He accepted the guilt of all sin. . . . In Him is God's love for man and man's love for God. . . .

"This is the secret of man's capacity to fulfil his human nature through love, to atone for guilt by his suffering, to experience joy in a world that is overburdened by sorrow. He has been given back the life of Christ—Christ's mind to adore with, Christ's love to love with, Christ's sacrifice to atone with. . . .

"*The great repression of our age is the repression of Christ in man.*"*

Fallen man "fumbles in the darkness like a blind man trying to learn the divine features through the touch of his finger tips"; and amazingly, in many non-Christian religions, he did learn much; "but the mystery of Christ, of the Trinity, and of man's place in that unutterable dispensation of love, can only be known by faith through the revelation of the Word."

Caryll had come from the huge mental hospital intensely

* Italics mine.

alive to the sufferings of its inmates. But indeed she was always alive to the sufferings of all the world, and in one unforgettable passage of this book she pictures Christ in His agony seeing, "for the second time in His human life—all the cities of the world and the glory of them"—only this time He saw behind that glory the hidden rat-infested slums, the black industrial cities, stunted and twisted little children in factories, all the battle-fields of the world, the secret dungeons and prisons, all the sufferings inflicted on man by man to the end of time. Many people talk only "notionally" of the Mystical Body, but to her it was intensely actual, and it meant Christ suffering in men and being consoled by men. Two of her most personal messages are given in this book supremely. "Again and again in human history those in whom Christ lives have been able to heal because they could not be healed." All Christians realize this about the cripple, the physically sick, the old and feeble—but Caryll saw the redeeming Christ also in lunatic asylums and in mental homes. The neurotic too can be a saint: "The one essential for sanctity is the capacity to love." And "sanctity is the only cure for the vast unhappiness of our universal failure as human beings."

This does not mean she was not concerned with remedies for neurosis—for we have seen how keenly she was. But she wanted, from the first, by telling the neurotic the truth concerning the power of his sufferings united to those of Christ, of his cwn possibilities of Christhood, to awaken hope and an effort at charity—"an outgoing from the narrow prison of self to share the common suffering of all mankind: the whole world's fear and labour and pain."

While in his prison of self the neurotic had felt always frustrated, never receiving the love he demanded from others; and the strange thing about this is that "what the neurotic asks is exactly what man was created for: to be loved illimitably," not by man but "by the God who created him.

"The beginning of integrity is not effort but surrender; it is simply the opening of the heart to receive that for which the heart is longing. The healing of mankind begins whenever any man ceases to resist the love of God."

Not all neuroses are the result of a man's own sin, and Caryll draws a parallel between the effort of the psychiatrist to heal a man by taking him back to his childhood and Christ's command to us to "become as little children." Only too often the treatment of the child has created the neurotic: tyranny and spoiling alike can damage the child's integrity, and in many an evil man we can see the spoilt child hardly aware of the havoc he is working. He remains the nasty child, "and what is there on earth *more* nasty than a nasty child?" But more frequently parents with the "utility mind" so common today have reduced their child to mediocrity by taking from him the wonder and mystery that are "his right and his necessity," the fairy stories and fables in which Christ is the Hero hidden under many different disguises, the coming through Christ to His Father and the world of spirit. Entry into this world is vital for the true growth of "that bright and beautiful thing, childhood."

When the child becomes the boy too many parents are concerned only that he should pass exams brilliantly, be able to earn a living in some dull profession; they are not themselves alive to the worth-while in life, fear enterprise, adventure, risk, have themselves accepted the dreary standards of an unpoetic world. The work he chooses should be, but most probably will not be "his own choice, not one forced on him as the one most likely to get him a good social standing or the most money," but "one which will enable him to serve God best and . . . be in itself, as work should be, a means of contemplation."

Caryll's experience at Frensham and with Dr. Strauss's boy patients had left her convinced that parents often frustrate their child by failing to see the Christ in him. By his own integrity and by seeing life aright the father would give to his son "the greatest help to being a success as a human being, even if he does not give him much help to being a success as men ordinarily estimate success.

"If a man is whole, his wholeness can be his gift to his child."

This of course is perfectly true, but the trouble about work is more complex. What applies to the outstanding artist may be true in theory about many boys. But the unfortunate parent lays himself open later to the son's reproaches if, untrained for any ordinary profession, he cannot earn enough to marry and in turn have sons of his own. Perhaps Caryll underestimated the vast problem in a civilization where craftsmanship practically exists no longer and even the artist can hardly earn a meagre living. That a father should not oppose a manifest talent is true enough, that he should foster it if he can, but Caryll's sympathy was wholly for the frustrated son, she had none to spare for the sincerely perplexed parent.

Then of course she did *hate* "the utility mind." And here she had a valuable lesson for many of us: the second great lesson of her book.

With all our efforts many neurotics will remain un-cured, many will even remain lunatics or hopelessly re-gressed men. "There are heroes of the last two wars who are crawling on all fours, playing with toys, learning to eat with a spoon, trying, less successfully than real babies, to learn to talk."

These sights many avoid who are yet considered charitable. Sometimes, says Caryll, "they are only too willing to give from a distance . . . to have sickness and misery . . . kept out of sight . . . decontaminated. Their unexamined motive is not to heal suffering but to disinfect it."

In the doctors and nurses at the asylum she had seen the man in the Gospel who was rewarded at the Judgment be-cause, whether he knew Christ or not, he had ministered to

Him. Saints likewise "cannot see men as derelicts . . . they can only see them as Christ, down on His face in the dust under the weight of the cross, needing another man to help Him carry it."

Supposing that we cannot give a cure, we can still give sympathy, and "this means sharing in another's sorrow, a real self-giving. Anything else can be given without involving self, but sympathy *is* giving self to suffer someone else's sufferings."

It must have been easier to see the Infant Christ in the baby Clare as with minute hands she took possession, sweeter to sink the self in serving her than to serve the suffering Christ whose suffering could not be taken away—in "so many sick who cannot be cured, so many unstable who cannot be changed—and most of all, so many whose suffering is in their mind, and so cannot often be alleviated. In all these the saint sees Christ. He sees Christ in Gethsemane, the Christ who asked in vain, not for His friends to take His suffering from Him (that they could not do) but that they would watch with Him, simply be there with Him and give Him themselves in compassion."

16

Art, Pain and the Mystic

GUILT TOOK LONGER to write than any of Caryll's earlier books, partly because it was a much more ambitious undertaking, demanding deeper thought and more gathering in of the material around her whether in mental homes or in the highways and hedges of life, partly because her own life was getting daily more crowded. Indeed, as we have seen, the expeditions to St. Bernard's alone brought more patients for social therapy, every book brought more requests for spiritual help.

Then too, although Caryll had always kept in touch with both parents it was only as they grew older that she felt they really depended on regular visits from her as an important element in their lives.

To a friend who wanted to see her more often Caryll wrote in June 1949, explaining why she could not make engagements to dine out:

My father is eighty, my mother seventy-five, and they live in the opposite ends of London. Each has to be visited at least once a week. Then I have an invalid aunt in Brighton, who would like a weekly visit but has to have a two-weekly one or less; there are several neurotic invalids who can't leave their homes, and several people in the mental hospital, also requiring regular and frequent visits. . . . My dinner when alone here only takes about 15 minutes to cook and eat! Also I continue to work while eating it—. Of course I know how pernicious it is to demand of one's blood to go simultaneously to the brain and the stomach—I must be setting up some frightful conflicts.

That autumn Caryll, Iris and Henry carried out a long-planned pilgrimage to Walsingham.

My husband had asked Caryll to read the MS of Father Keenan's *Neuroses and Sacraments*. Rather surprisingly, her comments came on notepaper headed Blue Boar Hotel, Cambridge:

The contents of [the book] are magnificent and it is just what is needed, first of all because it is the first book (I have seen) that offers the neurotic and even psychotic person not only hope but their own part in the Body of Christ on earth; this seems to me more important even than the hope of cure or relief.

It changes the whole point of view to these people. Secondly it does offer not what practically all other books do on this subject, just diagnosis, but a way of setting about a cure, which requires the patient's co-operation, but guarantees God's part—and does not claim infallible results.

I mean, the Sacramental life is not offered as magic or a pill, but in the really creative sense, and with the certainty of *either* curing the patient, or else showing him his honourable part in the Communion of sinners and making it acceptable to him.

All this is *so* important from the point of view of the neurotic or psychotic person, that the value of the book from that angle can not be exaggerated. But it is also, I think, an essential and greatly needed point in charity, which we all need to grasp if we are to really live out the love of Christ.

I could say much more, but at any moment shall be ordered by Iris and Henry to take up my pack and walk—sometimes when doing so, I regret it is not my bed. (I am on a very Chaucerish "pilgrimage" to Walsingham, combining conviviality with devotion.)

Iris tells me, rather surprisingly, that whenever they did leave their home territory—Nell Gwynn and the cottage— Caryll insisted on a first-class hotel. She would then annoy the management by asking for an assurance that her bedroom would be free from mice. Finally, to make assurance doubly sure, she would sprinkle oil of peppermint around her bed as a specific against these rodents.

Even with a comfortable bed, food and good drinks (certainly in that order), the pilgrimage from London to Walsingham was no light undertaking for a woman now in middle age and with Caryll's complication of illnesses. It had taken them nearly four days, and then Caryll said they must walk the final "holy mile" barefoot. They went single file, Caryll first, their shoes round their necks, reciting the rosary, Henry manifestly uneasy lest some passer-by might prove to be an acquaintance. After twenty minutes' walk a sign-post warned them that it was still one mile to Walsingham. At this point Henry gave up and put on his shoes, but the two women persevered barefoot to the bitter end of their pilgrimage.

Early in 1950 when pneumonia had laid her low Caryll wrote from her bed rejoicing:

"This solitude is lovely. All I really want is the Mass. But I have the Oratory in sight from my window, hear the Angelus and the Sanctus bell, and somehow seem to be surrounded by the Real Presence all the time."

On March 9th she wrote: "I only got up yesterday (after a whole *month* in bed) . . . I still have the blessed orders not to see any one. . . . It has been wonderful to be alone and able to put all my energy into my book and none into the frittering away of life that one usually has to."

Her vitality had been for a long time sapped by the hard

work, the unceasing demands, and she began with this illness a return—but for how short a time!—to the ardent tranquillity necessary, one would think, to the life of an artist. For Caryll was an artist, and the artist in her sometimes seemed to be putting up a fight against the aspirant to that total self-giving love which in her eyes was the beginning and end of sanctity.

Francis Thompson, a very different character, saw a similar problem in the more human terms of a fight between

> The life of flesh and life of song!
> If one life wrought the other wrong,
> What expiating agony
> May for him doomed to poesy,
> Shut in that little sentence be—
> What deep austerities of strife—
> "He lived his life." He lived *his* life!

For Thompson the struggle lay between normal human living and an existence in which vivid inspiration was too often replaced (or stimulated?) by drugs. Caryll's rhythms, like all her writings, were themselves the wine of life to her. She needed no drugs if she could only write. Gilson in his *Choir of Muses* questions whether the consummated saint could still be interested in his Art, and he can think only of Fra Angelico. It is strange that he did *not* think of Gerard Manley Hopkins. But I doubt anyhow whether the question at the supreme moment in an artist's work is whether he is interested in his Art or whether, as his subject fills him and overflows, his Art does not take possession of him totally, shaping his speech, filling his song, laying his colours on the canvas, or making of his life of service a living symphony.

Surely there is a deep truth in the words of Evelyn Underhill concerning the profound art with which most of the mystics write. "They ever seek," she says, "like the artists they

are, some new and vital image which is not yet part of the debased currency . . . and conserves its original power of sting-
ing the imagination to more vivid life."

Baron von Hügel studying St. Catherine of Genoa found
that he could infallibly decide which were her authentic
writings by the rhythm into which they fell. Is not Julian of
Norwich profoundly poetical, are not Catherine of Siena and
Teresa of Avila? Augustine's *Confessions* are a work of immense literary genius. I believe the reason we often fail to
see this from the angle of literature is the truly debased
nature of most of the translations—whether they be out of a
foreign language or clumsy adaptations of old English. Notice
the difference when a poet undertakes to translate St. John of
the Cross or a master of prose St. Augustine. The hacks had
their way too long with those saints.

Caryll's own view was interesting. She lists in *Guilt* a number of literary artists as having been neurotic or psychopathic,
who conquered or were conquered by their own instabil-
ity. She then studies some examples of those who sought to
fulfil their destiny as channels "through which the universal
experience of mankind is poured." This destiny they *can*
only fulfil "through the Man who abides in all mankind,
Christ." She goes on:

Genius admits of no compromise. The human being to whom
it is given must either be a saint, surrendering absolutely to his
Christ-destiny, or be broken by his genius. . . .

The neurosis or frustrating circumstance in the life of a
genius is always a conflict between the frailty of human nature
and the immensity of his destiny, but it is not always a sign
that he has been broken on the rock of his destiny. Sometimes
the conflict is the means by which he must fulfil his vocation
and enter into the communion with mankind which is its fulfilment.

Whether or not Caryll had (as I believe) a touch of genius, her art was like that of the saints, subserving and embodying a spiritual message. But she was acutely aware of how hampered she was in exercising it at all, and how in her overdriven life she had lately lost even the perception of natural beauty so deeply rooted in her being. Put together two passages, both roughly of this date. In a letter to a close friend we hear the natural plaint of the artist:

. . . I am incomparably better than I have been for months, and this altho' the inflammation in one lung is still hanging fire a little. I still have to have more treatment—but the wonderful thing is how the ability to enjoy beautiful things is simply flow-ing back into me. For more than a year my senses have been dead to beauty, and anything like music or even looking at a beautiful scene has only seemed to add to the effort of being alive almost unbearably, but I only realized how much this is so by the sudden wonder, like a miracle, of being moved and carried away the other evening by the voice of a Spanish woman singing on the wireless, a real Spanish voice, with that strange mixture of hardness and deep deep warmth and love, a won-derful inconsistency that somehow seems logical in a Spaniard—a mixture of fire and water—if you can imagine the miracle of water burning—you find it in the writing and the mind of St. Teresa of Avila. To my amazement I was just carried away and came alive in the beauty of this singing, and ever since, everything—flowers, light, poetry—has touched something in me that could waken and respond, going out to meet the beauty with something in myself, instead of shrinking back from the effort of response, blinking at it, as a person with aching eyes blinks at a strong light.

Also my own mind is filling with words—rhythms—stories, and I am now burning with impatience to finish my book, and write just for the sheer joy of poetry, words, etc.

One thing this illness has taught to me; it has made me realize that though God has given me gifts, I have never in all my life, for one single week, been free to *enjoy* them, they have always been violated, scamped, hurried, fitted in to other people's convenience, and never allowed to grow. They might never have come to much in the way of art, and now they certainly won't, for I am too old, and in spite of this little resurgence of life, too broken, to develop talents now, even *if* I ever could have—but one thing I am sure, they could come to great personal happiness, and they should—that alone is a real thanksgiving to God, and now I am going to achieve that, what remains to me of life, I am going to live happily. . . .

In *Guilt* she answered these words with the profounder voice of her whole life as a Christian:

There are those who must live, as it were, in other men's hands; whose success, even if it be of a spiritual order, must be paid for in a suffering of poverty far more terrible than material poverty, a poverty of not having themselves, not having anything of their own—not time, or solitude, or their thoughts, or even their senses: their hearing filled always with other men's troubles, their eyes with the face of other people's sorrows, all their words given to others without stint for their comfort, their touch the perpetual touch of healing and blessing.

She instances St. Francis de Sales, "accessible to all"; and also those who "in order to embrace humanity . . . may be obliged to withdraw from humanity. Scholars, poets, artists, scientists and contemplatives, whose lives are lived in terms of universal love. . . . To give oneself to the world, to take all mankind to one's heart, may be the loneliest of experiences."

It was to be a difficult year. No sooner was Caryll better than Iris got ill and Caryll had to nurse her. Her letters show alternations between an exasperated feeling that her friend had suffered a collapse brought on by the fact of her own illness, and terror lest there might be something seriously wrong with Iris. They both had to be X-rayed, and now Caryll wrote:

I who am *utterly* indifferent about my own X-ray (which is to take a look at a "patch," *not* TB) am simply physically ill from nervous anxiety at the mere idea of Iris having the X-ray in case some awful hidden thing is shown in *her.* . . . I keep putting her and your [child] and all of us into the Sacred Heart. But all the same my mouth is dry, my hands shaking, and I am so breathless from sheer nerves and have such palpitations that I fear the doctor who is to sound us at the Hospital will imagine my case to be far more serious than it is.

Doctors are not so easily deceived as all that. Iris had painful but not dangerous inter-costal rheumatism, Caryll got the warning to go really slowly, a warning that life as well as her own temperament made pretty futile. As soon as she was pronounced clear of TB came a longish visit from Clare, and we find her again writing at night to get the book finished—naturally enough "shaking with nerves and depression."

Going to the cottage to try to complete her recovery, Caryll was met by a telephone message to say that her father and her mother were both gravely ill. She went straight back to London, not even waiting to see Clare, who was arriving that day. Her parents were still living apart, "in the opposite ends of London," which added to the difficulties. She tells the story in a letter to a friend some months later: "The old man, who is eighty-three, got better, though his recovery must be regarded as only partial and precarious, but my poor mother became worse and worse. She had both cancer and consumption, and suffered quite terribly. Although day after day, for weeks and then months, I told myself I should find time to write a few letters, each day demanded of me more and more concentration on my mother."

After Mrs. Houselander was moved into St. George's Hospital "it became literally a day and *night* concentration."

Caryll and her sister shared some long vigils. As ever with Caryll, tragedy and comedy chased each other in her conversation. She told me both of her mother's sufferings and of her sister and herself utterly exhausted drinking brandy from a bottle and suddenly realizing that a magnified shadow of them both was thrown on the screen around the bed. "The hospital staff," said Caryll, "let me stay with my mother in the ward both day and night, and I only came away to have a bath and one or two hours rest in the morning."

As she got worse Mrs. Houselander suffered terribly— "more," Caryll said, "than I have ever seen anyone suffer before. . . . I practically lived in the ward." Her mother had not been to the Sacraments for many years, but now she went to Confession and received Holy Communion and the last anointing. Caryll could say, "She died in great peace and happiness; in fact I never in my life remember having seen her peaceful or happy before, but she was so from the moment that she was anointed until she died."

Caryll felt her mother's death more than one would have expected. "Something of oneself," she once said, "dies with one's mother." And despite all she had done and tried to do she suffered from a deep remorse at the thought that she had not been a good daughter: later on she had a sort of sick fancy that her own illness came as "Gert's" revenge.

Looking back on the months after her mother's death, Caryll varied in her memory of when she first suspected she had cancer. At one time she spoke as though she had guessed it the day of the funeral, at others as though it was many weeks later, after her expedition with Iris to Chartres. In all probability her memory was like that of most people: when something is known for certain, earlier faint guesses pushed aside by life's business, faint fears laughed away by what *then* seemed the voice of commonsense, suddenly take on the semblance of the knowledge we *now* have.

A talk with Caryll's doctor at Nell Gwynn House was illuminating. "She loathed," said Dr. Heyman, "any intrusion on her privacy." She was slow to come for a check-up, but "always went ahead" when he told her what she must do.

Caryll was used to ill-health, and she surely knew enough, had she been certain, to have gone to her doctor at once. But it was a month after Mrs. Houselander died that Iris and she set off to spend Christmas at Chartres. Caryll came home with influenza, which Iris caught from her and which in Iris turned to pleurisy. She was very ill, and Caryll had now another sick woman on her hands, this time with the full-time job of nursing her.

It was when Iris was getting better that Caryll told Rosamond of her fears, adding that she could hardly bear to go to the doctor lest it should upset Iris. This was hardly to be taken seriously, and Rosamond pointed out how infinitely more upsetting—if so mild a word could be used—it would be if she delayed too long.

"When I told her she had cancer," Dr. Heyman said, "she took it perfectly calmly. She realized she would probably never get over it." And looking back on all the time that followed he said, "She suffered *greatly,* but uncomplainingly."

The cancer was on the left breast—precisely where her mother had been operated on five years earlier. Her doctor sent her to a specialist who turned out to have studied under her uncle, and he secured for Caryll a cubicle at the Westminster Hospital. It was at the end of a public ward, and the other patients wandered in and out. She wrote to Dickie Olivier thanking her for the "radiantly lovely flowers" that had "made the first day so much more bearable" and went on:

I feel as if I had been here for months—I am already completely hospital-minded. The operation, which in this case I consider a *mutilation,* is already referred to by the nurses, fellow patients and self as "The op" and the question tossed to and fro between all the patients is "When is—or when was—*your* op, dear?" Meanwhile despite a determination to remain snobbishly aloof, the question of whether or not the cascara will work has become more important than whether or not the "op" will be fatal! I find myself clutching the relic of Blessed

Martin de Porres and praying wildly, not that my heart but that my bowels may be moved, before Sister approaches with the dread word "Enema" on her lips.

Caryll was greatly impressed by the reverence of the entire ward when the priest came early in the morning

without bell, Sister or ceremony at crack of dawn, and gave Holy Communion to self and the other RCs behind screens—coming almost furtively, as Christ said, "like a thief in the night"—but a thief to steal unrest and the darkness of the night. But what astonished me was . . . when "the ward" knew he was coming with the Host, though they are all non-Catholic, they became really reverent, offered us to choose any of their flowers to put on the table, and became quiet, a beautiful hush at last on the continual banter—but not a morbid one, something more like a silent smile of peace. The nurses were the same.

To Christine Spender she wrote:

You will be astonished to hear that, much as I dreaded the public ward—and I *did* dread it, more than the operation—I have now learnt to be glad I am in it, and if I ever come again, which is all too likely, I will choose it! But I have a cubicle in it, which gives a lot of privacy, though the other patients, who are all very friendly, walk in and chat to me constantly—but anyhow I don't have to be perpetually exposed to the public gaze—and my admiration and liking for human nature has gone up by leaps and bounds since I came here. There is, no doubt, a Communion with Christ through pain, which gives people the power of *His* love, regardless of what, if anything, they believe.

There is so much I want to tell you, but I can't write more today. Don't come here to see me; it's hopeless, the visiting hours are at awful times, and the visitors all clash; only two are allowed, but dozens come, though I've asked them not to—and it is all confusing and embarrassing and I am exhausted every time. I will let you know (on your P.C.!) when I am going home, and I will ask you to come and see me there, where we can talk.

On April 2nd Caryll wrote to Iris believing that she was to be operated on on the following day:

. . . tomorrow the troubles will be nearly over—we've got to the peak and I shall swing across it in a haze of ether, to come out into light on the other side.

Somehow or other this all fits into God's plan for us. . . . God now gives me the chance of being quite helpless, literally knocked out, and committed helpless into His hands. It is not for me to say "I must live" or "I must die" or to resist the humiliations and fears of the occasion, but simply, with Christ, "Into Thy hands"—and the result is, the terrible anxiety I have been feeling for you . . . is gone, though my grief at causing you to suffer has not. . . .

It seems to me this crisis had to occur, but it is a test, like with that old man in the Bible who was asked to sacrifice his son, a test to compel me, the half truster, to trust completely— and you will see, God will send the angel, not to stay the hand with the knife this time, but all the same to make it save the life of the "victim"! . . .

Don't let two or three days of anxiety break you, Darling, but let them give you such great trust that you will never be able to doubt the Love that is hidden in all suffering again, and so never be defeated by it.

By the time you get this letter anyway all will be well as far as my wretched body is concerned, and I hope and pray you will be happier.

Have a good stiff drink of my gin—and cheer up—when I see you again we will have gone through the tunnel into the light, and be able to have a few good laughs.

Your own

Caryll

But the operation was postponed. Already the delay had been too long, and Caryll heard a doctor say, "If it is inoperable the patient must be told." They asked her permission to use her as a "guinea-pig," the surgeon lecturing on her case to the students, and she saw that they viewed it very seriously.

She wrote to Dickie:

The lecturer asked several of them to describe and diagnose my case (in spite of the evasive answers to me of the doctors in the ward!!) —and they answered that it was "carcinoma of the breast in the *second* stage." Two of them said it was inoperable (the lecturer said he did not agree about that). . . . When I saw the house-surgeon in the ward again, I said, "Well, according to the doctors, my chances of life are small."

His only reply in obvious embarrassment was "Oh, take what they said with a grain of salt."

I said, "It would need a very big pinch of salt—but we are all in God's hands and He alone can know," to which he said, "Ah, that's just the right attitude for you to adopt!"

Of course I've only told Iris a garbled and witty (meant to be!) description of the lecture, omitting the alarming (to her) parts altogether.

Well it's true we are in God's hands, and, as I meant to say, and may have said to you before, the only prayer I can say now is "Into Thy hands, Father, into Thy hands"—and it is not only my wretched body and shivering soul that I am at last committing absolutely to the hands of Infinite Love, but, and this is so much greater a surrender, all those whom I love, you, Elizabeth, Iris, Clare, David,* Rosamond—above all those whom I presumed to feel dependent on my love.

I feel sure this act of surrender is asked of me, and I think, which I admit heartens me enormously, that it may be all that is asked (see how generous I am), and that so long as I make this surrender, and I *think* I really have, though now and then I get a moment of panic—I shall be spared to delight more than ever I have done before, in this world and those whom I love.

* Elizabeth was her godchild, David her name for Henry Tayler.

The operation was only the beginning of a heavy siege of pain. She writes to Christine Spender:

They say they have removed all the cancer. . . . But as it was already in the second stage, there is no guarantee at all that it won't return—the chances are about 50-50. After the operation the wound got infected and would not drain properly, and I had a week of real agony, which was helped by drugs, astonishing kindness and wonderful nurses and doctors, but couldn't really be made anything but agony for a large part of the time; then last Monday I had to go back to the theatre and have the wounds drained under an anaesthetic and a few more punctures made into the bargain. Now it's really getting better and I had the stitches out today.

Despite her physical misery Caryll was highly amused by one of the nurses to whom she mentioned her pain. "Oh that's not pain, dear," the nurse said brightly, "it's just post-operational soreness."

Rosamond—one of the tiny inner circle invited by Caryll to come—visited her soon after the operation and noted "her astonishing normality, cheerfulness and insouciance, although she looked like a ghost. Almost as soon as she came round from the anaesthetic she began to write again: I remember her sitting up in bed writing rhythms. And when she was slightly better she used to go onto a little balcony and have long talks about existentialism with a man from an adjoining room."

She was [Rosamond says in another letter] extraordinarily herself—talking cheerfully and with interest about everything *but* herself—very much about the wonderful charity and kindness of the nurses (two of whom she converted): in fact, she said she had never before seen such wonderful, tireless charity as among these overdriven, underpaid nurses: nothing was ever too much for them to do. They were very young, and went through their exhausting day- or night-long shifts with unfailing cheerfulness and sweet temper. (Caryll and Iris organized a midnight feast for the night shift: Iris smuggled in the food and the booze, and Caryll hid it in her locker.)

With all the pain and what might almost be called the minor operations of draining, punctures, etc., Caryll did not forget Iris's birthday, and got the nurses to buy the presents she could not this time choose herself. When Iris arrived that day she found the tiny cubicle full of red roses and birthday gifts. Caryll always loved to make a fuss of birthdays—to give many presents, to adorn the table. She was like Gilbert and Frances Chesterton in the "circumstance" with which she surrounded Christmas as well as birthdays, coming round a few days before with carefully chosen presents for each member of the family. And it was rash to express a desire: if Caryll had any money in the bank out came a cheque-book—for a dog which one of her friends coveted and for which she could not afford to pay £15; for a £15 cardigan that she knew Iris wanted. Rosamond believes that her only use for money was to give it away and is reminded of Wesley's saying: "I throw it out of my hands as fast as I can, lest it should find a way to my heart."

A few days later Caryll "developed a colossal abscess" which had to be lanced and "the skin graft they made to close the wound had broken down. They will probably have to re-graft it before I can have radium."

In May, after six weeks in hospital, she was discharged with orders to come in for deep-ray treatment daily. Caryll had faced calmly the possibility of death, but she was very far from wanting to die, and she told me at the time of her return home how trying and difficult to answer she found letters from pious friends assuming that her one desire was to be in heaven.

To Dickie she wrote of how she would continue to pray

for her little Elizabeth if she were to find herself in Purgatory—of an immediate Heaven she had no dreams—but she went on, "I honestly long to be told 'a hundred per cent cure' and to return to this life and celebrate it with gramophone records, giggling and gin."

To a young friend whose frequent fits of depression she tried to help she wrote a year later:

I agree with you indeed about the "importance of living." I go further: it seems to me that the very great thing is to be able to *enjoy* life. When I was in the hospital last year and they told me, as they did, that they were not at all sure that they could operate, I felt no fear of death, though I did not *want* to die, as I knew how lonely it would leave my friend, with whom I have lived for twenty-eight years. But what I *did* feel was remorse because I realized that I had never really *let* myself *enjoy* life—so many scruples and inhibitions and things preventing me from really enjoying the sheer loveliness of the world, the people in it, and even the material things in it, food, drink, the sun, spending money, etc. I imagine that will sound very low to you. But when my poor old mother died, in 1950, in St. George's Hospital, I went out into the park, opposite the hospital, and sat down and suddenly realized how *lovely* it was—the sky, the bare trees (it was November), the grass, the very touch of the air—and it suddenly swept over me, with a terrible pang, that my old mother had never really *enjoyed* life. She was always worried, always working, always thinking about money—never, or certainly hardly ever, sufficiently detached from self to enjoy the beauties and pleasures of this life. Then and there I made up my mind to enjoy my own, at the expense of my own vanity, self-love, anxiety (another form of self-love)—and everything else. When following hard on this I nearly lost my own life, I made only one resolution: if I was given another chance (as I have been), I would enjoy everything in life that I can, for as long as I can, and as wholly as I can.

17

Towards the End

Soon Caryll was leading her normal life again, complicated while in London by the necessity to save her father from knowing what had been the matter. He expected a daily visit which the extreme exhaustion following the treatments made horribly difficult.

Unfortunately that summer Caryll and Iris were in a really nasty accident. "The car turned over," Caryll wrote to a friend, "and was wrecked completely." Put into the prose of one not involved in the accident, this meant that the car was on its side, one door against the ground, the other jammed. Neither passenger appeared to be injured, but they were imprisoned for quite a while, unable to climb out, while other cars rushed past them. It seemed an eternity before a motorist as last stopped and came to the rescue. Iris went back to the cottage, but Caryll went to London, arriving very late and "suffering really severely from physical shock."

She describes as a neurosis the state of mental anxiety which followed and which she found so hard to shake off. But, astonishingly enough, it was only some weeks later she was discovered to have broken a rib. She was still undergoing treatments in which were included exercises to strengthen her arm on the side where the breast had been amputated. These gave her intense pain, but she thought this was still the result of the operation and did not complain. One sometimes gets the impression that she was so used to pain that the more or less of it appeared almost irrelevant. When the frequent treatments ended, she joined Iris at the cottage with orders from the Westminster Hospital to return for a monthly check-up, and the first X-ray taken revealed the broken rib.

It was with no high hopes that Caryll took up life again. "I'm not here for long," she said one day to Kate. "Don't tell Mrs. Wyndham."

And to Miss Gunn she said several times, "I'm so short of time. I know I won't get it all done."

To Douglas Begg, who had been her House Surgeon and was now at another hospital, she wrote: "I'm getting along all right, but would never be surprised to find myself back at the Westminster—if I do, how I shall miss you."

Probably her moods varied between the conviction she sometimes expressed that her illness would take exactly the same course as her mother's, whose cancer returned five years after her operation, and a hopefulness induced by the good reports she was receiving month by month.

For Father Diamond, of the neighbouring church of Princes Risborough, Caryll carved that year a wooden Bambino—a new-born baby which is still used for the Christmas crib. This figure was inspired by her love for little Clare. The autumn after the operation, Clare's parents were off to Baghdad and had decided to take her with them. Caryll wrote to a friend: "I need not tell you the fears that beset me—the journey—the distance—the political situation —the climate and so on. I am still praying, not by the day but by the hour and minute. . . . Clare is coming to stay with me when I get back to London until she goes, if—in spite of my positive bull-dozers of prayer—she does go."

Father Diamond had asked for the figure before Clare left, but Caryll could not start it while she was there "because she would certainly pick up the razor-sharp carving chisels with fearful results."

As soon as Clare had gone Caryll began the carving, worked unceasingly and then took it herself to Princes Risborough:

> I put the carved Bambino in the crib as an offering to God to get Clare back. I made it like a real infant, new-born, in swaddling bands, and I did it just as I remembered her at two weeks old. . . . Now I tell the Father in Heaven that He must look down and see that I have offered Him his baby Christ and for that He *must* bring us back our baby Clare to be brought up as "another Christ." It is hard to think that God *could* refuse when one simply puts the Infant Christ before Him as one's plea. I wait hourly then for the miracle—meantime the ferment in the Middle East grows more formidable daily. I had Clare photographed here before she went. The light wasn't good, but you get an idea. She is in your fair isle jersey because I was most familiar with her in that.

In April 1952 Caryll writes of "a piece of glorious happiness." She felt almost ashamed to tell her correspondent, who was herself being "bitterly tried"—yet it might comfort her too, it is so clear an answer to prayers, such as "those you are now offering; clearly God understands them perfectly." Her news is that Clare's mother is coming to England in about six months, wants Iris and Caryll to "meet her at the airport and take Clare for several weeks straight away."

The friend to whom she was writing had made the lovely dresses which Clare always wore at the cottage, some of which had been left behind. Caryll had felt she ought to give them to some poor child, Clare would surely have grown out of them before her return; yet they so brought the child back to her that she could hardly bear to part with them.

Then, meeting a friend who told her how her sister, with three small children, one just Clare's age, could not afford pretty clothes for them, she made up her mind and gave her these lovely things. She writes, "Well, when they were gone, and Clare's box nearly empty, I sat down feeling like someone might after a child's funeral—it seemed as if my flat, my heart, and my life were quite empty.

"While I sat there, the 'phone rang, with the news (from Iris) of Clare's return to us!

"Don't you think that it was God's answer, and that giving Clare's clothes away to a child in need was a prayer much more pleasing to Him than all my sobs and whines at His feet?"

Very soon after the operation Caryll had developed a new interest in the planning and erection of what came to be called Woodpeckers. For some time she and Iris had wanted to make an addition to the cottage—a little flat at the side for Caryll to work and sleep in. But for a long time local government permits were required for any building, and these had been refused. With some money left to her by her mother, Caryll decided to put up something that in their locality needed no permit—a prefabricated wooden bungalow at the end of the long garden. She planned to use it especially to help her many friends. Piero told me that, when he was seeking for a home, she offered it to him and his wife for an indefinite period, and there are many references in her letters to other friends invited or to be invited.

The new building—a prefabricated sanatorium chalet—was added to an existing summer house, proper foundations were dug and light and water laid on.

A photograph taken the summer of 1952 shows Odette Churchill, famous for her war work with the French underground, standing in front of a still uncompleted building, the erection of which had dragged on owing to the impossibility of negotiating the field in winter. Odette had read one of Caryll's books and wanted to meet her. She arrived to find a group of villagers at the gate of the farm who had got word of her coming and were eager to see her. Charles Scott-Paton had driven Odette down, and in the photograph of them all taken that day Caryll is smiling brightly and looks entirely herself. Odette showed her the little worn-out prayer book which had been her great stay and comfort in the German prison, and Caryll had an immense sense of how she had been upheld by the power of prayer throughout the world and had borne her own part in prayer and suffering to uphold others.

One of the strangest things I know is to meet someone who has endured all that Odette endured—the torture, the solitary confinement—whose heroism one realizes, and to find her so gay, almost frivolous, certainly possessed of the quality with "the lovely lilting name levity." Certainly her strength in that awful time must, as she said, have come to her from outside herself and would still be there did she need it again.

Woodpeckers reached completion that summer, and Caryll took a tremendous interest in the furnishing, going up to the Ideal Home Exhibition with Iris, and also to Heals, to choose the solid, rough-hewn table and seats for the brick pavement in front, the curtains, rush-bottomed rocking chair and rush matting for the floor. For the rest there was a camp bed, a small writing desk and a carpenter's bench for her carving. The walls were painted a dead glistening white—cold but rather attractive. Her books she left in London, putting up no shelves but just bringing down what she needed on each visit. "It made her miserable," says Rosamond, "to be in a room with much furniture or possessions of any kind. She liked Iris's flat best when it contained only mattresses and the five-shilling table, and was greatly upset when the rest of the furniture arrived."

But, very curiously, considering her conviction that her days were numbered, and also her distaste for gardening,

she had the bit of wild garden in front of Woodpeckers pro-
fessionally landscaped. The name Woodpeckers was given
to the bungalow from the gardener's remark that Caryll as
she carved sounded like a woodpecker tapping at a tree.

"Although," Rosamond writes, "the interruptions at Nell
Gwynn House drove her half-distracted, she missed the
stimulus of London. For her writing, that is: she did some
lovely carving down there, and there were times when she
thought of herself primarily as a carver: she loved wood, and
everything to do with the carving, shaping and polishing of
it—with all the tools that reveal its beauty. I remember her
saying to me that *all* wood, even when cut down and made
into furniture, is alive: it is only not alive when it becomes
touchwood, and crumbles away. And the life and grain and
colour of wood had a great fascination for her. She carved the
Madonna and Child (now wreathed, in summer, with white
roses in the hedge) out of an old cherry tree—the sway of
the figures taking the curve of the tree." This figure is
fixed on top of a tree trunk from which it seems to grow.
And the gardener made later, at Iris's request, a small
roofed shrine to protect it from the weather, adding on his
own a cross at the top and refusing to be paid for any of
his work.

"Caryll had," Father Alan Keenan writes, "a Franciscan
quality of seeing spiritual shapes in matter. She gave me a
Madonna and Child she had carved from the curve of an
apple branch, explaining that her carving had made visible
what was already there. Indeed her charity unlocked the
image of Christ in most unlikely people."

Clare had come back taller, thinner and talking Arabic.
This summer—now four, a little girl rather than a baby—
she became devoted to her grandmother and to Caryll: "She
wishes us to be together all the time so that she can be
glued to us both." Her grandmother she called "Lally,"
Caryll was "Sid"—taken from a radio programme which

usually began, "I'm your old friend Sid." Caryll records Clare as "above all maternal, and her dolls have to be bathed, have their hair and their clothes washed (and ironed) every day, at least once."

They had expected to lose her again before long, and Caryll continued anxious about the climate, the Arabs and their politics, Clare's own health and her religious education. But to her great joy Maurice Rowden decided to give up the job at Baghdad. Joan was to have another baby before long, and Iris and Caryll were soon asked to take Clare to the convent of their own choice—Goodings, the preparatory school for New Hall.

To her friend from the Westminster Hospital, Douglas Begg, she wrote rejoicing in the fact that "the nuns there and the Reverend Mother especially have none of the formalness that some nuns do; they are openly loving, and obviously the little children love them in return and are wholly at ease with them." She had delighted in the sight of a novice climbing a tree with the children.

As to Woodpeckers, "it is a dream for a child, everything in miniature, though the main room is big enough for work and comfort and has windows all round. But there is a tiny cooking stove and the general effect is like the Three Bears' Cottage—so Clare can make sweets and awful pies from unutterably dirty bits of dough, and be in and out of the garden too—moreover there is a little stream running through the garden, and when it is hot she gets in and out of that all day."

Just now and again for a few nights when her mother and other guests crowded the cottage, Clare would sleep at Woodpeckers with Caryll. This was a great thrill and excitement for both—and Caryll tends to talk in her letters as though it had become their home. But in fact both normally slept at the cottage and Woodpeckers was the guest house. Caryll urges Dr. Begg to come and stay—Woodpeckers could be given up to him for "real rest, and if you want it, solitude."

He asked her whether she was keeping up her visits to the Westminster. She assures him that she is, but also puts a problem felt keenly by the patients of today in relation to the system of almost any vast modern hospital. She begins by expressing her immense admiration for her own surgeon and for himself in their tireless work and patience. But she goes on:

"I would hesitate to mention any suspicious circumstances there, however, as my experience over my broken rib has taught me what to expect if I do—X-rays, more blood tests, more frequent visits, hours and hours of waiting about—and very little information at the end of it!"

The long waits, the literally sickening lack of confirmation or dissipation of one's fears, are hard for any patient—but for one who had heard her case expounded in relentless detail by a group of doctors the whole thing strikes the layman as reaching a high point of mental cruelty.

Sometimes the reticence may be inevitable, but knowing as we do today the powers of the mind's reaction on the body one cannot but feel that the vast anonymous silence *must* be physically, if only because psychologically, hurtful. And surely provision could be made for patients to be seen within at least an hour or so from the time they are told to come. These are my own thoughts, not Caryll's. She always remained devoted to her doctors and nurses and grateful to the hospital. And as for the things she did find trying, "one really ought," she writes, "to put up with anything, if it is going to benefit future sufferers, as no doubt it will. Yet," she goes on, "next time I have my doubts, if they are really serious I'll go to my own G.P., and if *he* confirms them, let the Hospital get cracking after—though of course I'll have to keep up the routine visits just the same."

Caryll was presuming on her apparently renewed health

to take up again the strenuous life that had been her norm, though of course Iris did the housekeeping and all meals were eaten at the cottage.

Before Clare went to Goodings Caryll took her daily, for a term, to school at Princes Risborough and brought her back in the evening—a long bus ride with a walk at each end. On her long summer-holiday visits the pattern of their lives seemed a renewal of the time at Nell Gwynn when Clare was a tiny baby: Caryll got her up in the morning and bathed her at night, while in the daytime Iris took full care of her, leaving Caryll free to write. But somehow, as Rosamond noticed, Caryll's pen never ran so well in the quiet of the country as in her London flat. She pressed her friends to come down, though sometimes feeling a number together rather a burden. She certainly never complained of interruptions of her work hours by Clare, who loved besides games and fun to be told stories and taught about God. One day Caryll discovered that Clare was keeping some small dead animal in a box, confident that it would rise again on the third day. She loved to tell one stories of things Clare had said and done like any doting aunt or grandmother. But she was getting very tired. She writes to a friend from Woodpeckers in the summer of 1953:

It is lovely here, but I would not say a rest for me. In order to answer even half the letters I ought to and to get my own work done, I have to get up at five o'clock in the morning to do two hours before Clare wakes, and to struggle to keep awake late into the night after she has gone to bed. The only time, however, that I really dislike in the twenty-four hours is Clare's bath time. She *loves* it, but somehow it seems an unbearable effort to me—I suppose because all the chores of the day have made me tired by then. But it is a thousand times worth it, and I would bath her three times a day and night to have her here.

In another letter to the same friend: "I have," she says, "been praying for you. I find that nowadays I cannot sleep much, but all the same when in bed I am too tired to write (as I always used to do at night).

"So this makes it possible for me to spend some hours every night praying for my friends . . . usually at four o'clock in the morning, an hour at which I always wake up, as certainly as if I had an alarm clock set for that time. . . .

"Incidentally, I must stop writing and make a school uniform for Clare's Teddy Bear, who is going with her."

Caryll started also to make a series of fascinating little dolls. They were to be what she described as a "good Catholic family," an enormous number of children, running in age from the twins in dark blue jerseys down to an enchanting "new-borner." These she carried out, but some of the intervening children, and the nurses, maids, grooms, gardeners, etc., who were to complete the household, were missing. It was to be just such a Catholic family, Caryll said, as she herself wished she had belonged to—families that one sees going up to Communion together. (But the *household* was surely typical of the atmosphere she had disliked in her schooldays!)

Besides the swing between hope and fear as to the outcome of her illness, Caryll seems to have experienced by turns an intense longing to go on living the life of this world and a reaching forward to the world to come. Summer holidays were over, and autumn was upon them:

> Milky the mist
> lying over our pastures
> and gleaming like pearl.
> It is October now.

This rhythm was in fact written in 1946, but it seems to fit one of the autumns that lay between Caryll's operation and her death:

> I walk among shadows,
> but shadows even
> are fires:
> lambent flames of leaves
> and yellow flowers
> and the last roses,
> and warmth with beauty
> is flesh and blood
> sacramental and holy
> for all our sinning.
> Though death walks at my heels,
> and welcome,
> this is the beginning,
> not the end of my story.
> I walk among shadows,
> O Liege Lord,
> my love,
> Shadows
> of Your bright glory!

From Nell Gwynn she writes again to Douglas Begg, himself now in hospital as a patient: she writes to him as what he is—a devout Christian although not a Catholic. She has been praying for him also at night, every night, and she trusts he will make a good recovery. She wants to correct his idea that it is as a penance she eats so little.

"I eat *all* I want to, sometimes more. Mind you, I do think we do all have to make penance for each other. The real way is, so I was taught and believe, absolute surrender to the will of God, and that ought definitely to include *enjoyment* when it comes our way. One ought to offer to God, not only pains and sufferings, etc.—but joy too." Douglas Begg, compelled by circumstances ("which is only a pagan word for God's will") to be inactive, has a magnificent opportunity. "The answer surely is that God wants you simply to 'offer yourself up' as Christ offers Himself up in the

Host in the Mass, for the whole world." This is also, she believes, "a time of preparation for a tremendous vocation. God will show you just what He wants of you and you will do it."

Turning to her own life Caryll continues:

> I was terribly glad to get back. We had visitor after visitor, and very little peace—but still when I built Woodpeckers I had it in mind that it might be a blessed refuge for city people who do not love London as I do, and I think it has been. But I am *very* happy back here, and not at all worried by London noises —as a matter of fact I like them much better than country ones, especially at night, the noises of hunting animals, owls, etc.— which frighten me more than I can say.

Here in London she is again writing eight hours a day and suffering from eyestrain as she has also to do a lot of reading for reviews and research.

Integrity, now alas dead, was an American Catholic magazine of originality and value. Founded by Carol Jackson and Ed Willock, it was at this time edited by Dorothy Dohen. Caryll wrote a number of articles in it; each issue was devoted to one subject. She wrote on "The Crown of Thorns" for the number on Mental Suffering, on "Care of the Mentally Ill" for that on Vocations, on "Christ in Men" for that on Human Relations, on our attitude to the old for that on Growing Old Gracefully.

Caryll and Dorothy began to correspond, and Caryll wrote in November:

> As you ask for suggestions I will make one, namely a number of *Integrity* on the subject of *Mercy.* The word "mercy" is one that comes into the press almost daily—"mercy killing," for example, and those who suppose that birth control is a form of mercy, not to mention lying to people who are fatally ill.
>
> I think an issue on this subject could include an article en-

titled "What is Mercy?" in which man's idea of mercy and God's mercy could be compared. Then "The Mercy of Christ"—then perhaps "Mercy Killing"—followed up by "The Mercy of the Saints" which could give one or preferably two sketches of a saint's life, and how it poured out mercy; for example, Blessed Martin de Porres on the physical plane, and St. Thérèse of Lisieux on the spiritual plane. Then perhaps "Mercy to the Living and Mercy to the Dead" bringing in St. Catherine of Genoa and the doctrine of purgatory. Finally "Mercy and Truth," bringing in mercy and its vital relation to justice, and on the most practical plane simply having the courage to tell the truth always and the compassion to tell it in the way more likely to help than hurt—e.g. the doctor to his patient—someone *asked* for advice to a sinner—not to mention the much more difficult point of being truthful to oneself and having that mercy on one's own soul.

In March 1954 Caryll writes again promising an article by April 2nd, choosing as her subject "The Mercy of God and the Mercy of Man":

This article would have to be more personal than I like because it would have to give examples from my own experience in hospitals and that of other patients. Actually it was in the cancer wards of two hospitals that I first realized that God's mercy works in a wonderful way through suffering, and how foolish, though well-intended, men are who think that they are more merciful than God and therefore have a right, perhaps even a duty, to end or prevent life.

Besides writing, through these months in London, Caryll had resumed Sprat work and was again trying to rally the organization, which always seemed to die away when she was not energizing it.

Her letters of advice and help were still pouring out. She records the reception into the Church of one of her nurses from the Westminster. Her old father was ill and needed constant visiting and she speaks of the consequent piling up of her other work. Also she is preparing birthday presents for Clare. She took tickets for the pantomime for Iris and Clare for the birthday—and could not resist going herself, although suspecting she was developing congestion of the lungs. (Where her own health was concerned I can only differ totally from Piero as to Caryll's possessing *any* common-sense.) Christmas was approaching, and it was no time to be ill. There was to be a children's party in the little flat. A godson and a nephew of Rosamond were among the children loved by Caryll. They often came to see her and would race each other down the long passages of Nell Gwynn in what she called "a charge of cavalry" to reach the flat. That evening carols were sung, vigorous games played and an immense tea eaten. Returning home, four-year-old Christopher burst into the drawing-room shouting, "A wonderful party! A wonderful, wonderful party!"

As her life drew towards its close I become more amazed than ever at Caryll's physical as well as mental energy. She seemed to have no reserves of strength to draw upon, yet always the strength to act; and she threw as much of this mysterious energy into making a success of a children's party as into handling a neurotic or writing a book. She told a friend that her *psi* faculty became strongest when she was utterly exhausted. One day a girl patient of Dr. Strauss, a persistent truant from school and "wanderer," came to tea bringing unexpectedly her mother and brothers and sisters. Too tired even to take in what they were saying, Caryll suddenly "saw" a band of gypsies. Up to now the treatment tried had not worked, but this gave Caryll the needed clue which led to complete success. It was only later discovered that the child was in fact descended from gypsies.

Christmas over, her pneumonia did drive Caryll to bed and produced the usual cries of joy at having solitude to

think in and time to write. In March she tells Dorothy
Dohen, "I am better—or so I think."

Reckoning all the time on the possibility, probability
rather, of a return of the cancer, she was yet planning for
further life in a world to which she was deeply attached.
And with all her complaints of the "chores" of country life
she was longing to add another burden. A young friend sent
her this spring a money gift, begging her to spend it on
drink or any other indulgence for *herself*. (The same friend
had once sent her champagne with such firmly limiting conditions that Caryll had to beg her permission to share it
with Iris.) Caryll wrote:

Yes, indeed I *will* indulge myself, not in gin, except perhaps a
very small amount, but in things I need, and the first of these—
this will amaze you—will be a basket for my dog! Yes, I *have* a
dog now: he was a direct answer to prayer. Last time I got down
to the cottage Iris said she had been thinking things over and
decided that if I wanted a dog I could have one, and she would
help me to look after it.

I began making enquiries, and then I had to go to London,
and suddenly I thought, if I don't get the dog before I go, I believe it may all fall through, so I knelt down then and there and
asked Our Lady to send one. Before I had finished the prayer,
plus one Hail Mary, the 'phone rang, and it was our local policeman whom I had told that I was looking for a dog. He said he
had one there, only six months old, and his master had brought
him to be put to sleep as he could not keep him: but the policeman said it was a lovely dog and very gay and lively, would I
give it a home? So it arrived ten minutes later in the police car,
with an escort of policemen, and its master.

It took to Iris and me at once, and is the most loving and
winning dog I have ever had. Iris has gone mad on it—it is really
"he" and is named Gregory (not by us, but we have to keep the
name he knows, we call him Greg). He is a mongrel, which I
like, a very pretty one, though bigger than I wanted, part wire-

haired terrier, part fox-hound, and astonishingly intelligent. I want him to have a basket so that he will have something he knows as his little home wherever I take him. He will have to come back to Nell Gwynn in the winter: what could be a more fitting present from you than his basket? Of course I will get other things too, because, truth to tell, I am needing *everything!* I even discovered moth in such old clothes as I have got the other day, and I haven't had time for the ghastly turn-out this will involve, so I don't know what more horrors I will find!

At long last Jones had a successor, and I think the coming of Greg was Caryll's last gleam of sheerly human joy. Ill though she was, they had, Rosamond told me, tremendous fun that summer on "my last visit to the cottage in her lifetime—in response to a letter delightedly telling me she had now got a dog and I must come and see him. When I went into her room to say goodnight, she confided to me that Greg always insinuated himself onto her bed, one paw at a time, during the night, and slept there—'But don't tell Iris' (who of course knew)."

A rhythm written a few years earlier gives one a guess at the special delight Caryll felt in rescuing even one victim of an indifference at least akin to the human cruelty for which she abases herself:

Confession to Animals

I confess
to the beast in the stall,
to the ox in the yoke,
to the lion in the cage,
to the homeless cat
and the lost dog,
to the cold,
the hungry,
the mangy,
the cowed,

and the wounded beast,
I am he who has wronged you.

I am he
who made the yoke
and the muzzle,
the chain,
the cage
and the whip:
who wasted the harvest
and damped the fire
and slammed the door.

I merit
pain in my body,
the lash on my back,
the hard bed,
the empty night,
and the meagre plate.

I am he who has wronged you.
The innocent
and the patient,
the lowly
and loving
beast.
You,
the loveliest least,
who groan together with Him
who made you.

Because of my sin,
you groan together with Him
who made you
for my delight.

18

Through a Dark Night

IN A LETTER OF November 19th, 1953, Caryll tells a
friend that she is writing an autobiography, and in one to
Lois Boardman in February 1954 she offers to send her
some meditations—*The Stations of the Cross,* which she is
publishing in the American *Messenger* and which became a
book under the same title. Her thoughts were concentrating
more and more on the beginning of her life and on the road
to death which was trodden by Our Lord and which He
treads again, with each one of us, in the measure of our
capacity. The autobiography ended up as *A Rocking-Horse
Catholic.* These two books were published after her death
as was another also belonging to her last years, *The Risen
Christ.* About *A Rocking-Horse Catholic* she wrote:

"In my view a study of one's childhood does tell more
than anything else about one's whole life.

"I mean that in the childhood lies the whole life, hidden
like the life of a flower or a tree in the seed. Certainly we
can't always read its secrets, but they are there.

"Indeed if we could open the book of everyone's childhood,
we should know the story of their lives so far as essential
things are concerned without anything else."

I have made use of this book in the chapters on Caryll's

childhood and youth. In it she leaves her life at the point of
the vision of Christ in man by which her whole later existence was shaped. She hardly expresses in it the deep contrition, visible in her other books and in her letters, for
the few years of her wandering, nor yet the conviction that
grew on her that God had chosen in His unfathomable
mercy to make her, through her experience, a more useful
instrument in His hands. Because she had known doubt she
could help the doubter, aware of sinfulness she could help
the sinner, tempted at moments to despair she could help
the desperate. And learning that Christ dwelt in all men she
learnt to make the supreme act of faith of realizing that He
dwelt in her.

In a church, assembled for the Stations of the Cross, Caryll
sees the crowd that always throngs her books, the people she
loved to observe; rich and poor, a couple in love, a young
soldier, a bowed-down old man, students, children, a tramp,
a business man and two little nuns, "like birds shaking the
rain off their black feathers."

"What a diversity of places these people must have come
from—luxury flats, tenements, small boarding houses, in-
stitutions, barracks, studios, colleges, doss houses, schools,
offices, convents. What sharp contrast there must be between
their different lives and circumstances. But they seemed to
be strangely at one here gathered round a crude coloured
picture on the wall of the church, 'The First Station of the
Cross.' "

The Stations of the Cross come to us chiefly from Scrip-
ture: Christ condemned to death by Pilate, loaded with His
cross, helped by Simon of Cyrene, wept over by the women
of Jerusalem, stripped of His clothes, nailed to the cross,
dying on the cross, taken down from the cross, laid in the
tomb. To these nine five more have been added by tradition
and the meditation of Christians—three falls beneath the
cross's weight, the wiping of Christ's face by Veronica, on

whose towel was imprinted the likeness of the Man of Sorrows, Christ's meeting with His mother.

But above all, says Caryll: "The Stations of the Cross are not given to us only to remind us of the historical Passion of Christ, but to show us what is happening now and happening to each one of us. Every human being alive is on the road to death. Each one meets himself on the *via crucis*, which is the road through death to life."

Caryll had an immense love for this devotion. She had carved and painted countless sets of Stations. There are some lovely things in those she did for this book, and I have another beautiful set in black and white. But she always said that she could not draw, and the best of her Stations are certainly those she carved. In this little book the meditations are what matter and the rhythmic prayer that follows each meditation.

"It is a showing," she says, of Christ's journey, "not simply of the way of sorrows which we are all destined to walk, but of the way of love which heals sorrow, and which we can all take if we walk in the footsteps Christ has marked out for us, and not only imitate Him but identify ourselves with Him."

At each Station we pray, "We adore Thee, O Christ, and we bless Thee, because by Thy holy cross Thou hast redeemed the world." This simple rhythmic prayer "echoes down the centuries, not in tones of fear and reluctance but as a cry of welcome, a tender cry, in the tones of a lover's greeting, to Him whom every man must meet on the way of sorrows, changed for him to the way of love."

In the traditional Stations with which she grew up we say, at the nailing of Christ to the cross, "Nail my heart to Thy feet"; and Caryll prays:

> Let us so bind ourselves
> that we will not only

adhere to You
in times of consolation,
in times of sweetness and devotion
and when life goes smoothly,
but yet more securely
in the bleak and bitter
seasons of the soul—
in the hard iron of the winters
of the spirit.

It is impossible to know when the cancer really did return, but as spring grew towards summer it was plain,
despite continued encouraging reports, that Caryll was very
ill. She spoke of herself as a hypochondriac and the doctors
told her she had rheumatism—which seemed likely enough
in the horrible summer of that year. The rain poured and
poured, the field became a swamp, everything felt damp.
Caryll ate less and less. Iris, who had been told to try to
get her to eat more, pressed food upon her. But Caryll, if
she forced herself to eat, was sick.

The strain grew between the two friends—each fairly
certain of the issue, each trying to hide her certainty from
the other. One day when Caryll was bathing, Iris could
get no reply to repeated calls and knocks. She begged her
henceforth to leave the bathroom door unbolted and to give
an occasional sign that all was well with her. And she would
hear the cracked and feeble voice singing the hymn of their
youth, "O Mary I crown thee with blossoms so gay."

There were times now when her mind wandered, and
sometimes Iris would find her lying asleep with her head
on the table or sitting on the floor at Woodpeckers leaning
against the cupboard. But she still got up and dressed, managed to get to Woodpeckers, to write her letters and even
some promised articles.

As she grew weaker the daily journey to Mass became obviously impossible. She had to remember her own teaching of our presence in the spirit at a Mass unceasingly offered somewhere at every moment of every day, of God's secret ways of giving the Bread of Life to prisoners and wanderers, the helpless and the sick. But the deprivation of the sacramental life was hard for one who had lived by it so intensely—and the inability to assist physically at the one perfect worship that lifts us into union with Christ's adoration of the Father as Head of the Mystical Body to which we all belong.

And then there was the fear of death which none but the most insensitive can escape and which Caryll had always felt. One day Iris met her coming across the field and Caryll said, "I've been doing a big think and I'm not afraid of death any more."

My husband and I were on our way to Australia, and there we received a letter from Caryll dated August 29th which showed a strange sudden ray of hope:

My dears Frank and Maisie,

I am really deeply ashamed because I have been so long in answering Frank's letter, about *The Rocking-Horse Catholic*. Actually I have been, quite literally, "under the weather"—in fact I have been feeling so ill that I had more or less made up my mind that I had no hope of living longer, and was trying to get the few overdue things written . . . before lying down to die! It did not even occur to me that I am *not* dying, I was concerned only with whether I could settle my affairs, leave them with neat edges and so on before the end.

But to my amazement when, having made my arrangements, I went to the doctor, determined to accept my death sentence with a stiff upper lip (all the rest of me is stiff with rheumatism anyway!)—the doctor told me that I am not dying at all! That I am not even suffering from cancer and that with a little patience and medical treatment I shall be alright and probably good for many years to come—but to stick to my own work and not to attempt physical work!

I was so relieved, as you can well imagine, just like a person in the condemned cell suddenly seeing the doors thrown open and told to go free! The only thing to spoil the picture slightly being that I am still so weak I can hardly crawl, and there is no sign at all of a blue sky outside the condemned cell— no, nothing but rain and mud, and I have hardly strength enough to cross the fields that isolate our cottage from the civilized world. I am given a new set of medicines every few days, but up till now none of them have had the slightest effect. But all the same it is good to know that I have every chance of survival and may still do some work, and may even feel alive in a little while!

I am very guilty about *The Rocking-Horse Catholic.* I read your friend's too kind criticism with deep interest, and am engaged on doing what I can about it, but I am afraid I won't be able to add to the grown-up part. I honestly think it would be artistically wrong to do so, unless indeed I tried to write a real autobiography. *If* I ever did that it would have to be much, much longer—*too* long, I think, and conceived wholly differently. . . .

Apart from other reasons against doing a full adult biography, it seems to me that I have not sufficient importance in myself to justify that. The people who might be interested would be very few. In a very short time after I am dead I shall be forgotten, and there are already in the world far too many rather tedious autobiographies by writers who have not achieved much, if anything, and which seem to be little more than lists of titled people they have met.

I shall introduce into such novels as I write in future many *interesting* true things, and characters which really are interesting, not because they concern *me,* but because they concern vast numbers of people who never seem to get written about at all.

Iris tells me that after her last check-up that spring Caryll was told she need not return for six months—and perhaps, while this really meant they could do no more for her, she had interpreted it as meaning she was clear of the disease. A doctor has told me that when this type of cancer returns there is absolutely nothing that can be done, so it seems not impossible that the hospital was hiding the truth from Caryll. With a patient disposed to go quietly this would have worked out better than it did with her. (Whether it is ever legitimate is another question.)

Her vitality of mind was as great as ever, and the problem was that, told she was not dying, she struggled to carry on a near normal life—a life near *her* normal. She wanted to meet Dorothy Dohen, who was in England, and a letter she wrote her shows something of the difficult atmosphere of these last months:

I would so gladly have come to London tomorrow, but it happens that I have been ill for a long time—partly, I think, owing to the awful weather—and when my friend heard me say I would come up to town and meet you there she rushed in like a mad tornado and tried to seize the phone. What with her shouting down what I was trying to say to you, and little Clare standing by longing to speak to you but too shy, it was like a madhouse here. I admired your calm but tremble to think what you must think of us. Now I will try to tell you more about getting here, for with monstrous presumption, I still hope you will be able to come and that it won't be *too* dreadful for you. . . .

When you come please stay for tea and supper—you can, if you want, go to London from here. The child will be out to tea, but she is nearly out of her mind in case she misses you; every day she packs all her clothes in a bag to go to America!

Lots of love and still hoping to meet. I have spent most of yesterday in bed in order to gather up enough strength to prove to my anxious friend that I can, and I really was rather under the weather.

"Rather under the weather" she returned to London, still speaking of her rheumatism and her hypochondria. Iris had

had to take charge of Greg, as Caryll was obviously too weak, but when one day Caryll took him out Iris noticed the stiff slowness of her walk. Back in London she dragged herself to Mass every morning—to within a week or two of her death.

At last, in October, Iris went to her own doctor, who was also Caryll's, and got from him the opinion that Caryll had not many months to live. Sheila Shaw, an old friend and companion at the First Aid post, was in London at the time and took Caryll in a taxi to the Westminster Hospital. As they drove back in silence, she realized that Caryll too knew with full certainty.

We arrived home a few days later, and I talked to Caryll on the telephone, thinking how hoarse and strange her voice sounded. My husband was the first to see her and found her sitting up in bed drawing herself as a rocking-horse Catholic—a faintly outlined, quaint little figure riding bravely into life.

God seems to give to all souls a measure of solitude before He calls them. It is man's share in His agony. I have witnessed it again and again, and Caryll, who always saw *our* death as redemptive in union with His, must have been making the offering asked of her during this time. She tried to avoid emotion with her friends, speaking still of nothing worse than rheumatism, but the brief gleam of hope had passed and she had now set herself resolutely to prepare for death. She must have known from her own sensations how short the time would be, at least for any physical effort. Increasingly she found any movement difficult. But she managed to put her flat into its usual exquisite order, she destroyed papers too private to be left for other eyes, she washed for the last time her glowing red-gold hair. Rosamond, coming in on October 7th, found Iris making her bed, Caryll in a chair in obvious pain before she got into it, never again to leave it.

The doctor had spoken of months, but when I saw Caryll I was utterly dismayed. My own father had lived fewer weeks than the months the doctors predicted—Caryll, I felt, was very near the end. We talked little, but I asked her, "Would you like me to ring up a priest and ask him to bring you Holy Communion tomorrow?"

She said how grateful she would be. On a sudden impulse I said to him, "Father, I don't want to be an alarmist, but if I were you I'd take along the holy oils."

Caryll grew rapidly worse that night, and when the priest arrived no doubt was possible that she was dying. Iris left the room that Father Thomas might hear Caryll's confession, but although she was able to kiss the crucifix she could no longer speak. Iris is convinced that she was still fully conscious.

I love to think, with the dying, of those marvellous prayers begging Our Lord, accompanied by His saints and angels, to meet the Christian, going forth from this world, the senses anointed and cleansed from sins committed through the body, the spirit renewed by a final absolution. Theologians are dwelling increasingly on the power of the sacrament of unction to prepare the soul, like a second baptism, for the immediate vision of God. And Caryll had had a long purgatory. "She suffered *greatly* and uncomplainingly."

There was little to do now except watch, for Caryll never spoke again. Her last words had been to Iris before Father Thomas arrived: "You must be very tired."

The dog Greg, still a puppy and usually over-lively, stayed in the room all through, quiet and well-behaved and laying no claim to his usual station on the foot of Caryll's bed. Soon after, whether from the pain-killing drugs the doctor was now giving her or the rapid progress of the disease, she sank into total unconsciousness. Iris was beside her constantly, and it seemed suitable that other friends should gather in the old familiar way almost as if for a party: Caryll's sister and niece,

Dickie bringing exquisite flowers, a neighbour from the country with roses from her garden, Rosamond and Sheila Shaw, Henry Tayler and Charles Scott-Paton. Two nuns who had been begging through Nell Gwynn House came to kneel at the bedside. Each night Iris kept vigil. It was only on the 11th that a professional nurse could be secured.

Rosamond had never read Caryll's rhythm "Ghosts and Memories." Reading it after her death, she recognized with a shock of surprise words which now came into her mind as clearly as if spoken by the insensible woman on the bed. They recur in the poem as the growing intimation of God's presence in a child's heart, and now perhaps came back to Caryll in her seeming unconsciousness so clearly as to echo in another heart:

> "Guess who I am?
> Guess who it is
> that loves you—"

For long now Caryll had been thinking of the Ghosts and Memories of her childhood. But in the rhythm a thread links childhood with death—the thread of her deepest thought: in man God seems to leave us, in man He comes to us:

> Home and father and mother
> were God.

But human desertion is in truth only a shadow, the reality is still there, but more deeply hidden. Through friendship, through human love, God had come to Caryll; through man He had come to heal the hurt man had inflicted. She had prayed in the poem for

> Hands
> that, laid on the head of the dying,
> transmit the infinite love.

And through the touch of human hands she met God on her death bed as she had learned to meet Him in her life. The poem ends:

> "Guess who I am?
> Guess who it is
> that loves you—
> you, who were the breaking of spring
> in my heart
> before the beginning of time:
> guess who I am,
> you,
> in the womb
> before the day star
> I have begotten you."

Caryll Houselander died on October 12th, 1954.

Epilogue

I cannot do better than end Caryll's story with her own words—some thoughts from *The Risen Christ* and an unpublished rhythm looking forward to the joy of our resurrection.

"Everything falls away from us, even memories—even the weariness of self. This is the breaking of the bread, the supreme moment in the prayer of the body, the end of the liturgy of our mortal lives, when we are broken for and in the communion of Christ's love to the whole world.

"But it is not the end of the prayer of the body. To that there is no end. Our dust pays homage to God, until the endless morning of resurrection wakens our body, glorified."

The Spirit Speaks to the Body on the Day of Resurrection.

> Come back to me,
> you beloved,
> who have gathered the beauty of the earth
> to the unchanging
> through centuries of change.
> God has put off the universe
> like a cloak worn threadbare,
> and made new his raiment.

Hands and feet and body
I love,
fallen into dust,
bring back to the sockets of your eyes
the earth's forget-me-nots,
the skies we knew together
and the dew,
you, beloved, who grew
out of the dust of the grave
in flower and leaf,
who blew in shining seed
upon the wind.

Come back to me,
you beloved,
who have gathered loveliness
through centuries of change
to the unchanging:
you who have gathered
multitudinous living
to the singleness of life.

And this through being dead.
Body I love,
fallen away into grey dust,
heart of my little love,
a handful of dust
grown in the blossom
of flowers upon the grave,
sown in windblown seed
all over the earth.

What beauty will you bring back to me,
eyes that were empty sockets,
conscious no more of the light?
You have gathered the skies
now, and blue of columbine
and the purple irises:

you have gathered the colour
of hazelwoods
and sable of dark seas
and the greenness of summer pools
in cool woods—
what loveliness
will you open for me,
opening eyes?

What gold has grown
into that fallen flax of your hair
that there in the grave
fell from your little skull—
what honeysuckle and wheat
and what movement
of wind and wave
will the locks of your hair
bring back from the grave?
Strength of beauty
is there now in the filigree
of your bleached bones,
little skeleton.
that were the pillars
of Christ's lowliest house—
will they bring me the living wood
of the almond tree
and the subtlety of the birch
and the rising sap
in the larch:
and your tongue,
will it sing with all the
winds and the wild birds' song?

When you died
they folded your hands on the crucifix
over your heart,
and composed your blameless feet
and buried you under the earth.

Come,
God's glory
burning in me
will burn in you
and you will shine in His light
as the moon in the light of the sun:
Come,
I will live in you
as the bridegroom lives
in the life of the bride.

Caryll's grave is on a hillside, overlooking a glorious sweep of countryside. There some American admirers of her books found it, and then came on to the cottage to see the room in, and the table on, which she worked. Ever since 1954 they have had a Mass said for her on the day she died.